RESIDENTIAL REHABILITATION:
PRIVATE PROFITS AND PUBLIC PURPOSES

*American Council To Improve
Our Neighborhoods*

SERIES IN HOUSING AND COMMUNITY DEVELOPMENT

BANFIELD AND GRODZINS:
Government and Housing in Metropolitan Areas

WINNICK:
Rental Housing: Opportunities for Private Investment

NASH:
Residential Rehabilitation: Private Profits and Public Purposes

KELLY AND ASSOCIATES:
Design and the Production of Houses

Other books are in preparation

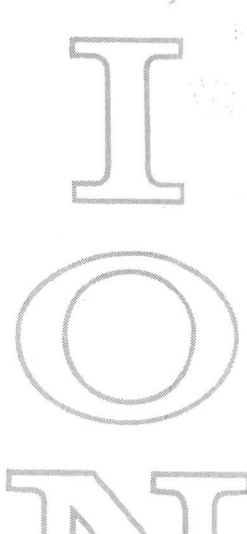

RESIDENTIAL REHABILITATION: PRIVATE PROFITS AND PUBLIC PURPOSES

William W. Nash
ACTION Research Program

DIRECTED AND WITH A PREFACE BY
Miles L. Colean
Consulting Economist

McGRAW-HILL BOOK COMPANY, INC. 1959
New York Toronto London

RESIDENTIAL REHABILITATION: PRIVATE PROFITS AND PUBLIC PURPOSES

Copyright © 1959 by the McGraw-Hill Book Company, Inc. Printed in the United States of America. All rights reserved. This book, or parts thereof, may not be reproduced in any form without permission of the publishers.

Library of Congress Catalog Card Number: 59-8555

ACTION *American Council to Improve Our Neighborhoods*
Series in Housing and Community Development

Andrew Heiskell, *Chairman; Publisher, Life Magazine*
Ferd Kramer, *Vice Chairman for Research; President, Draper and Kramer, Inc.*
James E. Lash, *Executive Vice President*
Martin Meyerson, *Vice President for Research; Williams Professor and Director, Center for Urban Studies, Harvard University*
Barbara Terrett, *Deputy Director of Research*

ACTION *Research Committee* Ferd Kramer, *Chairman*

C. J. BACKSTRAND
President, Armstrong Cork Company

FRITZ B. BURNS *
Builder and developer; founder of Panama City, California

MRS. T. S. CHAPMAN *
Past President, General Federation of Women's Clubs

THOMAS F. COOGAN
President, Housing Securities, Inc.

JAMES C. DOWNS, JR.
Chairman, Real Estate Research Corporation

BEN FISCHER
International Representative, United Steelworkers of America

PHILIP L. GRAHAM
President and Publisher, The Washington Post Company

JOSEPH A. GRAZIER
President, American Radiator and Standard Sanitary Corporation

HENRY T. HEALD *
Past Chancellor, New York University

ANDREW HEISKELL
Publisher, Life Magazine

GUY T. O. HOLLYDAY
Chairman of the Board, The Title Guarantee Company; past Commissioner, Federal Housing Administration

* Served on ACTION Research Committee during initial period of investigations for this series.
† Deceased.

ROY W. JOHNSON
Director, Advanced Research Projects Agency, Department of Defense; past Executive Vice President, General Electric Co.

PHILIP M. KLUTZNICK
Chairman of the Board, American Community Builders, Inc.; past Commissioner, Public Housing Administration

JOSEPH W. LUND
Executive Vice President, R. M. Bradley and Company, Inc.

ROBERT B. MITCHELL
Chairman, Department of Land and City Planning, University of Pennsylvania

DE LESSEPS S. MORRISON
Mayor, City of New Orleans

CLARENCE J. MYERS
President, New York Life Insurance Company

JAMES W. ROUSE
President, James W. Rouse and Company, Inc.

EMANUEL M. SPIEGEL †
Past President, National Association of Home Builders

CHARLES P. TAFT *
Past Mayor, Cincinnati, Ohio

RALPH WALKER
Architect, Voorhees, Walker, Smith and Smith

ROBERT C. WEAVER
State Rent Administrator, New York Temporary State Housing Rent Commission

v

Residential Rehabilitation: Private Profits and Public Purposes

ACTION *ad hoc* Committee on the Investor

Joseph W. Lund, *Chairman*
Executive Vice President, R. M. Bradley and Company, Inc.

(MRS.) CATHERINE BAUER
(WURSTER)
*Lecturer on City Planning,
University of California*

ERNEST J. BOHN [*]
*Director
Cleveland Metropolitan Housing
Authority*

THOMAS P. COOGAN [*]
President, Housing Securities, Inc.

ROBERT W. DOWLING [*]
President, City Investing Company

ALLISON DUNHAM
*Professor of Real Estate Law,
University of Chicago*

GUY T. O. HOLLYDAY [*]
*Chairman of the Board,
The Title Guarantee Company; post
Commissioner, Federal Housing
Administration*

EDWARD HOPKINSON, JR. [*]
Partner, Drexel & Company

M. K. M. MURPHY [*]
*President, Federal Home Loan
Bank of New York*

CLARENCE J. MYERS [*]
*President, New York Life
Insurance Company*

RICHARD U. RATCLIFF
*Professor of Land Economics,
University of Wisconsin*

DR. LEONARD A. SCHEELE
*President, Warner-Chilcott
Laboratories*

JAMES H. SCHEUER
*Chairman, Executive Committee,
City and Suburban Homes Company*

Ex officio
ANDREW HEISKELL [*]
Publisher, Life Magazine

FERD KRAMER [*]
President, Draper and Kramer, Inc.

[*] Members of ACTION'S Board of Directors.

This volume is one in the ACTION Series in Housing and Community Development made possible by a grant from the Ford Foundation to the American Council To Improve Our Neighborhoods. Some of the contributors to the Series are members of ACTION's staff; others are at universities or in private practice. The findings they present here are the product of their own selective process. The conclusions they reach have had the benefit of advice and comment from a wide variety of persons, including members of ACTION's *ad hoc* committees for the Series. Neither individually nor collectively, however, has ACTION's Board of Directors attempted to limit the authors in the facts they present, the conclusions they reach, or the recommendations they propose to solve or mitigate a particular problem. Whether prepared by staff or consultants, the volumes in the Series are uniquely the product of their authors. To say here that the authors' findings and views do not necessarily reflect the knowledge and attitude of ACTION or of any or all of the ACTION Board of Directors is also to underline the Board's intention that the Series should provide fresh points of view to some of the most complex and controversial problems of housing and urban development in America.

ACTION hopes that both the expert and the student will find the volumes useful additions to the literature on housing and community development. The principal purpose of the Series, however, is to inform and stimulate the growing body of influential businessmen, professionals, and citizen leaders whose opinions on many facets of urban life are having a profound effect upon the kinds of policy and actions required for the provision of adequate housing.

> Andrew Heiskell, Chairman, ACTION Board of Directors
> Ferd Kramer, Chairman, ACTION Research Committee
> Joseph W. Lund, Chairman, *ad hoc* Committee on the Investor
> Roy W. Johnson, Chairman, *ad hoc* Committee on the Producer
> Ben Fischer, Chairman, *ad hoc* Committee on the Consumer
> Philip L. Graham, Chairman, *ad hoc* Committee on the Government
> Guy T. O. Hollyday, Chairman, *ad hoc* Committee on the Community

Foreword

The ACTION Series in Housing and Community Development is the published part of a two-pronged effort of the American Council To Improve Our Neighborhoods (ACTION) to help bring about a higher level of living in this country's urban areas. It has been made possible by a grant from the Ford Foundation. These volumes analyze many of the facts about the present condition of American communities, particularly with respect to housing, and offer new conclusions about the problems and potentialities implied by the facts. The other part of this ACTION effort is made up of many activities through which ACTION and other groups are aiding communities and their citizens to meet present local problems and to realize future potentialities for sound urban growth. These activities put to the test the proposals of the authors and the members of the *ad hoc* committees for improving the nation's urban life.

Specifically, ACTION aims through this Series and its related program efforts to create a climate within which the choices available to the American people for improved urban living can be expanded in terms of a larger supply of housing, of better quality and at lesser cost. At the least, this means the realization of the following objectives:

1. The elimination of slums that cannot be economically rehabilitated.
2. The improvement of properties that can be economically rehabilitated.
3. The preservation of currently sound housing and neighborhoods by slowing down their rates of obsolescence.
4. The provision of new housing on both cleared and va-

cant land in sufficient quantity and in satisfactory quality to meet current requirements and the requirements of the huge urban growth foreseen in the years ahead.

5. The accomplishment of the foregoing objectives in conjunction with a high level of coordinated community services and in such a manner that all income, racial, and other groups in the population will be served.

6. The effective planning and distribution of urban functions in order to correct the costly imbalances which now exist among them both within the central city and between it and its surrounding metropolitan area.

These objectives cannot be accomplished without intensive effort to organize pertinent knowledge systematically and to clarify the aims of urban policy. Obviously, this Series cannot furnish all the information necessary to solve all the problems. But the authors of the volumes do provide a basis for policy. They do so by analyzing the current problems and indicating possible future changes. The summary volume, the over-all view, takes the major findings of each of these specific studies and presents them along with the suggestions which the ACTION *ad hoc* committees believe to be most promising for solving a number of critical current problems.

The framework of the Series is based on the primacy of the consumer in the housing market and in housing policy. Because the largest number of Americans live in urban communities, the studies deal only with cities and urban housing.

Most of the wealth of America is in its cities. And most of the wealth of cities is in residential structures and their related utilities and facilities. The value of dwellings alone stands at over $300 billion, a figure twice as large as the assets of the country's 500 biggest manufacturing companies. Not only is housing the largest single item in our national wealth, but that part of it which is newly constructed amounts on the average to more than a fifth of all our capital expenditures each year. New housing uses one-third of the lumber produced in the country, two-thirds of the bricks, at least half of most plumbing items, and three-fourths of all gypsum products. Yet new housing in any given year is only 3 per cent of all housing. These statistics prove that housing is among the most important commodities in our economy, but they do not prove that our supply of housing meets the requirements of all consumers nor that it is produced as efficiently as possible.

For housing, as for other commodities, the market place tends to govern the quantity, quality, cost, and distribution of the product. America is properly famous for what it produces. It is equally admired for the methods of production and distribution which its industries have developed. Particularly in the past 25 years, accomplishments in housing have been considerable, but either they are not considerable enough or the dissatisfied observers of, and participants in, the housing market argue their case more eloquently than people do about other commodities and services.

The very nature of housing makes almost inevitable that both the product of the housing industry and the mechanism of the housing market should come under criticism. Unlike most other economic commodities, housing is also a social commodity. As such, it is overlaid with all kinds of attributes that blur the lines between supply and demand, need and preference. In our system of values as well as in our vernacular, the house is the home. So long as it stands as the symbol of the family, satisfaction with it will take as many forms as the traditional sentiments which people attach to it.

But putting aside its social values, housing is still very different from other economic commodities. Its scale of cost, for one thing, is not matched by any other commodity. For most householders, monthly housing outlays represent their largest current expenditure after food and—if they buy a house—their largest single expenditure in a lifetime. Another of its distinguishing attributes is immobility. A pair of shoes or an automobile can be shipped from one part of the country to another as demand varies regionally. Most housing, on the other hand, is immobile; it is tied to its land. Still another example of difference is the fact that the market for housing is essentially one for an existing stockpile; even in years of highest new housing production, the stockpile still meets 97 per cent of the demand for housing. Coupled with the high level of expenditure always required for housing, it makes the market respond disproportionately to sudden declines in the economy and in consumer income. The Depression of the thirties, for example, while it greatly reduced the production of automobiles and other consumer goods, cut down the number of new housing starts proportionately very much more. Because housing is so vulnerable to economic fluctuations, it has rarely attracted large amounts of risk capital from individual firms.

Relatively few of housing's small businessmen have introduced technological advances into their operations. Where they have, the results have been remarkable, but the small scale at which most of them operate has generally precluded their investing in much more than an occasional market analysis or research in design. Their scale of operation also tends to foster labor practices which, while protecting the otherwise precarious position of workers in a seasonal and fluctuating trade, nevertheless contribute to production inefficiencies. But if the small businessman in housing sometimes operates at a disadvantage, he has nonetheless been remarkably successful in Washington. Since the 1930s he has persuaded the Federal government to underwrite the housing market with credit mechanisms and other benefits which eliminate much of his risk.

It is important to remember, however, that Federal policies which reduce risk in home building have not been adopted simply because housing has extraordinary persuasive spokesmen. Inducements to the construction industry and to the manufacturers of materials have become traditional compensatory measures when the economy slumps.

There is considerable irony in the fact that the very protective devices which surround the production and marketing of housing inhibit its industrial rationalization. As the risk goes down, so does competition, and competition is one of the essential ingredients for successful production and merchandising in America. Piece by piece, the whole setting for housing tends to magnify the inability of private enterprise to merchandise housing in the extraordinary way that the American economy merchandises its soup and soap, aspirins and automobiles. It is hardly surprising, therefore, that the consumer has come to place less and less attention on his dwelling and more and more attention on nationally advertised commodities to go into his dwelling or to use outside it.

This widespread shift in consumer values hits hard at every city's struggle to stay viable, for the state of our dwellings and the state of our cities are inseparable. Relatively minor deterioration and obsolescence in a city's residential parts can have major economic repercussions on the whole urbanized area. So can inappropriate locations of housing types and levels of density. If housing types determine the pattern of social organization and activity in the city, density determines the city's size and circulation. In different combinations they add up to a greater or lesser public investment in schools, parks, playgrounds, streets, and utilities and to a greater or lesser economic return to the private entrepreneurs who invest in, build, own, and manage housing or provide a range of services and commodities for its occupants. Next to their employment, where people live and the way they live constitute the most important feature of urban policy.

Within this general setting, the ACTION Series in Housing and Community Development deliberately combines research and policy-making activities to help clear away obstacles that stand in the way of the kinds of communities that will meet the requirements of new quantities and qualities—aesthetic as well as economic and social—in American life. Throughout the preparation of the volumes there has been unique interplay between the researcher and representatives of the key groups which make public and private policy for the housing market and for urban development.

For all the studies, I sought to associate with the Series the ablest persons I could find. Some of the authors, although informed on housing matters, had not previously written about them. Their points of view, I felt, were likely to be uncluttered by old attachments. I asked other persons to participate in the Series, however, because they so clearly were experts in the field.

My method of organization for the Series was this: The primary agents whose decisions determine how effectively housing and community services respond at any point in time to the often conflicting demands and requirements that are made upon them were identified as the investor, the producer, the consumer, the government, and the community. For each of these major areas of housing involvement and interest, ACTION'S directors set up an *ad hoc* committee whose responsibility was to suggest feasible courses of action which stemmed from the subject matter dealt with by the researchers for the separate volumes.

Thus, within the broad category of investment, the *ad hoc* Committee on the Investor considered the problems of rental housing and rehabilitation. In his study, *Rental Housing: Opportunities for Private Investment,* Louis Winnick uncovers many of the deep-seated forces which have produced a significant decline in apartment construction. He sets forth reasons why life insurance companies have abandoned their rental-housing programs and why apartment developers have become so dependent on government mortgage aids. But he also outlines an impressive list of factors which point to a broader demand for urban apartments in the future. The committee's second area of interest, the economic feasibility of rehabilitation, had its inception in the great stress on rehabilitation expressed in the urban-renewal provisions of the Housing Act of 1954. In *Residential Rehabilitation: Private Profits and Public Purposes,* Miles L. Colean and William W. Nash present a comprehensive examination of the rehabilitation market and the individuals who operate successfully in it. Based on intensive field investigation and factual accounts of operations by well-known rehabilitators in a number of cities, the study explores investment opportunities in housing rehabilitation and discusses the role local government can play in stimulating rehabilitation either inside or outside official urban-renewal areas.

The Committee on the Producer accepted the challenge of proposing ways to achieve the potential opportunities for technological change in the design and production of housing. As a basis for these proposals, Burnham Kelly and a team of associated experts at the Massachusetts Institute of Technology analyze the blocks which prevent the housing industry from taking advantage of a new way of life and cost-saving features offered by new design and technology. Their book, *Design and the Production of Houses,* explores the roles of the builder, the labor union, the manufacturer of building materials, the architect, and the public official and points out ways in which their combined efforts can introduce many forms of improved design and technological innovation into future home-building operations.

Problems with which the Committee on the Consumer dealt are interrelated with all the other studies in the Series, as the committee faced the issue of whether the behavior of the consumer can be altered to induce him to place a higher value on housing and the neighborhood amenities which complement it. Nelson Foote, Janet Abu-Lughod, Mary Mix Foley, and Louis Winnick collaborated in the research and writing of *Housing Choices and Housing Constraints,* which brings together knowledge about the values people attach to their housing and the degree to which they appear to be realizing or sacrificing those values. In his chapters, Foote presents some original and thought-provoking material on the organization of the dwelling unit for the kind of urban life now developing in most American cities.

Because housing is a commodity whose social value makes it a matter of national interest, it was necessary to explore the role the Federal government plays in its production and consumption. The Committee on the Government, therefore, was concerned largely with how housing credit policies of the Federal government impede or stimulate desirable competitive practices in the housing market and provide necessary protective devices for consumers who for reasons of age, income, discrimination, or incapacity cannot compete successfully in the market. Charles M. Haar, in *Federal Credit and Private Housing: The Mass Financing Dilemma*, gives a comprehensive account of the twenty-year evolution of Federal housing credit programs and provides a stimulating reappraisal of their impact on the housing market.

Finally, the studies which came under the view of the Committee on the Community explore both the responsibility and the limitations of local government in the achievement of a higher standard of urban life. Here the principal issues were ones of governmental structure as it affects the standard of housing in metropolitan areas, and of levels of expenditure for housing and related facilities required to reach a set of tentative goals throughout an urban area. Edward C. Banfield and Morton Grodzins are deliberately quizzical and provocative as they explore the first issue in *Government and Housing in Metropolitan Areas*. They look carefully at the political impediments to large-scale structural changes in metropolitan governments; examine the lack of logic underlying many current schemes for reorganization; point up some values of the "chaos of governments" in metropolitan areas; and offer a "model for action" looking to governmental change on a scale needed in terms of improved housing and possible in terms of political realities. In the second study prepared for the Committee on the Community, John W. Dyckman and Reginald R. Isaacs explore the questions of our ability to pay for required investment in cities and the organization of our economy necessary to realize urban goals. In *Capital Requirements for Urban Development and Renewal*, they translate national expenditure totals into specific changes in the urban environment and convert specific local programs into a national bill of goods.

The final volume—the over-all view of the ACTION Series—brings together the principal points in each of the other volumes and puts them in the setting of the total housing market and public policy. The consolidated suggestions of the five *ad hoc* committees, which appear in the over-all view, thus become the preface for action.

As the committees reviewed the research materials presented to them, they sought to suggest policies and activities which if implemented by public agencies, private groups, or institutions under the stimulus of ACTION might reasonably help achieve the major objectives for the Series. The steps the committees recommend are an attempt to establish a level of aspiration for housing and urban development against which private and public decision makers can formulate policies and programs that with more ingenuity and flexibility than has been shown in the past will enable the housing market to function to its limit in satisfying the value we place upon its product. The combined report of the committees, which appears in the last volume of the Series, includes a plea for the empirical testing in many communities of a wide variety of new practices.

In a field such as housing and urban development, in which only a small amount of research has or is being done, any effort is a pioneering one. Those who make it do so not only with the expectation that it will provide a fresh outlook for scholars and policy makers, but with the intention that it will provoke the next push forward. This Series, whose preparation began in February of 1956, is heavily indebted to several important predecessors: The Twentieth Century Fund's comprehensive analysis by Miles L. Colean, *American Housing: Problems and Prospects;* the scholarly research of Ernest M. Fisher and his associates at Columbia University's Institute for Urban Land Use and Housing Studies; and Coleman Woodbury's collection of perceptive essays for *The Future of Cities* and *Urban Redevelopment.* Moreover, this ACTION Series looks forward to being complemented by one which the Commission on Race and Housing is sponsoring.

Barbara Terrett, Deputy Director of Research at ACTION, shared the responsibility of administration, criticism and editing. Among many other persons whose knowledge and experience I called on frequently were Neal J. Hardy, director of the National Housing Center, and Arthur S. Goldman, director of marketing for *House & Home* magazine. Both of them were endlessly generous with their time and counsel. William L. C. Wheaton, a collaborator on the final volume, gave constructive review to several of the other volumes, as did Herrymon Maurer, the editorial consultant for the Series. Most of all, I am indebted to the authors of the separate volumes for the excellence of their contribution, and to the understanding and wisdom of the ACTION directors and *ad hoc* committee members. In particular, Ferd Kramer, ACTION Vice Chairman, who heads the Research Committee, Andrew Heiskell, Chairman of ACTION's Board of Directors, and James E. Lash, ACTION Executive Vice President, provided helpful criticism without which the Series would never have been developed.

Martin Meyerson
ACTION Vice President

Preface

Our standing stock of housing is an enormous resource. The value of the residential structures in our urban communities, exclusive of land, has been estimated (as of 1955) to be $320 billion, or nearly one-quarter of all national wealth.[1]

From its magnitude alone, this vast investment merits attention and concern. From its bearing on the general welfare, in terms of the health, safety, comfort, and happiness of the people, its meaning is not surpassed by any of our other assets. In terms of the business generated through real estate and financing transactions and property repair and improvement, its importance is hardly less. It provides a large source of local tax revenue. It is at once the glory and despair of our cities.

In spite of the size and significance of our residential property, we know far too little about it. We have had but two complete housing censuses in our history, and these show us the situation only as of given points of time. Of the whole dynamic process by which the elements of the housing supply change, or are changed, during their usually long and varied span between construction and collapse or demolition, our data are hardly of more than a tentative and experimental sort.[2]

The present study endeavors to illuminate one part of this process: that of the ways in which existing dwelling structures are, on a commercial basis, kept from deterioration or restored

---

[1] Raymond Goldsmith, "Postwar Capital Market," *Financial Research and the Problems of the Day*, Thirty-seventh Annual Report, National Bureau of Economic Research, Inc., New York, May, 1957, p. 34.

[2] See U.S. Bureau of the Census, *1956 National Housing Inventory*, in which data on "components of change" become available for the first time.

to useful condition. Considering the area of *terra incognita*, this may seem to be a very limited exploration. It is indeed limited; but it is an essential one nonetheless.

In a market economy, the test of feasibility is profitability. If we find that the tasks of maintaining and improving the existing housing supply and of adapting it to altered environmental conditions can make for good business and satisfactory investment, then we may point the way both to an important economic opportunity and to a means for reducing governmental burdens. Or, if we find that the business opportunities are unexploited, then we may seek the reasons and undertake to suggest remedies. Out of this exploration, we may in the end hope to find a rational basis for public policies aimed, on the one hand, at improving the economic potentials of rehabilitation and, on the other, at defining the areas in which the community may determine that private effort must be supplemented by some form of public action.

These are the general purposes of this survey. In the absence of any comprehensive body of data or of the means for obtaining such (if indeed it were available for collection), it has been necessary to adopt the method of making case studies. This method has limitations insofar as reaching definitive broad conclusions is concerned, but it has the advantage of revealing the down-to-earth problems encountered by practical men trying for practical solutions. It also is able to show the characteristics of the properties affected, the physical and financial operations involved, and the organizations participating in what are considered to be fairly typical activities throughout the whole range of property values.

In spite of the limitations imposed both by the case-study method and by the small number of cases reviewed, some significant findings are to be noted. The smallness of the number of cases is in itself noteworthy. In spite of the fact that success has often been attained in the instances analyzed, it was not easy to find cases, whether profitable or not. While no claim is made to comprehensive coverage of the cities that were visited, the conclusion seems warranted that residential rehabilitation can hardly be identified as yet as a distinct form of business. Organizations mainly devoted to it are few in number and their activities appear generally to be scattered and intermittent or conducted along with other forms of business. It also seems clear that the extent of such work now being carried on, whether on a professional or on an amateur basis, is far from enough to keep pace with the steady march of obsolescence and deterioration.

On the face of it, this is an amazing situation. Here we have some 38 million single-family houses and unknown millions of structures with two or more apartments, all in some stage of the aging process from that of first-year's maintenance to that of hopeless disrepair. In between there are vast potentialities for the preservation or augmentation of the original investment, for halting the process of decay, and for restoring value. More than this, there is the economic and social desirability of utilizing the housing supply in the most efficient way possible, which certainly means avoiding its waste and maintaining its utility until the location is ripe for a new and more profitable use.

Yet these circumstances have not, as might be expected, called forth an industry. Why is it that what apparently offers such a fertile business opportunity has borne so little business fruit? An effort has been made to get answers from the persons most directly involved, the rehabilitators themselves. Here the common complaints are of difficulties in obtaining financing and of lack of cooperation from or confusion of policy among the governmental agencies with whom they must deal.

These problems are unquestionably serious. Although the survey was conducted at a time when mortgage money was especially tight, there is little doubt that a money scarcity is chronic in this area of activity. Lenders have often been accused of lack of boldness and imagination. The same accusation has been leveled at the Federal Housing Administration. In all fairness, perhaps these qualities should not be expected in financial institutions. If boldness is too much to expect, however, perception at least may be asked for. It should be possible and, if any progress is to be made, it certainly will be necessary for lending institutions to grasp the potentials of rehabilitation and to look beyond the "as is" to the "can be."

Examples of perception tinged even with boldness are to be found. Many institutions, of course, have made loans to aid the process of revival; and there are instances of organized consumer effort. One of the most interesting has been the joint effort of lending institutions working through the Voluntary Home Mortgage Credit Program,[3] under which private funds have been made available to home-mortgage borrowers in out-of-the-way places. This technique, now several years old, might readily be adapted to the provision of funds for mortgages or property-improvement loans in deteriorated urban areas. The possibilities of doing something along these lines are to be demonstrated in the District of Columbia, where the local savings and loan associations are creating a substantial pool of funds from which loans will be made to help property owners meet the standards of the District housing code.

Encouraging as is this kind of action, the onus for blight or the responsibilty for its elimination cannot be placed on the financial institutions. They must have an environment in which it is possible to function; and if the present environment is bad, a better one must be at least in prospect. This can be provided only by public authority. One of the most depressing

[3] An arrangement, first incorporated in the Housing Act of 1954, permitting lending institutions to consult together under Federal auspices and make allocations of funds without violation of the antitrust statutes.

aspects of our older urban districts is their neglect by local government. When municipal budgets are short or expenses curtailed, it is usually the older areas that suffer first, in the lapse of trash collection, the disregard of pavements and lighting, the failure to provide or to maintain playgrounds, and the indifference to other services. The default in municipal housekeeping cannot help but lead to bad personal housekeeping. In fact, it makes good personal housekeeping virtually impossible. More than this, it creates an infectious discouragement that makes maintenance and repair seem hardly worthwhile to the resident and financially hazardous to the lender.

The first insurance against blight is good municipal housekeeping. The second is to have on the books, and to enforce, ordinances in respect to building requirements and property repair and occupancy. There is much to be said for maintaining what a former mayor of New York referred to as "the outward order and decency," and this at least should be done. It is much better, however, to go further to prevent the indiscriminate subdivision and crowding of living quarters, the neglect of repairs, and the accumulation of clutter. Unless the municipality does these things, it is safe to say that decay will advance and rehabilitation will be discouraged and defeated.

It is surprising how difficult it is to persuade municipal governments and the voters who elect them that civic housekeeping is a profitable enterprise. Because it provides the environment essential to confident action on the part of property owners and investors and because it contributes to the conservation and even the enhancement of values, good civic housekeeping helps assure the maintenance of municipal revenue. The arithmetic is simple and incontrovertible, as the scattered instances in this survey reveal. Nevertheless, it would be hard to find a community of any size in this country that could be graded "A" on this score.

The study brings out another type of obstacle to rehabilitation that is produced by government. This is the confusion and lack of coordination in policy and operations among the agencies with which the rehabilitator must deal. Zoning officials are often at odds with redevelopment officials. Local officials become involved in protracted disagreements with Federal officials on the plans for an area and, where highway construction is involved, with state officials as well. Enforcement of local codes is often in several uncoordinated agencies, which in turn may not be coordinated with those dealing with street work, trash collection, and so on. Again, we have the problem of the failure of the local governing body to provide an environment in which rehabilitation may proceed safely, confidently, and practicably; and the more sophisticated the rehabilitator is, the more certainly he will avoid the risks that this sort of confusion creates. Under the circumstances, the surprising thing is not that there has been so little organized rehabilitation but that there has been as much as there has.

Related to this is the further problem resulting from standards that are wholly out of line with what people can afford. Officials and welfare enthusiasts are often inclined to be impatient with gradualness and to insist on a subjectively derived ideal to be reached at a single jump. The success of the rehabilitation efforts in Charlotte has been largely attributable to the realism of the approach. The results do not create a photogenic spectacle, but the effects on the families directly involved and on the community as a whole are immeasurable. By and large, however, the fact seems to be that rehabilitation has little appeal either to administrators or planners. It is unspectacular in itself and its success requires the doing of a lot of unspectacular things. It does not fit readily into the pattern of Federal subsidy. It often seems simpler and more satisfying to take the bulldozer approach and clear the whole mess away.

Obviously, the whole task of maintenance and renewal of our cities is not to be accomplished by the dramatic course of total clearance and total rebuilding. Clearance has its important place; but it will be wastefully costly, except where the existing situation is clearly beyond less drastic treatment or where there is the clear opportunity for a new and better paying use for the land. For the rest, dependence must be placed upon the maintenance, improvement, and adaptation of existing structures.

This is the hard fact that municipal authorities must face. Failure to face it can only increase the extent of the deterioration and the difficulty of the remedy. If, on the other hand, the issue is firmly confronted, an environment encouraging to rehabilitation activity can be created. Such a confrontation would involve:

1. A sincere acceptance of rehabilitation as a vital feature of a sound urban economy.

2. The maintenance of municipal services (particularly trash and garbage collection, street paving and lighting, and police protection) in declining sections of the city.

3. The installation and maintenance of small parks and playgrounds in these sections.

4. A firm zoning policy which establishes logical uses and avoids spot changes that contribute to the process of decay.

5. Realistic housing standards (which can be stiffened as progress is made) vigorously enforced.

6. The same realism in establishing standards for the insurance of mortgages in the older urban areas.

7. Coordination among governmental agencies dealing with planning, zoning, highways, and code enforcement.

A program of this sort should provide a stable and orderly framework within which private action could be operative. It is reasonable to assume that private investment would proceed with less hesitancy under these circumstances and that private business initiative would respond to the opportunities so created.

Rehabilitation has another aspect—the human aspect—that is often given too little attention. Neighborhoods, even rundown neighborhoods, often have meaning to their residents. Personal associations, attachment to a church, a sense of community, all involve intangible values worth preserving where they are found or may be stimulated. Rehabilitation may preserve and strengthen these values. Clearance never can. Desirable and unavoidable as it may frequently be, large-scale clearance is always disruptive of community feeling. It contributes, at least temporarily, to the rootlessness and impersonality of urban life. A well-established program of rehabilitation, on the other hand, is an influence for stability, for continuity, for identification. It is worth while on this score alone.

Miles L. Colean

Acknowledgments

This book could not have been written without the extensive help I received during its preparation. My major debt is to Miles L. Colean, whose knowledge, judgment, and patient direction gave the book purpose and form. I am also grateful for the advice and guidance provided by Martin Meyerson, ACTION Vice President and Director of the ACTION Research Program; by Barbara Terrett, Deputy Director of Research for ACTION; by Louis Winnick, whose informal conversations strengthened my economic assertions; and by the members of ACTION's *ad hoc* Committee on the Investor, directed by Joseph W. Lund of Boston, whose suggestions clarified many aspects of the business of rehabilitation. Thanks are also due to William L. C. Wheaton and Chester Rapkin of the Institute for Urban Studies of the University of Pennsylvania for their critical reading of the manuscript during its formative stages. And of course there could have been no book without the cooperation and materials provided by rehabilitators, officers of financial institutions, and public officials, only some of whom are mentioned in the text. Finally, I am grateful for the editorial assistance and understanding of Dorothy W. Nash, who uncomplainingly endured the composition of the manuscript.

William W. Nash

Contents

Foreword, by Martin Meyerson ix

Preface, by Miles L. Colean xix

CHAPTER 1	The Background	1
CHAPTER 2	Prestige Rehabilitation	8
CHAPTER 3	Rehabilitation for Middle-income Families	47
CHAPTER 4	Rehabilitation of Low-rent Housing	85
CHAPTER 5	Locating and Estimating Rehabilitation Projects	129
CHAPTER 6	The Financing Problem	145
CHAPTER 7	Rehabilitation as Part of Public Programs	163
CHAPTER 8	Expanding the Volume of Rehabilitation	186
Appendix A	Other Case Materials	199
Appendix B	Studies of the Economic Feasibility of Rehabilitation	217

Rehabilitation Bibliography 259

Index 269

Chapter 1

THE BACKGROUND

Every discussion of the nation's housing problem includes the potential share rehabilitation has in meeting our total housing requirements. That housing rehabilitation has become an integral part of public policy was highlighted by The President's Advisory Committee on Housing, which reported in 1953 that neither redevelopment nor rehabilitation and conservation could separately wipe out slums and check the spread of blight. Their report called for a program to "... remove houses and clear areas of our cities which are beyond recall" and "restore to sound condition all dwellings worth saving." [1] Government looks to rehabilitation as a method of providing the maximum number of standard houses for American families at the minimum economic cost.

The present capacity of the housing industry to supply new housing is formidable. The industry on the whole has been able to meet the dollar demand for new housing and still help governments in their publicly sponsored programs. The homebuilding industry produced on the average over one million units a year from 1949 through 1958, and the dollar volume for nonfarm residences in 1957 alone was slightly over

[1] *A Report to the President of the United States,* The President's Advisory Committee on Government Policies and Programs, December, 1953, p. 1.

$17 billion.[2] The industry also filled a growing demand for home improvements and repairs, variously estimated at from $6 billion to $14 billion a year.

In spite of these immense expenditures, the need for better housing still appears to outstrip our present performance. Some of the estimates for the required annual rate of construction during the period 1955–1960 range from 1.4 to 2.1 million units,[3] and all these imply a large concurrent volume of rehabilitation. What is needed is information on rehabilitation's potential in tapping new markets as yet barely touched: the house too sound for demolition, the neighborhood with unutilized purchasing power, or the substandard neighborhood where the residents have only a few dollars a month to spend but can obtain better housing standards through a partnership of private industry and public aids.

ACTION's over-all study of impediments in the housing market was designed to provide guides for public and private policy. The portion of the program represented by this volume studies the economic feasibility of rehabilitation to the private investor and to the financial institutions which share the risk. It also examines the significance of the economics of rehabilitation to the residents of rehabilitated housing and to governments in their housing and urban-renewal programs. The term "rehabilitation" generally includes everything from a badly needed coat of paint to virtual reconstruction. However, the primary emphasis of this volume is on rehabilitation which tangibly adds to the value of the structure in rents and potential selling price.

[2] U.S. Bureau of the Census, *Statistical Abstract of the United States: 1958*, p. 746, and Housing and Home Finance Agency, *Housing Statistics*, April, 1958, p. 19.
[3] *American Housing Statistics: Conditions, Supply, Demand*, American Council To Improve Our Neighborhoods, New York, 1956, p. 28.

Rehabilitation as a Business

Houses which are centuries old, found in the world's major cities, testify to the long-standing practice of rehabilitation. But the literature of the nineteenth century on the subject mentioned only the restoration of expensive homes with historic value rather than the business of more modest rehabilitation.

One of the earliest written evidences of remodeling homes for general family living appeared in a magazine called *Suburban Life*, first published in 1904. The magazine extolled rural living and offered practical advice on commuting, gardening, and home remodeling to any reader contemplating a move to the suburbs.[4] *Suburban Life*'s remodeling articles were the only signs of a rehabilitation business until World War I sent war workers scurrying to the cities, creating a monumental housing shortage. Speculative investment involving mass conversions became extremely profitable.[5] But rehabilitation went relatively unheralded in consumer and trade magazines until the late 1920s.

The parallel with today's activity is striking. The home-improvement movements of today were preceded by the Home Modernizing Bureau of National Industries, Inc., formed in April, 1928. Its motto was: "To increase property values, beautify the city, promote healthful living, make happier homes." Modernization was the appeal to homeowners: tear off the gingerbread trim, bring plumbing and heating up to date, and take full advantage of modern electrical equipment.[6]

[4] See Charles E. White, Jr., "The Transformation of an Old House," *Suburban Life*, vol. 11, December, 1910, pp. 359-360.
[5] Arthur Binns, a Philadelphia realtor, reported that many of his rehabilitation predecessors began working in this period.
[6] See "Modernizing Number," *Building Age*, vol. 5, January, 1929.

The business of rehabilitation was well known by the time the Great Depression clamped the lid on the economy. It continued at a slower pace throughout the 1930s, concentrating on conversion to small, low-rent units but with some home remodeling by lending institutions, designed to improve the sale of foreclosed properties.[7] Stimulus was given to remodeling work in this period by the advent of Federal Housing Administration Title I loans in 1934.

World War II saw the events of World War I repeated, with the Federal government through its National Housing Agency recommending rehabilitation as a means of economically filling wartime housing needs. The building boom following the war has been greater than that of the 1920s. Pressures to renew cities, improve houses, and provide better shelter for low-income families have been asserted with a vigor which only prosperity will allow.[8]

Outline of Investigation

This survey employs case studies based upon sixty-four interviews in ten cities conducted during late 1956 and during 1957 with public officials, bankers, and rehabilitators of wide experience.[9] The interviews were supplemented by twenty-six questionnaires from rehabilitators largely in cities other than those covered in the interviews. Also, the residents of rehabili-

---

[7] See discussion of selected activities of the Home Owners' Loan Corporation in Arthur Goodwillie, *Waverly—A Study of Neighborhood Conservation*, Home Loan Bank Board, 1940, 97 pp., illus., plans.

[8] See Appendix B for a fuller discussion of the rehabilitation movement in the last three decades, as told through rehabilitation studies of the past.

[9] The breakdown was 28 interviews with responsible public officials, 9 with bankers, and 27 with rehabilitators. The cities were Boston, New York, Newark, Philadelphia, Baltimore, Washington, Charlotte, Durham, St. Louis, and San Francisco. Washington and Philadelphia received the greatest attention.

tated dwellings in selected areas of Philadelphia and Chicago were sampled in a consumer study conducted jointly by ACTION and *Fortune* magazine in 1957. Additional consumer interviews were undertaken by the author in Washington, D.C.

It was decided to confine attention to those cities where the size and condition of the housing stock made rehabilitation particularly important, and to center-city rehabilitation of deteriorated dwellings, rather than outlying suburban remodeling. Interviews concentrated on commercial rehabilitators with a number of diverse operations to report rather than on homeowners with only a single remodeling experience. Because actual construction techniques are well covered in trade journals and other publications, only those structural problems which vitally affect the economics of the business were included in the text.

Some unavoidable but probably not significant biases have resulted from the approach used. Certain cities were selected for concentrated attention, but other cities with important efforts were not included in the study. This difficulty was not fully compensated for by the responses to questionnaires mailed to other cities. Rehabilitators, moreover, were more willing to give cost figures for their successes than their failures, only the most successful analyzing their losses. Cost figures even for successful projects were exceedingly difficult to obtain. Few rehabilitators keep detailed cost records, and the absence of accepted accounting procedures makes it difficult to compare the costs of different projects.

An exploration of all the side roads of the rehabilitation process was not possible. Some of the problems, important enough to justify independent studies, are the mortgage experience with older properties, the changes in potential rents of existing properties following additions of different types of community facilities or land uses, and architectural studies showing possibilities for blending new and existing properties.

In spite of its limitations, the study brings a new approach to the subject. Earlier studies usually examined the feasibility of remodeling individual structures to fit some predetermined set of physical standards (see Appendix B). This study investigates rehabilitation for different income groups, on both an individual structure and a neighborhood basis, examining the physical standards which are achieved by private investors under varying conditions of consumer demand and public activity.

The collected materials were assembled into three groupings based on family income and rents paid, using 1957 figures as a guide. The first describes some typical cases of rehabilitation for families with incomes over $7,500, and the capacity to pay shelter rents of $125 or more. The next describes rehabilitation for families with incomes between $3,500 and $7,500, who pay shelter rents between $50 and $125 a month. The third covers rehabilitation for families whose incomes are less than $3,500 a year, and who pay rents of less than $50 a month.[10]

The remaining chapters cover methods employed in locating a suitable market for rehabilitation, the process of estimating project cost, and a discussion and analysis of the role government plays in the rehabilitation process.

---

[10] The divisions used in the study do not correspond to a three-part statistical division of nonfarm families by total money income in 1956. If this had been done using census data, the low-income category would have included families with incomes somewhat higher than $3,500 and the upper-income category would have started at approximately $7,000. These figures were altered to bring the categories into line with definitions used by rehabilitators. (U.S. Bureau of the Census, *Income of Families and Persons in the United States: 1956*, ser. P-60, no. 27, April, 1958, p. 21, table 1.)

Two appendixes cover complementary case materials not complete enough to include in the text, and analyses of rehabilitation studies undertaken within the last thirty years. The purpose of this study is to highlight the economics of the rehabilitation process, and to demonstrate how businessmen and government officials can use rehabilitation to combat a part of the urban decay and raise the general standard of housing in our communities.

Chapter 2

PRESTIGE REHABILITATION

Prestige rehabilitation is the most striking form of modernization. The exteriors of these rehabilitated dwellings suggest high incomes, and the interiors are packed with modern conveniences. The result is particularly dramatic when rehabilitation takes place in areas which have been through an appreciable decline and where the incursion of prosperity contrasts sharply with the surrounding poverty.

Prestige rehabilitation will be defined here as residential rehabilitation for families with incomes in excess of $7,500 a year who are willing to pay shelter costs either in rent or in owner's expense of more than $125 per month. There are established areas of prestige rehabilitation in many cities: Boston's Beacon Hill, New York's Sutton Place, Washington's Georgetown. All these areas have characteristics in common. They were once living areas for the affluent, or near affluent, which over the years have declined in condition and value, and then have had much of their original value and character restored through renovation. The same process of decline and restoration can be seen for individual houses in stable, high-rent areas. However, this latter form of rehabilitation is so similar to the bulk of middle-income work, except for differences in physical standards and design, that it will not be covered in this discussion.[1] In the following pages we shall scrutinize specific instances of recent prestige rehabilitation in the central areas of Washington, Philadelphia, and San Francisco in order to identify the circumstances under which this form of investment can be profitably undertaken.

Foggy Bottom in Washington

Foggy Bottom is a low-lying area in the Northwest section of Washington, located west of the White House and south of Pennsylvania Avenue. In its early days, only small parts of Foggy Bottom had the prestige given other sections of Washington or that usually accorded current-day rehabilitation areas. It was laid out in 1768 by Jacob Funk as a rival Potomac River port to upstream Georgetown. Although some mansions were built along the river front and near the White House on the east, a greater part of the housing was built in the nineteenth century for workers in Washington's breweries, along her docks, and in the nearby gas works.[2]

The Bottom was not a glamorous place at the turn of the century. Behind a screen of acceptable houses, small alley row houses, devoid of conveniences, were occupied by low-income families. The alleys were narrow, unpaved, and unlit. These unsightly hovels, close to the White House but hidden from conscience's view, were to become the target of civic-minded bodies, which fought for the Alley Dwelling Law and the Board for the Condemnation of Insanitary Buildings.

[1] See Appendix A for examples of prestige remodeling in stable areas.
[2] Historical material from an article in the *Washington Post* by Edward T. Folliard, Mar. 27, 1949.

These same hovels were also to become one of the prime investment outlets for twentieth-century rehabilitators.

First, however, improvements to the environment had to overcome the public's distaste for the area before rehabilitation could begin. The Federal government undertook Lincoln Memorial in 1922, and shortly thereafter, Constitution Avenue, bordering the magnificent Mall between the Memorial and the Capitol. Then, in 1947, the State Department moved its offices to the area, adding a prestige significant in the minds of Washingtonians.

Other important changes included an enlargement of George Washington University, some scattered apartment construction in the late twenties, and the replacement of unsightly gas tanks by a complex of office and apartment buildings now called Potomac Plaza.

To the north of the Bottom, just across Rock Creek Park, Georgetown had been enjoying a lively resuscitation since the early thirties, but its success had increased local property values. The condition of the remaining unimproved houses was markedly below that of the first houses improved. Even with a high-income market inflated by rising standards of living, the supply of structures suitable for rehabilitation had become limited, and interest turned elsewhere.

It would be too simple to say that Foggy Bottom's rehabilitation was entirely due to the overspill from Georgetown, but this was certainly a contributing factor. If Georgetown was close to the center of Washington, Foggy Bottom was closer. If persons were willing to live in tiny houses in Georgetown, they should be willing to live in similar houses in Foggy Bottom. The selling price might have to be considerably lower, but the initial acquisition cost of the unimproved property would be lower as well.

One of the first projects was started on a triangular block in the southern end of the area. It was near the places of employment of a large number of potential consumers and was isolated from the blighting influences of the rest of the area by heavily trafficked streets. The first house was sold in November, 1952. These earlier projects were done in larger, better preserved houses along the main streets, and it was not until Dr. and Mrs. Jonas B. Robitscher began working in the area in 1953 that dwellings in the alleys were remodeled. The Robitschers thought that if the worst slums could be eliminated and a pleasant view provided for the patios of the main-street houses, rehabilitation could move ahead more rapidly than ever. Other rehabilitators grasped this notion with alacrity.

Green's Court and Snow's Court were started in 1953 and Hughes Court was begun in 1954. New investment corporations were being formed, and a conservative estimate places the number of structures rehabilitated by 1958 at between 300 and 350. Added to these were new apartment and office buildings, and the total activity provides a visible impact from any street corner in the Bottom.

Two specific rehabilitation projects will be considered in detail. One was a project undertaken by inexperienced investors with the professional guidance of Charles Norris. The other was a project undertaken by Dr. and Mrs. Robitscher without prior experience or professional guidance. The sharp contrast between the number and size of problems faced by the Robitschers and Norris in their work clarifies the differences between the work of nonprofessionals and professionals, their expectations concerning the future of Foggy Bottom, and the roles played by local housing and renewal officials.

REHABILITATION UNDER PROFESSIONAL GUIDANCE

In January, 1955, Norris sold five row houses in partly revived Hughes Court to a group of three men forming the Wiland Corporation. The houses were only 12.5 feet wide. Light was provided by kerosene lamps, water by an outdoor hydrant, heating and cooking facilities were a wood stove for each house, and the units had backyard toilets.

The Wiland Corporation gutted the buildings and built new homes into freshly tuck-pointed shells.[3] They put in new plumbing, heating, wiring, air conditioning, compact kitchens with built-in cabinets, tiled baths, concrete basements, hardwood floors, interior fireplaces, a brick patio fenced with cypress staves, and complete interior decoration. An architect with experience in Georgetown designed the houses, and the entire job was contracted.

This project took considerably longer than originally anticipated. Surveys, easements, and clearance of title had to be handled carefully because of the many problems involved with properties of this kind. Building permits were not easy to obtain. The Alley Dwelling Law of 1914, which prohibited construction in alleys, had been repealed, and a 1934 law calling for the gradual elimination of alley dwellings was then amended. However, the status of alley rehabilitation was not clear, and special permission was needed until a clarifying amendment to the Zoning Regulations was passed in May, 1956.

[3] Gutting the buildings is initially more expensive but avoids the unexpected, which could ultimately cost much more. See Francis Lammer, "Rehabilitation Has Taken Three Forms in Philadelphia," *Journal of Housing*, vol. 12, no. 2, February, 1955, for an example of expenses that could have been avoided by gutting.

The first three houses in Hughes Court sold within ninety days of completion for $16,500 each. The fourth house, begun after the first three were completed, was sold at about the time the work began, and the fifth sold shortly thereafter. The initial acquisition cost of the units was about $4,000 each (with the settlement costs, architectural fees, and building permits included). The work cost approximately $9,000, and with the buildings selling for $16,500, the $3,500 profit equaled 21 per cent of sale price (see Table 1).

TABLE 1. Typical Breakdown of Costs on Hughes Court Property

Property (settlement, permits, plans, etc.)	$4,000
Labor costs	3,860
Plumbing	900
Electrical	375
Heating	350
Air conditioning	260
Floor and tilework	600
Materials	1,900
Roofing and skylight	100
Appliances	250
Painting	200
Fence, grading, patio, and barbecue	100
Financing expenses	140
Total	$13,035
Sale price	16,500
Profit (21% of sale price)	$ 3,465

Source: Wiland Corporation. Cost figures do not include real property taxes paid during the period the property was held.

Financing the operation was difficult and made selling the properties equally difficult. Most lending institutions were not interested because of the project's alley location and doubtful future. When mortgage commitments for buyers were finally obtained from a local savings and loan association, they were so low that the Wiland Corporation had to take deferred-purchase-money mortgages, which were still held by the members of the development corporation in 1957. No construction loans were used, since the money was provided by the Wiland Corporation.

The mortgage picture has improved in Foggy Bottom since these early projects. Edward Britt of the Home Building Association, Norris's recent financial source, says he welcomes rehabilitation business. Britt says he has had better experience with Foggy Bottom rehabilitation mortgages than with many mortgages on new suburban properties. He lists several reasons. First, the small houses are economical to run, with low utility charges and repair bills. Second, transportation expenses are low because the Bottom is in the core of the city. Third, the families are somewhat older and financially more responsible. And last, the down-payment requirements are relatively high so that only families with high incomes or large savings, compared with the price of the house, can afford to buy in the Bottom. However, this is a view which is far from typical in lending circles.

In merchandising the houses in Hughes Court, Norris had to forget the usual selling methods and invent new ones. He had designed the houses and planned his sales campaign with particular buyers in mind. What did Hughes Court offer a consumer? Norris offered the following property description:

> As you enter the house you step into a small foyer, facing the staircase with the wrought-iron stair rail; on the north side is the kitchen, small but compact, with handmade pine cabinets, a steel wall oven and table-top stove, garbage dispose-all, deepfreeze-top refrigerator, and a good counter and storage space. The corner brick fireplace is a big feature, as are the pegged oak floors.
> *West View of the Patio.* This highlights the barbecue fireplace

which is already in regular use. Note the electric outlets to the left of the French doors so that coffee can be brewed or bread toasted if you want to breakfast as well as dine out here.[4]

The center-city location was, of course, an important selling feature, and to dramatize this, Norris placed a sign on Virginia Avenue near the entrance to Rock Creek Park Freeway which leads to the Maryland suburbs and the bridges to Virginia. The sign said, "If you lived here, you'd be home now." A nearby traffic light piling up the cars during the evening rush hours gave the drivers a good look. The newspapers carried articles about the sign, and people began to think more seriously of Foggy Bottom's advantages.

The buyers were not young families with children but couples and single persons "who immediately recognized that there wasn't any other place where they could find the independence and stability of homeownership with such inexpensive maintenance, convenience of location, and association with historic background as in these little, charming town homes." [5]

Few families with children live in remodeled Bottom houses because they are small and because the District's public schools have a Negro enrollment of over 50 per cent. Of fifty-two households in Foggy Bottom, only two had school-age children. Each household had a joint income in excess of $8,000; one-half were employed by the government and the remainder in varied professions. Only three of the families had lived in the suburbs immediately prior to moving to the Bottom. Ex-

---
[4] Charles L. Norris, "How to Market Rehabilitated Property," *Modernizing Homes for a Profit*, National Association of Real Estate Boards, Washington, pp. 23–27.
[5] *Op. cit.*, p. 27.

actly half lived in the center city and the remainder were new residents in Washington.

REHABILITATION BY NONPROFESSIONALS

Dr. and Mrs. Jonas B. Robitscher rehabilitated twenty-two houses from 1953 to 1956 while living in Foggy Bottom. While profits were not great, their investments made more than would have been possible through other available outlets. Their gross profits amounted to somewhat less than $40,000; however, most of these profits were tied up in second mortgages.

The first seven houses were done as a single project in Snow's Court during 1953 and 1954. Snow's Court was an expression of the idea that if the interior of the block could be successfully improved, the exterior could easily follow suit. This particular court had a special advantage, since twenty of its buildings were owned by a single individual. Complicated title problems were thus avoided, and enough houses were obtained in a single purchase to ensure a substantial core of improvement. Other houses on the edge of the court continued to be occupied by lower-income Negro families.

The Robitschers did their own designing but employed an architect to check their plans and prepare working drawings acceptable to the contractor and the District building inspectors. The plans and designs were similar to those later used in the Hughes Court project. The interior was gutted and a completely new structure built into the shell. As a second step in the rehabilitation of Snow's Court, the Robitschers completed a row of nine additional houses.

The nine houses cost $27,000, were remodeled for $80,050 (a total investment of $107,050), and sold for $135,000. The assessment rose from $400 to $4,000. The $28,000 profit equaled 20.7 per cent of the sale price (see Table 2).

TABLE 2. Breakdown of Costs on Snow's Court Property

Acquisition costs		$ 27,000
Remodeling costs:		
Electrical wiring, fixtures	$ 2,700	
Brick work	9,000	
Air conditioning, heating	8,700	
Landscaping	600	
Roofing	3,000	
Ironwork	450	
Screens, weather stripping, Venetian blinds	800	
Plastering	6,000	
Insulation	500	
Plumbing	10,000	
Formica, sinks, linoleum, medicine cabinets	1,650	
Refrigerators and stoves	2,100	
Painting	4,000	
Steel and concrete	1,250	
Sanding floors	900	
Tiling	1,200	
Lumber	12,000	
Labor (carpenters and day laborers)	12,000	
Insurance	1,200	
Hardware	1,500	
Architect	500	
Total		80,050
		$107,050
Sale price		135,000
Profit (20.7% of sale price)		$27,950

Source: *ACTION Rehabilitation Questionnaire*. (Cost figures do not include property taxes or the cost of equity investment during the period the properties were held.)

The Robitschers needed $30,000 in cash to carry out the two-step project. Fortunately, they were able to assume existing mortgages on the houses, which defrayed a small part of the total cost. The remaining cash was raised by borrowing from relatives and friends, and by raising additional loans using bonds and life insurance policies as collateral. This was barely enough to complete the initial purchase of the houses and meet the contractor's first payment. The contractor

Snow's Court, Washington, before work began.

wanted four equal payments during the construction period, the last of which he agreed to defer until after the completed houses were sold. The two middle payments were met by selling two of the houses at cost for cash several months before they were completed and occupied.

Small first mortgages were obtained for the buyers only

after the project was completed, and the Robitschers had to co-sign for these. The mortgages averaged $7,500, with terms of fifteen years at 5 per cent. They had to take back second mortgages for the difference between an average equity of $3,500 and the amount of the first mortgages. These were with terms of eight years at 5½ per cent and represented most of the profits from their work. Even though financing became

Snow's Court, Washington, after project completion and sale.

easier after this first project, their starting capital was already tied up in mortgages so that they could not undertake any more work without selling the second mortgages at discounts of 5 per cent or more, thus reducing their profits. Since they were not willing to do this, in a sense they "remodeled themselves out of the remodeling business."

Their first financing was obtained from a Georgetown savings and loan association that had put some funds into rehabilitation projects there. Later, they were able to find both mortgages and construction loans from another association. At no time, however, did these loans total more than 50 per cent of the final selling price of any house, selling prices which grew larger each year.

The Robitschers' relations with the district government were described as difficult.

> Most of the health officials, zoning board members, and building inspectors let us know in one way or another that they didn't think the houses in Foggy Bottom were worth remodeling and were very unsympathetic to our plans. No district official has offered to add street lights, improve sidewalks, put in a park, or otherwise help the area, although almost half the houses have now been renovated by private individuals.[6]

The Robitschers were particularly troubled by three aspects of their contacts with the local government. First, the properties were condemned shortly after they were purchased, and frequent inspections caused costly delays in the progress of the work (not to mention the expense of boarding up the houses not under construction). Second, the Zoning Board of Appeals was initially unsympathetic to attempts by area property owners to block the path of commercial parking lots adjacent to their newly rehabilitated units, but later upheld the residential character of the community as the neighborhood improved. Third, the taxes were increased on the improved properties but not on adjacent properties. Thus, the owners of unimproved properties could watch their values

[6] *ACTION Rehabilitation Questionnaire.*

rise without contributing to, and in fact detracting neighborhood improvement.

Although the Robitschers' work was modestly pr(cannot be concluded that other inexperienced reha necessarily could have overcome the problems they met. At almost any point in the process their success could have turned to failure.

ENTER: URBAN RENEWAL

The local government faces many decisions in Foggy Bottom. New Federal construction and a major north-south inner-loop highway are planned for the near future. But the government of the district has its most delicate conciliatory role in integrating the different plans and aspirations of neighborhood interest groups in an urban-renewal program. The area is now zoned to allow apartment construction up to eight stories, but renewal policies may cause a change.

Two groups with different visions for Foggy Bottom's future have disagreed on the issue of urban renewal, with the local government in the middle. The groups might be characterized as "professional" and "nonprofessional" rehabilitators. The nonprofessionals are those who have had no experience in real estate investment prior to their first rehabilitation project, make their living in other fields, and possibly may make no further real estate investments. The professionals were, are, and always will be real estate investors by training and experience.

The nonprofessionals through a specially formed Foggy Bottom Restoration Association petitioned the local government for, and received, urban-renewal-area designation for approximately half of the Bottom.[7] The reasons behind the request are best stated by Mrs. Robitscher:

> Why do we want a renewal plan when rehabilitation is advancing at such a rapid rate without it? Because we have discovered that in spite of all the efforts that individual remodelers exert there are always holdouts who would rather preserve the slum status, and land speculators who press for commercial zoning in a downtown residential neighborhood. We have also discovered that remodeling in a blighted area is a major problem since the banks and mortgage companies consider half-blighted neighborhoods too risky; so we remodelers need the government-guaranteed mortgages which are available for officially designated urban renewal areas.[8]

The group sees the future of Foggy Bottom as an in-lying residential neighborhood, well endowed with community facilities and with a minimum of traffic-producing land uses such as apartment buildings and parking lots.

On the other hand, the urban-renewal-area designation was questioned by many local property owners and professional real estate investors. The *Washington Post and Times Herald* (December 8, 1954) said of their opposition:

> Some owners, according to remodelers, are reluctant to remodel or sell to remodelers because there is a feeling in the neighborhood that the nearby multi-million-dollar Potomac Plaza project will bring additional apartment construction to the area, thus increasing land values.

The conflict between the two groups can best be illustrated by the story of a single property. Mrs. Robitscher said that she

---

[7] The Foggy Bottom Renewal Area and the George Washington University Renewal area were designated at approximately the same time and cover about one-half of the Bottom. Under the Housing Act of 1954, urban-renewal-area designation necessarily precedes the availability of FHA mortgage insurance.

[8] Supplied by Mrs. Robitscher. (The types of mortgages referred to are those insured by FHA under Section 220 of the National Housing Act, which permits mortgages up to 97 per cent of the first $13,500 of appraised value, 85 per cent of $13,500 to $16,000, and 70 per cent of $16,000 to $20,000.)

and her contractor were offered a large, main-street house for $9,000. The house was purchased by another investor and was put back on the market for $11,000 before they could buy it.

This move might be explained by the reluctance of professional investors to see the remodeling of houses on larger lots which might be more profitably used as apartment or—assuming a zoning change—office sites. Thus the professionals strive for the highest prospective yield from the site while the nonprofessionals trade some of the future gains for more immediate returns, from what they consider a more rational use of the land.

The local government will have to reconcile such differences and at the same time determine the sort of urban-renewal program that will meet the future needs of the community as a whole. The task is admittedly great because it involves the problems of rising land costs, increasing costs of government operations, declining revenues, disruption of neighborhoods, and the redistribution of part of the Negro population, but even greater progress than has been accomplished to date is needed. One Washington rehabilitator claimed that the city's indecision was the worst obstacle to renewal efforts. City officials, however, remain convinced that moving ahead without studies of the possible effects of various programs might create chaos.

What have been the effects of the government's delay in Foggy Bottom? There has been no single effect beyond an uncertainty about the Bottom's future. Urban-renewal designation in the Bottom will be hailed as a tremendous success if the city's renewal plan can tread the narrow line between the conflicting points of view of neighborhood groups. However, it is unlikely that there will be much action until the

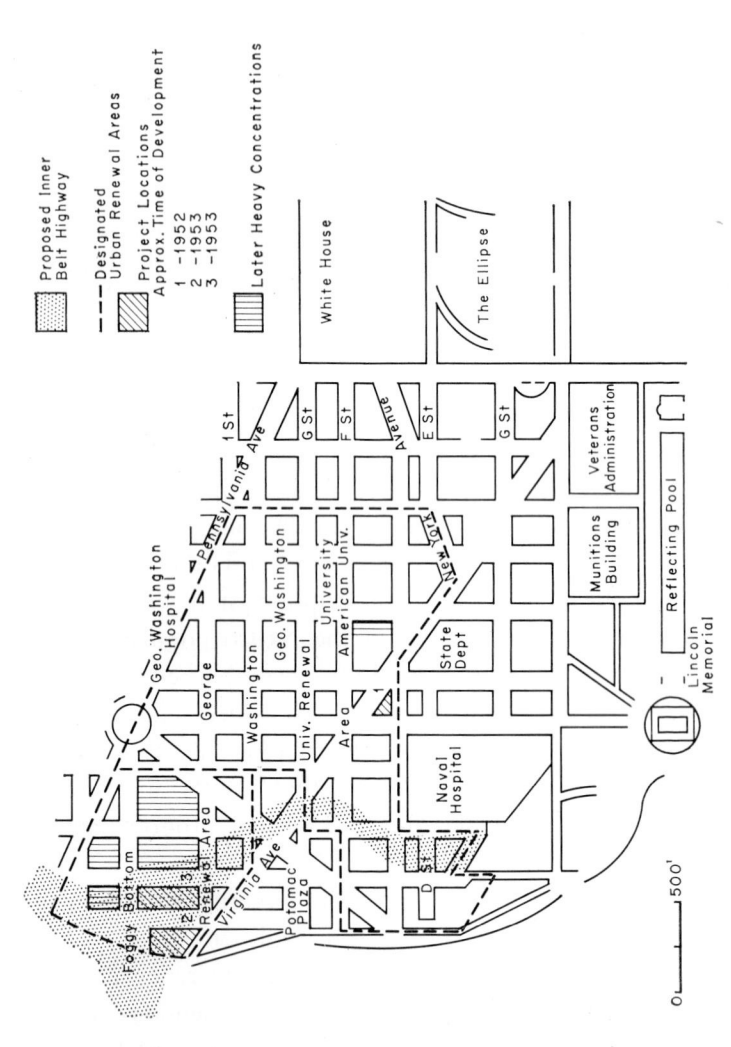

Map 1. Foggy Bottom—private rehabilitation and public plans.

relocation problem and some complicated planning problems are solved.[8a] This might take as long as five years.

Through the experience of two rehabilitators working in one area, most of the aspects of prestige rehabilitation have been touched upon. Prestige rehabilitation is economically feasible for an individual investor wherever there is a market for the finished product, but the picture can be complicated by the presence of competing land uses and the possibility that the market for prestige rehabilitation will not accord with public policy predicated on a long-term plan for the community's future. The feasibility of each project is determined by a congeries of factors, public and private. The answer may differ for the long and the short run, according to the particular interest of the investor or public official who raises the question.

Upper-income Rehabilitation in Philadelphia: A Comparative Case

Although the rate of prestige rehabilitation has been much slower in Philadelphia than in Washington and the areas of rehabilitation more concentrated, the beginnings extend back before World War I. While there has been a recent tendency for rehabilitation for middle- and low-income groups to spread throughout the city, prestige rehabilitation is still concentrated in two clusters near the main downtown parks. Prestige rehabilitation was probably given its impetus by owner-occupants who remodeled to live in the heart of the city.

Here, as in Washington, there is no single large-scale com-

[8a] Not the least of these planning problems is the construction of a highway which threatens to wipe out a good part of the recently remodeled dwellings, the land acquisition cost of which is greatly increased by continued remodeling activity (see Map 1).

mercial rehabilitator responsible for the bulk of the work, many people with many backgrounds having contributed their share. One of the two areas most affected includes a mixture of sales and rental rehabilitation in the southwest quadrant of the central city near the Schuylkill River, and illustrates the rules of area selection used by most rehabilitators. The second area, in the southeast quadrant of the central city, demonstrates incremental growth. It was built piece by piece, with each new project eliminating the least desirable features surrounding the already completed portions.

FITLER SQUARE AREA

The area near the Schuylkill surrounds Fitler Square, a small park no larger than one-half a block, having a few benches, a few trees, a drinking fountain, and a concrete turtle for climbing children. The section is an extension of the Rittenhouse Square area, the focal point of center-city upper-income families. The Fitler Square section is isolated from the main stream of center-city traffic because central Philadelphia narrows near its downtown, cutting off many of the through north-south streets. Fitler Square lies west of the most westerly through north-south street. Moreover, east-west street traffic is channeled north and south of the area over the Schuylkill River bridges.

Most of the two- and three-story row houses were built shortly after the Civil War. The smaller houses, located in narrow, cobbled alleys, are usually "bandbox" houses, three stories high, each story containing a single room. Steep, winding staircases join the floors. Most of them have had a shed added to the back containing a small kitchen. Yard toilets were common. The large houses lined the main streets. Many were built as mansions extending one hundred or more feet from

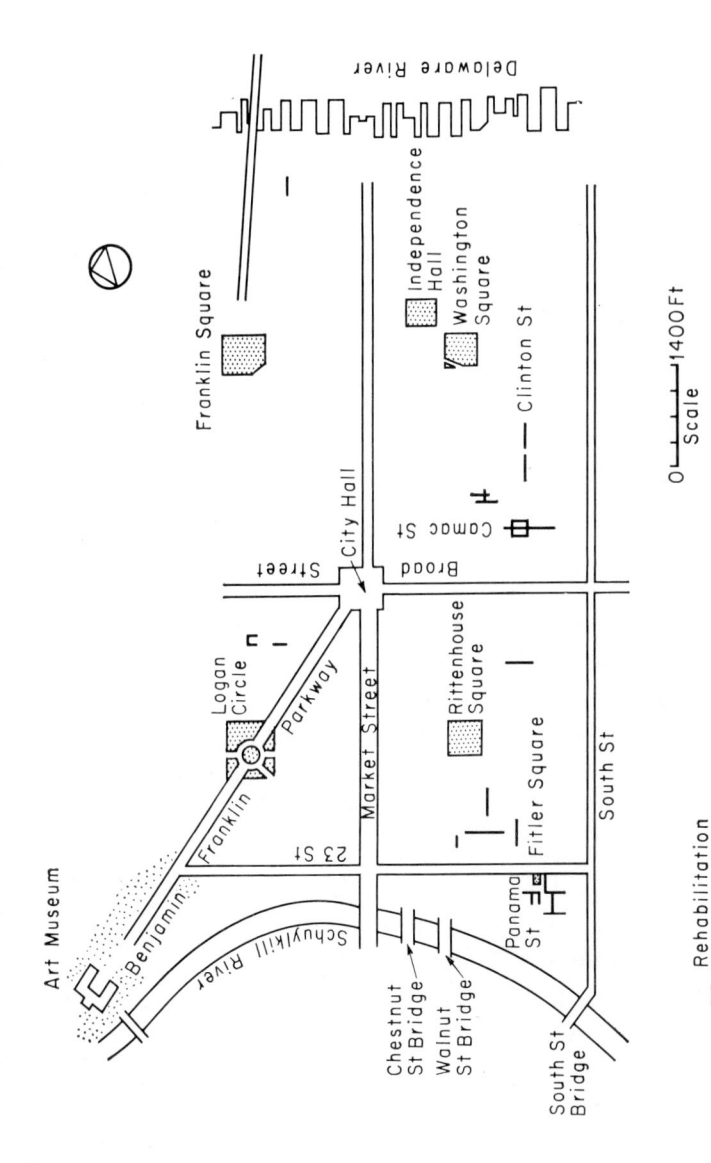

Map 2. Rehabilitation in central Philadelphia—1957.

the front of the lot. For the most part, these large old houses do not permit sales rehabilitation and have been converted to high-rental efficiency apartments. However, a few have been purchased by single families, and some have had the first floor turned into a private garage, leaving the remaining two floors for living space.

David Williams was one of the early rehabilitators in the area who, along with Mrs. Halsey Manning and Brinton Young, rehabilitated fourteen of the houses on Panama Street beginning in 1942. He later moved the locus of his operations to other areas, but his methods remain unchanged. Rehabilitation is his business and he does most of the tasks in the process himself. He purchases the house, redesigns it, supervises construction (using his own crew of carpenters and plasterers for the rough work and subcontracting for the plumbing, heating, and wiring), acts as his own salesman, and finally obtains mortgage commitments for prospective buyers. Typically, he buys the house for about $5,000, puts in $8,000 to $10,000 in repairs, and sells it for $15,000 to $16,000.

The houses on Panama Street were old but structurally sound. They were small, many of them bandboxes, but could be enlarged to suit the needs of a childless couple. The street itself was cobbled and so narrow that a car's tires scraped the curbs in passing. Today, the brightly painted houses leading down the street from Fitler Square offer an Old World charm that is rarely found in American cities.

Williams guts the buildings judiciously. First the ceiling plaster comes down, for even where not cracked, removal is necessary to permit inspection and repair of joists. Floors are sanded and refinished rather than replaced. Wall plaster is left on if possible and covered with a new coat after wiring and plumbing work is completed. The cellars are deepened and cemented. Each house gets new plumbing and heating, new wiring, new windows and doors where necessary, and a bright, pastel face. Williams tries to save any interesting feature which will have historic appeal for potential buyers: interesting mantels or solid old doors. Doorknockers are prized, and if the building possesses an old fire insurance emblem, it is proudly kept in place.

Mrs. Manning's early designs of façades and patios have become standards for other rehabilitators throughout the city. Window boxes and bright pastel surfaces brighten the fronts, and brick terraces reached from the living rooms through French doors give the rear of the units privacy and charm. These patios are small, since Williams and other rehabilitators usually add a cinder-block extension to house a kitchen or enlarge the living room. The extension might include a second story to provide a small bedroom or space for a bathroom.

As in Washington, finding financing was difficult even when money was easily obtainable for new residential building. Usually the construction and original acquisition are financed out of Williams's own pocket; the only contact with financial institutions has been in connection with mortgage commitments for buyers. Savings and loan associations and private trusts have been the most sympathetic to his operation. Usually loans are for 50 to 75 per cent of the selling price at 6 per cent interest, for periods of between ten and twenty years (see Table 3).

The purchasers of these homes, like their Washington counterparts, have been mostly childless couples in their middle years. Some have lived in suburban communities while their children were growing up, and moved back to the city after the children left home; but most have had no children and have never left the city. The rental units are often occupied by young, childless working couples whose joint income allows them to pay the higher rents of in-city houses. Most of the families, like those in Washington, are professionals working in the center city and availing themselves of the cultural and recreational facilities of the center city.

TABLE 3. Breakdown of Typical Costs on Williams Project, Philadelphia

Acquisition cost			$ 3,500
Remodeling costs:			
Excavation and foundation	$ 800		
Plumbing and kitchen	1,800		
Heating	1,200		
Carpentry	2,700		
Plastering	700		
Painting	500		
Electricity	225		
Roofing and insulation	380		
		8,305	
Total		$11,805	
Sale price		13,800	
Profit (14.5% of sale price)			$1,995

Source: "Fighting Blight at a Profit," *House & Home*, October, 1953, pp. 161–164.

There has been little contact with the local government, since no urban-renewal plans are underway in the Fitler Square area.

One interesting aspect of the Fitler Square area has been the construction of a group of 20-foot row houses selling for about $17,000 a half block from Panama Street. Earl James of the Robert J. Nash Realty Company, which built them, said they sold rapidly to the same kinds of families who bought the rehabilitated units. New construction was possible because the site had been a lumber yard, keeping land costs low, and because rehabilitation experience in the area helped pinpoint the potential market.

CAMAC STREET AREA

The other major prestige-rehabilitation area centers around Camac Street in the southeast quadrant of the old city. It is composed of a network of small, lightly trafficked streets. The predominant form of rehabilitation in this complex is done by individual owners who have contracted for remodeling. (The work of individual owners has been the basis of a flourishing antique trade in fire emblems, door knockers, and coach lamps.) A few of the larger houses have been remodeled by commercial investors as rental property. More recently some of the small houses have been remodeled by nonprofessionals who rent them to other families.

Charles La Grossa is a center-city realtor who has done very little rehabilitation himself but indirectly has made an important contribution to the rehabilitation of Camac Street. He purchases an unimproved house for between $1,500 (in the early days) and $4,000, and then sells it to a private family who wants to live in a center-city home. In selling the house, La Grossa describes how the house might be improved, tells what work needs to be done, and estimates the approximate costs of bringing it up to an acceptable standard. He also gives the prospective buyer a list of remodeling contractors who have worked in the area at reasonable prices. If the sale goes through, he will help the buyer obtain financing and check occasionally to see that the work is going well.

His direct profits from each rehabilitated structure are restricted to his commission on sales and his fees for arranging financing. He may also receive a small commission from the contract remodeler doing the work. However, these are not the only profits arising from his efforts. Since a majority of his brokerage business and property investments are concentrated in this area, he also benefits through increased value of property he owns and through higher brokerage commissions.

His contribution to rehabilitation has been unique. On his walks through the area he spots obstacles to renewal and plans for their removal. For example, an unsightly junk yard lay across the street from some newly rehabilitated houses. La Grossa helped buy the yard, clear it, and put a taxpaying parking lot on the site instead. When houses are too large for sales rehabilitation but tarnish the general aspect of the neighborhood, he will try to find a buyer to improve the building. Since the area has had no real shopping facilities, La Grossa with a few associates purchased a group of lots large enough to house a neighborhood market. Of course this was profitable to themselves, but more important, it contributed to the renascence of the neighborhood.

One of the rental rehabilitators in the area is Milton Hollander, who has acquired more than twenty large row houses since World War II. Most of his rehabilitation work is located on Clinton Street, a tree-lined block in central Philadelphia near the attractive grounds of the Pennsylvania Hospital. The houses are of brick construction, 3½ stories in height, many 20 by 120 feet in size, and built over a hundred years ago for large families with comfortable incomes.

The condition of the buildings was basically sound. Hollander estimated that no more than 10 per cent of the woodwork was rotted. He was continually surprised by the rich variety of details beneath the grimy surfaces of walls, floors, and staircases. In one case, a layer of cement had been laid over a beautiful wood floor. He found marble fireplaces covered by brick, sliding oak doors sealed into the walls, or brass fixtures tarnished beyond immediate recognition. Very often these items could be inexpensively reclaimed, adding to the attractiveness of the finished apartments.

Hollander converted each structure into six apartments: two on each of the first two floors, and two out of the third and fourth floors. The apartments contain two rooms, kitchen and bath. The common hall space is well lighted by brass fixtures, highlighting polished staircases to the upper floors. Each apartment has at least one marble fireplace and all-new kitchen and bath fixtures. The apartments on the top floor are quite unusual. The fourth floor has sloping eaves rising from the front and rear of the house. Hollander had the fourth floor cut away from the front and rear to a point towards the center of the house where there was 7 feet clearance from floor to roof. This formed a balcony large enough to be used as an extra room. The balcony is reached by the old attic stairs.

One of Hollander's assets is the warm relationship he has built up with his foreman, with whom he works closely on every phase of the job. The cost estimates are a joint process, supervision is shared, and although Hollander does the interior designing, his final plan is made only after they have jointly scrutinized the probable costs of several schemes. As on most of these projects, Hollander uses his own crew for everything but the most technical jobs such as plumbing, heating, and electrical wiring.

The actual rentals of the properties are somewhat below the price set for prestige rehabilitation, but the quality of the work and the nature of the finished product are in the luxury category. The average rent is approximately $100 a month plus gas and electricity for a one-bedroom unit. Typical cost figures for one of Hollander's houses are $16,000 for acquisition and $21,000 for rehabilitation. The gross rent runs about

$6,480 a year, with a net rent after operating expenses including debt service on an $18,000 mortgage of $2,740, thus yielding a rate of return of 14.4 per cent on his remaining equity.

In merchandising his units Hollander decided to direct his campaign to working couples employed within walking distance of his units. Since the apartments are located in the insurance district and next to the Pennsylvania Hospital, he sent advertising flyers to the personnel offices of these firms as well as advertising in the classified sections of the local papers. Apparently the flyers had unexpected effects. Many of his tenants said the flyer's contents had reached them by word of mouth.

His working-couple tenants have joint incomes between $6,000 and $10,000 and no children. These families are somewhat younger than those purchasing rehabilitated houses. Their equity position and current incomes are not as strong. Where prestige rental units are more costly, many of the families living in them seem to be willing to stretch their budget to cover the added costs rather than live in more modest housing, thereby saving the equity needed to buy.

Like many other rehabilitators, Hollander thinks the government can help most by encouraging more liberal financing. Hollander obtains a mortgage commitment to purchase and remodel the property at its improved value before acquiring the property. When he first began, he was lucky to get 60 to 65 per cent of the appraised value of the improved property as a mortgage, which amount might actually be only 50 per cent of the investment in the property. The amount of the mortgage relative to his costs has increased with his experience, and once or twice he reports receiving a mortgage for per cent of his investment.

Philadelphia's local government does not face the same problems as Washington in devising a program for center-city renewal. The demands for apartment and office buildings are ⟨be⟩ing met largely outside renewal areas. But every rehabilitation project further contracts the supply of housing available ⟨for the⟩ rapidly expanding Negro population. The city favors ⟨rehabi⟩litation and would like to help with more community ⟨facil⟩ities and urban-renewal-area designation, permitting FHA ⟨22⟩0 financing, but it must move slowly until the supply of ⟨Ne⟩gro housing can be expanded through new construction or until further racial integration of neighborhoods meets with broader public acceptance.

One renewal area located near Independence Hall was begun in 1956. The project complements a series of parks being constructed to set off Independence Hall as a national shrine. The advantage of Federal park facilities was too good an opportunity to be bypassed by public officials and private investors interested in the long range development of the city.

A Rental Rehabilitator Gets There First: San Francisco

There are comparatively few large, high-rent units supplied through rehabilitation in either Washington or Philadelphia. The market for apartments of two or more bedrooms is met through new construction. In a few cases in other cities, rehabilitated units have captured the market for large apartments before new apartment construction could begin.

An example of early and profitable rental rehabilitation is a unit done on San Francisco's Telegraph Hill by Architect John Campbell. The structure is located on a steep slope falling ⟨awa⟩y down-street from both the entrance of the building and ⟨to⟩ward the back of the lot, giving the effect of a small one-⟨st⟩ory frame house on the front, with three stories in the rear, the bottom story being a basement at ground level. Originally the building had two railroad apartments on each floor, with rooms opening off a long, narrow hall. The rear rooms were darkened by a wooden service porch with a staircase descending to the yard. Downtown San Francisco, rising before the distant backdrop of the bay, could be seen from the back porches.

An antiquated kitchen on Telegraph Hill in San Francisco.

The purchase price was $14,000; remodeling provided two units on the top floor, one large two-bedroom and two-bath unit on the second floor, and a single efficiency unit in the ground-level basement at a cost of $20,000. Campbell used a construction loan for the actual work and later refinanced the building with a $25,000 first mortgage at 6 per cent. The gross rental return is $575 a month, or $6,900 a year. Assuming an operating ratio of 60 per cent of the gross rent, the net rent would be $2,750 a year. Since Campbell has an equity of $9,000, this yields an estimated return on the equity of 30.7 per cent.

There is little doubt that the high rate of return is attributable in large measure to the excellent design of the units themselves. The long hall remains but has lost its dinginess and

Good design makes the antiquated kitchen a modern living room.

sense of narrowness through the use of pictures, and by enlarging the entrances to sunlit rooms. What had been three bedrooms and a kitchen in the top-floor apartments is now two bedrooms, with a large living room, opening on a patio through wide glass doors, and a kitchenette and bath carved out of the third bedroom. Fireplaces were added to the living rooms. The clean lines, paneled walls, modern equipment and light fixtures, and the view create a total effect that is little short of spectacular.[9]

The project was an unqualified financial success. New construction would entail a greater capital outlay and probably yield a smaller net percentage return on investment because potential rents are limited in the early days of neighborhood renewal. However, if the potential rents were rising rapidly, new construction soon might be more profitable than rehabilitation.

When Is Prestige Rehabilitation Economically Feasible?

Rehabilitation is feasible if there is an effective demand for units in a specific location at rents or sale prices permitting suppliers to fill the demand.

LOCATION

An area undergoing prestige rehabilitation must create its own environment isolating it from the blighting influences of its low-rent surroundings. Where such an environment exists in the form of an already advanced rehabilitation area or a bastion of high-rent housing, selecting a project site is relatively simple. A rehabilitator planning a new project area ordinarily utilizes existing natural barriers such as parks, major streets, or public facilities as boundaries. These boundaries separate the daily activities of high- and low-rent neighbors. They permit the tenants of the new project, no matter how small, to go to and from work, shopping centers, and recreational activities without unpleasant social contacts. Ideally a new prestige area is bounded on one side by a well-patrolled

---

[9] Material on Campbell derived from "Look Behind the Dirt and Find a Gold Mine," *House & Home*, October, 1954, pp. 106–108, and from *ACTION Rehabilitation Questionnaire*, 1957.

park, on another by a speedy public transit line, on a third by an efficient block of stores, and on the fourth by a public school. Failing such unusual circumstances, the minimum requirement is access through an attractive corridor to all the uses essential to daily life. The importance of "natural" barriers lessens as the difference between the rents of newly rehabilitated units and those of its neighbors diminishes.

SELECTING THE STRUCTURE

Once the rehabilitator has decided on an area of likely investment, the next problem is selecting a structure or structures. Acceptable physical condition and the location of the structure depend upon the amount of rehabilitation already completed. Much more careful attention is usually given to the condition of the structure in the early phases of a rehabilitation movement, because the rehabilitator's repair budget is limited by a relatively low selling price and the physical standards needed to sell the units are higher than later in the movement. Interior reconstruction is a normal feature of prestige rehabilitation, and considerable latitude in interior conditions is possible. But the exterior walls and foundations are another matter, and rehabilitators try to find a sound shell. Tangible salvage value inside and out is treated as an unexpected bonus.

The selection of the structure is a function of the economics of the rehabilitation area. A relatively poor structure may be acceptable if the relationship between the acquisition cost and the potential sale price truly reflects the amount of repairs needed to bring the structure up to community standards. In Georgetown more and more marginal structures were rehabilitated as the rising selling price pulled away from the acquisition costs. Finally, however, the price gap narrowed as the potential sale price leveled off, thus making commercial rehabilitation more difficult. A great deal of the work done in Georgetown today is being done by contractors for private owners.

Obviously, the key element in structure selection is the eventual selling price, a relatively simple figure to find if the trend is well advanced. A rehabilitator in St. Louis adds 10 per cent to the average market price of comparable houses in the neighborhood. Other rehabilitators are content to take the average price of similarly improved houses. If there is any doubt of the price being sufficient to cover the cost of the work and still leave a profit, some rehabilitators offer a potential buyer the option of buying the house unimproved and remodeling it himself or making a contract to purchase and improve the house for him.

DESIGNING THE PROJECT

Most prestige rehabilitators employ an architect experienced in remodeling to ensure the use of design features appealing to prestige buyers. In all cases the completed units mirror the homes of the community leaders past and present. In both Washington and Philadelphia the completed house has a traditional exterior and a modern interior. Brick walks and stoops, iron hand rails, shutters, coach lamps, and door knockers of the Federal or Colonial period are commonly found on the exterior.

The rear yard becomes a garden or patio, usually with a brick pavement and either a brick wall or stave fence to assure privacy. If there is enough space, a barbecue, fish pond, or fountain is popular. Unless the brickwork is very new, painting the exterior facing in pastel shades gives the house a fresh look and can hide minor defects. On the interior, the floors must be in good condition although they need not be new. Pegged hardwood floors are popular. Open planning is used even in a small house to give the unit the feeling of space. If the house is small, it is preferable to have a large living room with a dining area delineated by a different floor level, hand rail, or low room divider.

The walls in all rooms are usually painted in unobtrusive solid colors. Wood paneling with built-in book cases and cabinets are frequently supplied. A fireplace is usually essential. Baths and kitchen equipment are modern but special gadgets are rarely provided. An air conditioner or at least wiring for one is important if the climate demands it.

The picture of the prestige consumer's requirements that thus emerges is confirmed by interviews with buyers. The buyer wants a house which will provide the latest proven mechanical equipment, and a design suited to the basic structure of the house. He wants a sense of space without the discomfort of maintaining it. He wants a central location that offers cloistered privacy but hints of green space.

Tangible evidence of the kinds of families seeking center-city houses is available in a survey of center-city residents made in Philadelphia, Chicago, and New York through the joint cooperation of ACTION and *Fortune* magazine. Well over three hundred families were interviewed in the summer of 1957, over 100 in rehabilitated dwellings. Even though the sample was small, it indicated that the average family income in center-city rehabilitated structures is $10,000,[10] that 70 per cent of the families are only one or two persons, and that the median age of the family head is forty-four years. The predominant family types are young childless couples; middle-aged couples whose children have married and moved away; and single persons, many of whom are widowed, separated, or

[10] Luxury-apartment dwellers had a modal income of $15,000, showing that a good rehabilitated unit is a comparative center-city housing bargain.

divorced. Fifty-one per cent of the households were married couples. About 40 per cent of the two-person or larger families have more than one wage earner. Although the occupational specialties are quite varied, 47 per cent of the wage earners are in professional or creative fields, another 29 per cent are working in business and industry in a managerial capacity, and fully 19 per cent are not in the active labor force. It is interesting to note that wage earners in the creative fields—writing, art, music, etc.—numbering 29 per cent, far outstrip the 9 per cent found in a similar sample of center-city residents of luxury apartments.

Significantly, a large majority of the people living in rehabilitated houses, 77 per cent, lived in the center city before moving to their present homes. Only 9 per cent had lived in the suburbs immediately prior to moving to their present homes, and the remainder, 14 per cent, lived beyond the standard metropolitan area, many of them overseas. Fully 53 per cent of the families had never lived in the suburbs.

Adults seem willing to put up with neighborhood conditions they believe are unacceptable for children, in return for center-city amenities. Parents who can afford a choice seek traffic safety, a place to play (not necessarily a public playground), and safe companions at home and in school.[11] These are essentially neighborhood factors having little to do with the design and condition of the family home, and their importance increases with the size of the family. Thus center-city resuscitation for upper-income residents relies on small families wanting better quarters than are currently available.

[11] Chicago was the only city which had a noticeable number of children in the center-city rehabilitation area where interviews took place. This area is insulated by the lake front and a park, across which are the grounds of a private school attended by most of the children.

FINANCING

As noted before, financing center-city rehabilitation has been a difficult assignment. Financing the construction phase is variously handled; frequently the owner's capital is used without recourse to any loans. This is the least complicated procedure but limits the scale of the project and incurs opportunity costs by tying up funds for sixty to ninety days. If the rehabilitator can assume an existing mortgage on the unimproved house, this will allow him more capital to go further. However, the assumed mortgages in prestige areas are usually too small to do more than defray a small part of the construction costs.

Short-term loans are frequently used. The kinds of loans and the terms of the contract vary considerably, depending on the applicant's financial position and rehabilitation experience. FHA Title I loans have not been extensively used for prestige rehabilitation, because the original condition of the structures requires repairs far in excess of the maximum allowable under Title I loans ($3,500 for a single-family house).

Rehabilitators consider mortgages which can be transferred to the prospective buyer the most desirable method of financing. The ideal arrangement is a commitment for 80 per cent of the improved value of the houses, issued by the financial institution to the rehabilitator, either in a lump sum at the time of acquisition or in installments corresponding to the payments to contractors. However, the chances of getting this type of financing are slim. There has been no use of FHA-insured loans (which would permit a high loan to value ratio) for center-city areas. Usually the face amount of the loan is considerably less than 80 per cent and is not issued until the work is satisfactorily completed.

Obtaining mortgage commitments for prospective clients is an important part of the selling process. The equity requirements can be higher for the prestige market, but sales would be greatly eased if center-city rehabilitators could offer a better set of terms than those now typically available. Rehabilitators have to be prepared to take back second mortgages even when their clients' equity payments are comparatively high. The first mortgages, usually made by savings and loan associations, are for between 50 and 75 per cent of the final selling price. Interest rates vary between 5 and 6 per cent, and the length of loan runs from ten to seventeen years. A typical first mortgage on a house selling for $16,500 in 1957 would be an $8,000 to $9,000 mortgage at 5½ per cent for fifteen years. Second mortgages usually are for five to ten years, at interest rates of 5½ to 6 per cent. Since there is a ready secondary market for these mortgages, the rehabilitator does not need to hold them if more promising investments are in the offing. However, discounts up to 20 per cent are not unknown.

How could financing possibly be improved for prestige rehabilitation? Lenders have been reticent in supporting center-city rehabilitation, because the duration of the market for remodeled units is uncertain. As in Foggy Bottom, however, when the improvement trend was well-established and the area promised to hold its value for a number of years, financing at better terms was more easily found. The problem, therefore, is how to assure lenders that early remodeling projects indicate a decisive trend toward neighborhood improvement.

Several factors such as favorable market studies, citizens' activities, concerted programs of public improvements, and FHA insurance might convince lenders that their support was justified. Therefore, either a formal urban-renewal program or the elements found in a renewal program will be needed to obtain financing for an area's initial rehabilitation projects.

Conclusions

Of all the forms of rehabilitation, prestige rehabilitation, in spite of its hazards, offers the most chance for success to the inexperienced investor. In fact, little risk is involved if prestige rehabilitation has an appeal in the city under consideration. The experience to date would indicate that the demand would be high where the commuting distance to the suburbs is great, and where there are large numbers of childless, high-income families living in the center city.

An inexperienced investor can further safeguard his initial venture by hiring an established rehabilitator to invest his money for a commission. If he does not want to become involved with another rehabilitator, he can hire an architect who is familiar with remodeling work to spend a day investigating selected properties in the area where rehabilitation is well advanced. An architect can give a fair approximation of the structural condition and probable cost of remodeling the units for sales purposes.

The experienced investor who wants to begin prestige rehabilitation has even better roads open to him in gaining rehabilitation experience. He can sell an unimproved house in an established rehabilitation area and supervise the project for the new owner. He can wait for houses to be remodeled by purchasers, for their own use, in enough numbers to indicate a clear demand and a general price level before undertaking his own operation. Or he can talk to more experienced rehabilitators and perhaps go into partnership with them on a few projects. All methods clearly indicate a diminution of risk is possible, *if* the potential investor has the capital to consider rehabilitation: usually 50 per cent of the estimated costs if the project is not located in an urban-renewal area.

Whether a city should encourage prestige rehabilitation with urban renewal making FHA mortgage insurance available is a matter of public policy which will vary with the housing conditions of different communities. While remodeling substandard units for an upper-income market contributes to the urban environment of the community, it reduces the number of dwelling units available to low-income families.

With or without public support, prestige rehabilitation will continue to offer profits comparable to those of new construction to the careful investor who accurately judges the market. Increasingly congested highways and diminishing suburban tax advantages are just two factors which could vastly increase the future potential of center-city rehabilitation. A policy of public encouragement designed to lessen the mortgage risk involved in these investments, however, is vitally needed to convert this potential into concrete opportunities.

Chapter 3

REHABILITATION FOR MIDDLE-INCOME FAMILIES

As defined earlier, middle-income rehabilitation embraces those families with incomes between $3,500 and $7,500, paying between $50 and $125 per month or its shelter-cost equivalent.[1] However, considerable overlap from other categories blurs the sharp limits implied by the definition. The one-room luxury efficiency renting for $125 a month or the eight-room derelict for $55 a month accentuate the problem. Obviously, qualitative considerations such as the condition of the unit and the neighborhood must be used in sorting rehabilitation cases.

Within this broad grouping, rehabilitation takes many forms. Probably the largest dollar volume belongs to the contract remodeler updating private homes for the owner-occupant. In a strict sense, contract remodeling cannot be considered a form of speculative rehabilitation, since the investment and the accompanying risk is borne by the homeowner. Yet some discussion of contract remodeling will be

[1] Census statistics show that in 1950 the median gross monthly rental was $42.50 for the nation as a whole. (Gross monthly rental includes utility costs.) The rent index had risen from 108.8 in 1950 to 137.1 in March of 1958, indicating that the median gross monthly rent had then passed the $50 mark. (*Statistical Abstract of the United States*, U.S. Department of Commerce, 1958, p. 332.)

47

undertaken before considering commercial remodeling because of its importance to urban renewal and neighborhood conservation.

Contract Remodeling

Contract remodeling usually takes place when homeowners feel their houses have deteriorated or become obsolete to the point where remodeling is needed to preserve the structure's economic and social value. Unquestionably, prosperity has been a major factor in promoting a heavy volume of remodeling in many older neighborhoods.[2] But even in less prosperous times, families buying an older house will ordinarily put in some repairs before contentedly settling down. Usually the longer an owner intends to stay, the more repairs he will make on his new home.

Some years ago it was common to hire several contractors—one for plumbing, one for painting and decorating, etc. Now the homeowner can call just one firm and arrange for the entire job. The one-stop remodeler subcontracts much of his work, but by maintaining total supervision and a portion of the work, he can offer a "complete home-modernizing service." This can be less expensive as well as less troublesome for the homeowner, since the amount of overhead is reduced by one-firm control.

Lenders have found the remodeling business a growing outlet for their investment funds. However, because they are aware of shady practices by the "suede-shoe boys," they prefer

[2] The famous "Back-of-the-Yards" movement in Chicago did not include home remodeling among its aims until after the incomes of neighborhood residents had been increased by wartime and postwar prosperity. The early years, following the start of the movement in 1939, were spent in improving the health and labor conditions of the local families. (Saul Alinsky, *Reveille for Radicals*, University of Chicago Press, Chicago, 1948.)

to approve the remodeler who will do the work before they issue the loan.[3] Meanwhile, local and national organizations of remodeling contractors are attempting to bring stability and fair practices to this highly competitive business.

An Example of Contract Remodeling

Philip Shifrin is a Chicago contract remodeler whose firm, Sandra Engineers, has grown rapidly during the postwar building boom. Mr. Shifrin lists three essential talents for a contract remodeling firm: "First, you must have someone to merchandise the work. Second, you have to have an idea man and designer. Third, you must have a cost estimator."[4] Shifrin's background as a builder, combined with a flair for selling, gives him the very skills he mentions.

Vigorous selling distinguishes the contract remodeler. Shifrin sells through telephone, personal, and mail solicitations because he believes newspaper advertising is effective only if a six-month or longer campaign can be budgeted. Mail and telephone listings are obtained from Reuben H. Donnelly's Cross Reference Service, and Shifrin has found that "The best sales neighborhoods . . . are those in which the family income is $4,000 to $6,000 a year."[5]

[3] Such offenses committed under FHA Title I loans are being vigorously prosecuted. In a release of the Housing and Home Finance Agency dated July 18, 1956 (OA-1049), Albert M. Cole said: "The fact is that the Justice Department has obtained 450 convictions and 890 indictments for home repair rackets since April 1954, many of them for cases that occurred before the current safeguards were erected." This statement was in response to an article, 'Beware of the Home Repair Racketeers,' in a then-current issue of the *Saturday Evening Post*—one of many articles appearing about that time in popular magazines.

[4] Philip Shifrin, "How I Sell Modernizing to Home Owners," *Practical Builder*, vol. 20, no. 10, October, 1955, pp. 4–7.

[5] *Ibid.*, p. 7. These neighborhoods tend to have a high proportion of homeownership and continuing neighborhood pride.

Shifrin will call on the family expressing interest and will try to conclude the sale with one call, including cost estimates and a financing program. If he has any doubts about costs, he will tell the owner he is taking the estimate back to the office to try to whittle it down—a good public relations device and at the same time a safety precaution for himself. Financing is arranged with one of three lenders unless the client prefers to obtain financing on his own. Most of the loans are FHA-insured through Title I.

The job is done as quickly as possible in order to minimize the inconvenience to the client. A major part of the work is subcontracted but complete supervision is maintained. Shifrin relies on his reputation for honest dealing and sound construction as his best advertisement. Over the years many satisfied customers have sold thousands of dollars of work for him. The client who brings him new business receives a gratuity. (He tells of one woman for whom he did a $200 job. Over the years she brought in several contracts including one for $7,000, and he installed a set of Venetian blinds for her free of charge.)

Aggressive selling, a sense of design, and good financing contacts are necessary to make the remodeling business profitable. Careful cost estimating is essential to avoid losses. Remodeling contractors prefer a "cost plus" contract which permits unexpected expenses to be added to the bill. Where many homeowners prefer a firm contract, as is often the case, uncertainties about costs must be covered by a safety factor in the contract.

A brief glance at the business reveals that contract remodeling is economically feasible for any businessman who has the requisite skills and capital. The homeowner is really the one who must answer the question of economic feasibility, since much of this work may be uneconomic in strictly dollar terms.

Commercial rehabilitators compute feasibility on the basis of the formula, acquisition cost plus repair cost plus profit equals sale price. If every homeowner who remodeled his home used the same formula (without the profit figure), a great many—perhaps a majority—would find that the value of their house had not increased enough to compensate for the cost of the work. This is no reason to doubt the integrity of the remodeler or the intelligence of the homeowner. In the one case, the businessman is selling the consumer a package which costs the contractor around 20 per cent less than the consumer must pay. On the other hand, the consumer buys a product which will give him satisfaction over the coming years, without worrying about a selling price which, if he does not sell, will never be subject to test. Only if the consumer hopes to increase the value of the house beyond the cost of the work would the question of feasibility be raised and answered by the simple four-part estimating formula.

Commercial Rehabilitation for Middle-income Families

Middle-income neighborhoods circle the city and extend outward through the suburban fringe with a few small pockets resisting the pressures of time and maintaining themselves in evolving urban centers. Unlike upper-income rehabilitation, there are no one or two distinctive neighborhoods in which all the investment opportunities for middle-income rehabilitation are found.

Commercial rehabilitation has been successfully undertaken in many parts of the city. There has been a continual hope that the middle-income family would return to downtown areas, and some rehabilitation companies have begun to make this appeal with varying degrees of success. Farther out, neighborhoods that are beginning to lose their value, as reflected in declining relative rents, may have so strong an appeal to their residents that, if some tangible improvements are made, the residents may be willing to stay at higher rents than before. Local citizens' groups or vigorous commercial rehabilitators occasionally have started an improvement campaign in such neighborhoods. Still farther out, there are stable neighborhoods where the housing for the most part is well maintained, where the demand for housing is still firm, but where a few houses every few blocks may have begun to deteriorate. Commercial rehabilitators have purchased some of the neglected units for a price reflecting the repair costs, and have profitably remodeled and sold the units.

There are houses or apartments in every neighborhood designed in earlier days for the typical family of that period. Even in the newer suburbs some pockets of older housing no longer suit today's families. These apartment houses or large old homes are very often suitable for profitable conversion into smaller apartment units. Such work was possible even during the Depression.

The demonstration house of the Rochester (New York) Gas and Electric Company illustrates rehabilitation of the "worst house in a good neighborhood." Elmer Klavans's work with large elevator apartments in Washington and Newton Farr's work with large old homes in Chicago show what conversions can accomplish with obsolete housing in essentially sound neighborhoods. The work of Peter Turchon of Boston, John Havens of Columbus, and the Powelton Village Development Associates in Philadelphia demonstrates how private rehabilitators or neighborhood groups can help in the improvement of areas in various stages of decline. Harry Turek in New York converted condemned buildings on the edge of a low-rent area into middle-income units in spite of the surroundings.

Fritz Burns in Los Angeles went into a low-rent area to demonstrate how middle-income rehabilitation could pay and found that prestige rehabilitation could pay even more. And lastly, the Society of Friends managed to bring middle-income families into a Philadelphia slum area.

Overcoming Deferred Maintenance: The "Worst House in a Good Area"

The Rochester Gas and Electric Company, under the direction of the supervisor of its Architect and Builder Department, Gaston L. Breckenridge, undertook a remodeling project primarily to stimulate home modernization among property owners and secondarily to show the profit potential to investors. Breckenridge is quoted as saying,

> The project proved to local property owners that old neighborhoods can be revitalized. Many residents near the remodeled home changed their minds about moving to the suburbs.... And the open house helped change the thinking of landlords who had been *dragging their feet* as far as modernization was concerned.[6]

The house was eighty-six years old at the time of remodeling. It is located in an average middle-income neighborhood of frame, detached houses set on fair-sized lots. Selling prices in the area in 1956 averaged between $8,000 and $10,000. The one-story demonstration bungalow needed a good paint job, a new roof, new plumbing, redecoration, and replanning. Breckenridge was able to purchase the house for only $4,500.

Very little was saved in doing the remodeling. All that remained of the original house was the framework, floors, basement, roof, and a gas furnace that had been newly installed before purchase. The Rochester Gas and Electric Company

[6] "First Round Won in Slum Fight," *Electrical World*, Oct. 8, 1956, p. 47.

hired an architect, a contractor, and a real estate firm for the design, work, and sales respectively. The entire job cost $11,895.51 and took exactly one year, including the one-month public demonstration period (see Table 1).

TABLE 1. Cost Breakdown of Rochester Gas and Electric Company Project

Acquisition cost		$ 4,500.00
Rehabilitation costs:		
Building permits	$ 4.00	
Architect's fees	25.00	
Sales and advertising expenses	700.00	
Carpentry	1,237.50	
Masonry	745.22	
Plumbing and bath	679.00	
Kitchen	350.00	
Heating (furnace kept)	230.00	
Electrical	593.09	
Painting and papering	495.50	
Plastering	650.00	
Property taxes for period held	54.00	
Allowance for unpaid managerial labor	100.00	
Other	1,532.20	
		$ 7,395.51
Total		$11,895.51

Source: *ACTION Rehabilitation Questionnaire.*

The house was sold to a family with a $4,500-a-year income for a price of $12,500. This provided a modest profit of $604.49, a profit which could have been higher if the venture had been undertaken with profit in mind. Not only would the sales and advertising expenses have been less, but a higher sale price might have been possible. During the demonstration period, twenty-five offers were made for the house, the highest of which was $14,200.

The final buyer made a $3,000 down payment and received an FHA mortgage for $9,500, with a twenty-five year term at 4½ per cent from a local savings bank. Breckenridge reports that the rehabilitation job had the desired effect. By October, 1956—two months before the house was sold—three major remodeling jobs and twenty-five smaller remodeling jobs had taken place in the neighborhood. As of the spring of 1957 there was a decided increase in the amount of contract remodeling, although no large-scale commercial rehabilitation was in progress.

Working in Stable Areas Approaching Decline: Converting Single-family Houses

Newton C. Farr, a Chicago realtor, reported the rehabilitation and conversion of two houses in the Kenwood area on the South Side of Chicago.[7] These houses were on either side of Farr's home. They are large frame structures that had been built almost seventy years earlier for large middle-class families. By 1952, however, many families were moving away to escape aging housing, traffic congestion, and increasing neglect. For several years there has been a movement among Kenwood residents and those of the Hyde Park area (including the University of Chicago) immediately to the south to save the area from urban blight. Farr's work complemented the neighborhood-preservation movement.

The brick and frame house at 4733 Woodlawn Avenue had fifteen rooms and three baths. It was converted to six apartments: three one-bedroom apartments on the first floor; two apartments on the second floor, one of which had two bed-

---

[7] Newton C. Farr, "Don't Tear It Down—Build It Up," *Rehabilitation as a Business*, National Association of Real Estate Boards, Washington, 1952, pp. 65–70.

rooms; and a two-bedroom apartment on the third floor. Each apartment received a new kitchen and bath and complete redecoration. They rented for an average of $106 per month including utilities. Mr. Farr contracted all the work and financed the project with his own funds. A statement of repair and operating cost shows the house was purchased for $15,118.69, required a total investment of $34,545.72, and returned $6,480 annual gross rents and $2,656.30 net rent.[8]

The three-story frame house at 4747 Woodlawn Avenue was built in 1886. The remodeling costs were somewhat greater because a new heating plant and roof were required to service the five apartments built into the house. The average rental for these apartments was $122.50 a month with utilities, reflecting the added remodeling costs. The house cost $19,980.46, required a total investment of $43,637.90, and returned a net rent of $2,135.48.[9]

In both these cases the profits were slim—approximately 7 per cent and 4 per cent of investment respectively. They would have been higher if gas and electricity could have been made the responsibility of the tenants and if substantial mortgages had been obtained.

Many large old homes like these have become neglected because space and maintenance expenses are too high even for wealthier families. If there is any market in the neighborhood for smaller units at modest prices, conversions make investment sense. Conversion is usually facilitated by extensive use of existing plumbing lines, by adapting center hall entrances and stair wells to sensible space divisions, and by turning large yards or outbuildings into off-street parking.

Intelligent conversions meeting all the standards of housing

[8] *Ibid.*, p. 67.
[9] *Ibid.*, p. 70.

and building codes are more desirable than over-crowded, poorly designed rooming houses. Farr's main motive was to stop just such a boardinghouse incursion into what is still a desirable neighborhood. Obviously his attachment to the area made him satisfied with the low profit margin resulting from enthusiastic and perhaps overly extensive rehabilitation. Other instances of reutilizing obsolete residences and business properties through rehabilitation and conversion can be found in the practice of property managers responsible for a uniform or increasing flow of net income.

Converting Rental Apartments in Washington

Washington, D. C., with its population swollen first by war and thereafter by continuing government activity, has experienced a pronounced suburban building boom. Larger families with school-age children comprise the major market for new housing. Many of the families remaining in Washington are small, one- and two-person families who find little need for apartments designed for larger households. The demand for efficiency apartments has far outrun the supply.

It was this change in the pattern of market demand which convinced Elmer Klavans and other investors to convert middle-aged apartment buildings built during the boom of the twenties and scattered throughout the city. From 1948 to 1956 Klavans converted and rehabilitated forty-eight apartment buildings, acting as contractor for the existing owner in all but a few projects. The Northwest section where Klavans has done most of his work is north of Foggy Bottom, next to Rock Creek Park, and south of one of the most desirable residential neighborhoods within the city. Some of the features Klavans considers desirable in a potential property are an existing elevator shaft and disposal chute, apartments large enough to allow partitions to be added rather than moved, not too much exterior gingerbread, and good plumbing, heating, and wiring. Naturally the rehabilitated buildings did not always possess these features, but none cost more than thirty cents a cubic foot to acquire.

Klavans takes a personal interest in the design of the building, offering suggestions to the client or his architect on how the best effect can be created at minimum cost. The actual remodeling work ordinarily takes from thirty to seventy days, with Klavans' regular crew supplemented by subcontractors. The repairs typically include adding partitions to form new units, all new kitchens and baths, a coat of colored binder plaster over all walls and ceilings, fresh doors and repaired windows, refinished floors, redecorated halls with indirect lighting, and new floor coverings, and, as a final touch, rebuilt entrance and lobby in an elaborate modern style. Plumbing and wiring are repaired rather than replaced, and a new elevator shaft and disposal chute are added only if they are not already in the building. The stairs are never moved. In one job done for a Washington realtor the finished building had its net income more than doubled after full occupancy was obtained.

Klavans lists three essentials for successful apartment rehabilitation: a good basic structure, a good work crew, and good financing. A good basic structure is a function of the purchase price which anticipates unexpected difficulties that may arise during construction. Known construction problems, of course, mean a lower purchase price. Unexpected problems which have not been compensated for in the purchase price can make a project run over its budget. Care is taken, therefore, during the design and estimating stages to visualize the side effects of any specific improvement. In considering the conversion of an infrequently used stair well into an elevator shaft, for example, the rehabilitator must consider whether or not tearing out the old stairs will weaken the structure or disrupt utility lines and result in added cost that will upset his repair budget. Elmer Klavans keeps detailed cost-control records to avoid repeating costly mistakes in building selection and remodeling. In fact, he likes to point out that he employs four bookkeepers but no secretary.

The second asset, a good work force, assures that the rehabilitator can quickly finish the work and put the building on the market. Delays during construction add directly to construction costs (if the contract is on a cost plus profit basis), and indirectly reduce profits by diminishing gross rents while the building is unoccupied. Klavans keeps a basic work force which supervises any subcontracted labor hired for a specific job. His foremen are paid a percentage of profits to ensure rapid work, and during a good year they can expect to earn as much as $10,000. Klavans said contractors will take work at cost or even sustain a small loss if necessary, to keep their crews busy during off periods. During slack periods Klavans engages in commercial remodeling.

It is widely felt that satisfactory financing for this kind of work, or any rehabilitation, for that matter, would be a mortgage covering 80 per cent of the estimated value of the completed project and permitting generous construction advances.

Private Neighborhood Renewal in a Declining Area

The Powelton Village Development Association, Inc. (PVDA), was founded in the beginning of 1956. In an advance prospectus dated March 12, 1956, the Association listed as its purposes: ". . . making good rental housing available to people on an open-occupancy basis and to buy, develop, and improve properties in the 'Powelton Village' centered in the Powelton Redevelopment Area of West Philadelphia." The Village area covers twenty square blocks in the extreme eastern portion of the area bordering on the Schuylkill River. Most of the houses are detached and semidetached masonry structures built in the last half of the nineteenth century, and some are still inhabited by the original upper-middle-income families. The streets are wide and lined with fine old trees. The area has been sliding downhill in the past several years partly because the old residents resent the influx of Negro families and partly because the houses and the area no longer meet family needs. As families have left for suburban havens, their homes have been converted into apartment houses. The overflowing campuses of Drexel Institute of Technology and the University of Pennsylvania provide a ready market for small, cheap rooms and for family-sized units.

Many houses have withstood the ravages of time and maintained their graceful lines, even though their interiors were turned to various purposes. Some of the best-cared-for houses in the area are now fraternity houses, nursing homes, and carefully converted apartment houses. Many other houses have unfortunately fallen into the hands of unscrupulous landlords who are busily milking the properties at the expense of the university students and the remainder of the area's residents. One other class of landlords, widows, has had a disastrous effect on the area. On one block alone in 1956, six out of twenty-four houses were owned by elderly ladies who had no other means of support than the rental income from their houses. All but one of them had made some minor changes and were renting out poorly designed and equipped apartments or rooms. The effect was almost as telling as the most unscrupulous landlord's neglect, and yet the owners were barely eking out a living. There are, however, enough well-tended houses in the area to give it an individual personality which many people feel is worth saving. Many of the Negro families who have moved in in recent years have spent thousands of dollars remodeling the smaller houses into attractive homes.

The founders of the Powelton Village Development Association represent a racially mixed group of homeowners and interested outsiders. Many of the officers and directors of the Friendship Cooperative Houses—a group active in the area since 1946—have taken part in the Powelton Village venture. The Friendship Cooperative had previously purchased and remodeled $125,000 worth of houses into modest apartments, renting for between $40 and $85 per month, since 1946. The policy of the Friendship Cooperative to rent to anyone without discrimination has been carried over into the new organization.

The initial issue of stock was $100,000 and was fully subscribed in a little over one year. The money has been spent to buy and remodel structures around a nucleus formed by the Friendship Cooperative Houses. Houses are to be purchased regardless of condition, but repairs are budgeted to allow a small profit within their rent limits. The PVDA plans no structural alterations (fortunately most of the units in the area are structurally sound), but they do plan to move interior partitions, replace windows and doors, add partitions to create new apartments, and add whatever plumbing is absolutely necessary. By maintaining high maintenance standards and budgeting for continual improvement, they plan to bring their entire holdings up to a relatively high standard gradually and still remain within a limited rent category. As an ancillary part of their activities, new purchasers with intentions to remodel will receive advice and help from the Association, which will profit through the general improvement of the area.

Typical of the PVDA operation is a masonry structure purchased for $13,500. The building contained six completed apartments but required $8,000 in repairs to bring it up to standards set by the group. The gross monthly rent is $480, or an average of $80 per apartment. Their operating costs run approximately 65 per cent of the gross, resulting in a net return of 10 per cent on their gross investment. The typical mortgage for a structure of this type would cover no more than 50 per cent of the investment and run between ten and fifteen years at 5 to 6 per cent. However, even a small mortgage has been helpful, and the Association's profits are considered quite satisfactory.

Private neighborhood rehabilitation is in keeping with the current philosophy of urban renewal. The PVDA is a citizen effort financed completely by private individuals and aimed at the total improvement of a clearly defined neighborhood. Yet the group's resources are too limited (and further reduced by low-ratio mortgages) to compete with the comparatively powerful economic forces destroying any remaining neighborhood charm. Larger capitalization, with more liberal financing and full cooperation from the local government, is needed before organizations like PVDA can conduct a significant renewal effort.

Large-scale Rehabilitation in Declining Areas

Peter Turchon of Boston (President of Homes, Inc., with offices in Newton, Roxbury, and Cambridge) is one of the outstanding figures in the rehabilitation field today, having been in the field longer, done more work, and been more successful than most if not all other American rehabilitators. His specialty is remodeling two- and three-family houses for sale to a single owner who can reduce his carrying costs with rent from the remaining units. Most of these houses were built thirty to fifty years ago in Boston's working-class neighborhoods, neighborhoods which are now "conservation areas" in the parlance of redevelopment officials. Peter Turchon's work is considered by local people as just the kind of treatment these areas need. One of the local newspapers has characterized Turchon as "America's one-man urban renewal program."[10]

Turchon's firm began rehabilitation work in 1926 and remodeled several million dollars worth of property for Boston-area banks during the thirties. He kept about one hundred men employed during these years and developed remodeling techniques which still prove invaluable in his work. Long before 1957 he was remodeling at the rate of 500 structures a year, carrying on a sizable brokerage service, and building new suburban homes.

Peter Turchon buys seventy to eighty houses at a time, at auctions, probate court sales, and private sales. (Often sellers approach Turchon, knowing of his reputation for quick sales and purchases.) One collection of houses cost him $447,000 in cash. He will probably try to purchase as many of the houses near a recent acquisition as possible to capitalize on any rise in values resulting from his rehabilitation activities. In spite of his rapid purchasing, the houses are appraised before buying. The house is bought regardless of other conditions, location, or potential market, provided it has no costly structural defects. Turchon firmly believes that ". . . there is value in *every-*

[10] William E. Dorman, "A Millionaire Advises—Don't Ignore the 3-decker," *Boston Sunday Herald,* undated (reprint).

thing because we've seen that every house looks like a palace to someone." [11]

Costs are estimated on a basement-to-roof basis, and no repairs are made which will not add to the eventual sale price.[12] Of course, acting quickly means only rough estimating can be done, and Turchon relies on profits from the whole volume of his activity to compensate for losses that might be sustained on some of the individual structures.

His repairs on a three-story structure include the cleaning of basements, yards, and halls, repairs and replacements to roof and siding (painting and patching are often enough), extra outlets and often increased wire service, new electric fixtures, paint for the common halls, and complete redecoration, with a new kitchen and bath for the future owner's apartment only. The completed structure is sound and clean but lacking in any expensive frills.

The firm keeps a staff of between twelve and twenty-five people to do general repair work. About half of the work is subcontracted, with every job contracted that can be handled without unexpected complications—electrical work, plumbing, tiling, and about half the heating, painting, and carpentry. Turchon's firm is active enough, however, to keep these subcontractors constantly employed, making them practically part of the staff.

One of the selling features for Turchon's houses is the continued interest he takes in the property and its neighbors. If the new owner wants to redecorate the other apartments, Turchon will sell him materials at wholesale prices or even less

---

[11] "Biggest Modernizer Buys and Improves 500 Houses a Year," *House & Home*, October, 1954, p. 114.

[12] He is careful not to yield to an artistic impulse because in 1926 he purchased a house for $8,000, did a beautiful repair job for $7,000, and then could only sell the house for $13,000, sustaining a $2,000 loss.

than his own cost and send a man to advise the owner on the job. Tenants can obtain free materials if they will supply the labor to improve their flats. Turchon occasionally supplies other neighboring homeowners with materials at cost to make improvements, reasoning that any improvement in the neighborhood will increase the value of properties still held in the area and serve as good publicity for his firm.

Typical bathroom before the Turchon treatment.

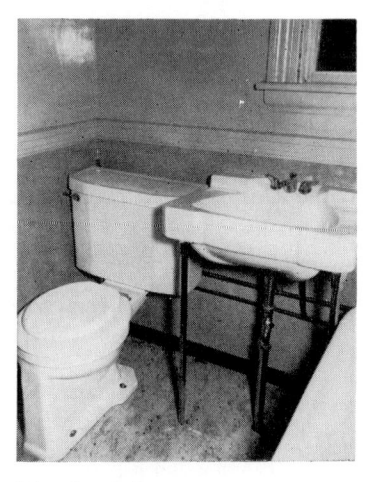

Turchon's improvements—modest but neat.

An example of a Turchon rehabilitation project is in Dorchester, an inlying suburb of Boston. Eight three-family houses were purchased from an estate for $75,000 cash. Then twelve adjacent houses were acquired before any repairs were made, because prices rise rapidly once work begins. The twenty houses cost a total of $201,000.

Cleanup crews moved in as soon as occupancy was obtained. They removed twenty loads of accumulated rubbish from one cellar alone. Then the carpenters began to modernize the owners' units and carry out the rehabilitation process described above.

The houses were offered to the original tenants before putting them on the general market. The first house sold for $10,900 and the last house for $13,900. Repair and merchandising costs averaged between $2,000 and $3,000 a structure, making the profit only about 3 per cent on total project costs. This is typical of Turchon's returns on his rehabilitation projects.[13] A sample cost breakdown of a house purchased in January of 1957 and sold ninety days later is given in Table 2. This is not a house from the project described.

TABLE 2. Cost Breakdown of Turchon Project, Boston Area

Acquisition costs (cash)		$10,500
Rehabilitation costs:		
Title and recording fees	$ 65	
Sales and advertising expenses	400	
Cleaning, before and after	140	
Tile work, baths	140	
Tile work, kitchen	105	
Heating	133	
Electrical outlets and fixtures	68	
Painting and papering, interior	830	
Roof repairs	114	
Exterior painting	550	
Miscellaneous	636	
		$3,181
Total		$13,681
Sale price		14,200
Profit (3.8%)		$519

Source: *ACTION Rehabilitation Questionnaire.*

Three per cent return is without much appeal for the normal investor, but two factors make Turchon's activities

[13] Dorman, *op. cit.*

profitable. First, Turchon's volume is so vast and the turnover so rapid that 3 per cent profit on individual projects adds up to a sizable annual yield. Second, the firm buys and holds choice commercial properties which were part of the estates or holdings purchased in volume for rehabilitation activities. Turchon says he has accumulated an enviable portfolio of commercial and residential rental properties with their value increased by nearby renewal. The profits from these properties are largely plowed back into the rehabilitation operation, but when rehabilitation is no longer economically feasible the commercial portfolio is expected to yield a rich return.

The rapid sale of such large volumes of property is facilitated by sound merchandising and the abiding conviction that multifamily homeownership is the only sensible housing solution for a market of lower- and middle-income families whose head is often between twenty-six and thirty-six years of age. Turchon says that: "When a young man buys a two- or three-family house the extra income helps him *pay more* of the mortgage faster than if he bought a single house." [14] The whole advertising approach is directed toward the motto, "Pay like rent." Advertisements always tell the owner's carrying costs after the rents have been deducted from the debt service. Here is a typical ad extracted from one of his 1957 circulars:

>**106 Stoughton Street, Dorchester**   3-Apt.
>(from 589 Columbia Rd. to 59 Pleasant St.)
>Three-family home of 5/5½/5½ rooms with 3-PIECE BATHS, WHITE SINKS, COMBINATION RANGES, WARM-AIR HEAT for first floor. Fireproof asbestos shingles on exterior provide ideal insulation. Rents: S-1, $42.00; S-2, VACANT, redecorated for buyer; S-3, $35.00. G.I. $600 down. Mtg. $9200. 4½%, 20 yrs., $13 per month.
>   *$9800*   V A C A N C Y

[14] *House & Home, op. cit.*

Obviously, offering such firm terms requires excellent cooperation from local lenders and appraisers. From 1946 to 1957 Turchon relied almost exclusively on Veterans Administration financing for his rehabilitated-home buyers. The easy VA terms allowed the firm to offer low down payments as well as low monthly carrying costs to purchasers. Turchon says easy terms are the key to selling those modernized homes.

Homes, Incorporated, offers its mortgages to a wide selection of Boston banks and building and loan associations. The firm is so dependent on ready financing that it has always made a point of protecting the lender against default. Peter Turchon is proud of the fact that no financial institution lost a penny on houses sold to his customers during the Depression. When a buyer cannot meet his payments, Homes, Incorporated, will take a low-interest second mortgage or make a direct loan, allowing the homeowner to meet his obligations. This policy has won high praise and continuing cooperation from local lenders. President Charles Sloan of the East Cambridge Savings Bank has said, "Modernizing old houses takes imagination, capital, drive, and integrity. Peter Turchon has them all. His business is good for the buyers and safe for the banks." [15]

Nonetheless, Turchon's rehabilitation activities declined in 1957 because VA mortgages with their generous terms lacked purchasers, and Turchon's customers cannot afford the high down payment required on conventional mortgages. During the period when terms stiffened, sales of modernized homes declined, and Turchon went to work on commercial proper-

[15] *Ibid.*, p. 116.

ties. When VA credit was eased in April, 1958, Turchon began home remodeling again.[16]

Turchon's relationship with the local government has been cordial; in fact, he serves Boston as an unpaid consultant on urban renewal. In this capacity he has convinced city officials that sharply increasing assessments on improved properties could retard the market and limit private remodeling. Also, he has been able to have street trees planted on some of the barren blocks recently restored to decent condition as a stimulant to further renewal.

As we have seen, Peter Turchon's business involves mass purchasing, wholesale remodeling, rapid merchandising, and protected investments for lenders. The advantages to rehabilitation on Turchon's scale are that it is possible to amass a profitable portfolio of rental properties, to receive wholesale discounts on materials, to gain valuable repair experience,[17]

---

[16] Turchon believes that "Private enterprise *cannot* do the job without Federal protection for bank mortgages given by home buyers. The secret of success could be long-term, *low* interest mortgages to reduce cost and to *convert renters into buyers*. This is the cheapest and quickest way to save neighborhoods." (*ACTION Rehabilitation Quesionnaire.*)

[17] Here are some of his remodeling suggestions from an article in *Popular Mechanics*, October, 1956, pp. 170 and 171.

"*Roofs*—Patch rather than replace the roof, using asphalt shingles for slopes and tar for a flat roof.

"*Exterior repairs*—Don't replace wooden siding; paint it. Point masonry and replace rotten wood. Tear off a sagging porch if the appearance is impaired. Generally, limit outside changes; they become expensive.

"*Structural changes*—Go easy but replace essentials; rotten wood, repair masonry, replace faulty drainage systems. Often the sway can be removed from a frame house by jacking it up one or two turns a day (after disconnecting all plumbing lines) and replacing rotted beams.

"*Interior Walls*—Repair cracks in plaster and use wallpaper over it which will hide such defects as waving or bulging walls; large patterns are best.

"*Ceilings*—If the old ceiling is bad, dry panel nailed to furring strips to keep a trained and continually employed work force, and to receive favorable attention from lenders, government officials, and the press.

Can other rehabilitators in other cities duplicate Turchon's business? The essence of the Turchon method is to have the added rents from multifamily homes keep housing costs well below the usual costs for equivalent units. The main factor limiting emulation is a ready supply of inexpensive two- or three-family houses in acceptable neighborhoods. Triple-deckers are cheap and numerous in Boston, having been built to house the immigrants of the early part of the century. They have become old-fashioned, with obsolete plumbing and wiring ill-designed for heavy use of appliances. If a city has a large supply of two- to four-family units available, and if careful adjustments are made for local design preferences and ability to pay, Turchon's activities might be duplicated.

---

directly over the old plaster will be inexpensive. Lower the ceiling a foot or two if ceilings are too high.

"*Floors*—Sand hardwood floors, clean and repaint soft wood floors or cover with linoleum. Use asphalt tile in the kitchen and bath.

"*Kitchen*—Kitchens should be done with particular care. If the equipment is old it should be replaced. Metal wall cabinets or unpainted wood cabinets may be used. Use enamel if the walls don't wave, but if they do, fur it out and use panel-type tileboard. A picture window only costs $80–$120.

"*Bath*—Leave old equipment if possible. Replacement is costly and often unexpected plumbing expenses arise. Ceiling tile and new wall covering often achieve gratifying results at low cost.

"*Wiring*—New fixtures, repaired wiring, if safe, and generous use of outlets fit the house to modern standards.

"*Heating*—If the heating is inadequate, a hot-air floor furnace or an oil unit with hot-air outlet into the living room will do a passable job. Cold walls or floors should be corrected by insulation."

Selling Financing Terms with a Rehabilitated House Attached

John F. Havens of Columbus, Ohio, began his rehabilitation activities in 1951. He sold or rented 500 remodeled units by the early part of 1957, 100 of them in 1956. Typically, he remodels a house costing $4,000 and either sells it for $8,000 or rents it for $60 per month. The units are located in modest middle-income neighborhoods and are sold to families from the same or similar areas whose average family income is between $3,000 and $4,000 a year. An essential part of his selling tools is an effective financing arrangement. In 1957 he financed approximately 80 per cent of his sales himself, requiring a 15 per cent down payment and 6 per cent interest on a ten-year land contract for the balance.[18] The other 20 per cent were financed by mortgages insured under Section 221 of the FHA statute.[19] Continual government activity coupled with the low equity investment for both Havens and his purchaser that the mortgage affords has convinced Havens to use Section 221 as extensively as possible.

Havens purchased a house on October 1, 1956, for $4,200. The purchase was financed by a $3,000 ten-year mortgage at 6 per cent, obtained from a local building and loan association. The repairs cost $1,767 and the property was sold on January 2, 1957, for $7,200. The sale was financed by a

[18] A land contract is an agreement between buyer and seller whereby the seller agrees to transfer title after the buyer has met the full purchase price through mutually agreeable monthly payments including interest.

[19] This section provides for special insured financing for families displaced by government construction and urban-renewal activity. The mortgage may equal 100 per cent of value to a maximum of $9,000, run for forty years or three-quarters of the remaining life of the property, and bear interest of 5½ per cent. There is the added advantage of assured purchase at par by Federal National Mortgage Association.

$1,500 down payment, and a land contract for the balance costing the purchaser $65 per month. The profits on the sale were $1,233 (see Table 3).

TABLE 3. Cost Breakdown of Havens Project, Columbus, Ohio

Acquisition cost		$4,200
Rehabilitation costs:		
Interest on loans	$ 35	
Building permits	16	
Sales and advertising expense	350	
Cleaning and watchmen	42	
Carpentry	240	
Masonry	110	
Plumbing and heating (contracted):		
Bath	65	
Kitchen	120	
Heating	105	
Electrical (contracted)	24	
Painting, papering, plastering, roofing	620	
Allowance for unpaid managerial labor not elsewhere listed	40	
	$1,767	
Total		$5,967
Selling price		7,200
Profit (17% on sale price)		$1,233

Source: *ACTION Rehabilitation Questionnaire.* The figures do not include real property taxes paid during the period held.

Havens's rehabilitation activities are greatly curtailed by the act of tying up his equity in land contracts in order to give better financing. Use of the special FHA-insured financing can release his equity by offering even more liberal terms and thus permitting a greater volume of work.

Harry Turek—East Side of Manhattan [20]

In 1952, Harry Turek purchased three boarded-up tenements on East 82 Street which had been condemned several years before. He paid $75,000 for the three buildings, each of which was 25 by 75 feet and five stories in height. He considered razing the buildings and building a new structure, but since the zoning ordinance requires fireproof construction and prohibits more than 65 per cent lot coverage (the existing structures covered 75 per cent of the lot), he rehabilitated the existing buildings at a cost of $175,000. He converted the buildings into a single apartment house at an average cost of $5,300 per unit, with thirty-three three-room-and-bath apartments renting for an average of $121 per month.

Turek employed an architect to design virtually a new building. Only the rear walls and the party walls were left standing. He managed also to salvage the joists and framing members, but even the front walls were torn down as the building was gutted for a fresh start. Turek employed his own work force for everything except plumbing and heating. Three months were needed to build an elevator apartment building into the three empty shells. The thirty-three units were distributed six to a floor and three in the basement.

Turek was able to get a $170,000 construction loan from a mortgage corporation to finance the work, and a savings bank gave him a $200,000 mortgage when the apartments were partially rented. The terms were quite favorable even for the time—4 per cent interest and 3 per cent amortization. The

---

[20] Groff Conklin, "The Builder Makes a Profit on Rehabilitation," *National Association of Home Builders Correlator*, vol. 8, no. 10, October, 1954, pp. 13–15.

building grossed $48,000 a year and netted a return of $16,600 on equity of $50,000 (see Table 4).

TABLE 4. Cost Breakdown of Turek Project, Manhattan

Acquisition cost	$ 75,000	
Repair costs	175,000	
Total investment		$250,000
Mortgage (4% on $200,000)	$ 14,000	
Taxes ($200,000 assessment)	7,200	
Insurance	1,000	
Oil and steam heat	2,500	
Superintendent, maintenance (basement apt., $40 per mo.)	5,000	
Total		$ 31,400
Gross rent		48,000
Net rent (on $50,000)		$16,600

Source: Conklin, *op. cit.* The allocation for maintenance is substantially lower than that for similar projects.

Turek's structures were located on a treeless block of tenements some of which still had hallway toilets and no central heating. Their poor condition kept the acquisition costs low, and their vacancy permitted construction economies associated with new construction, untrammeled by tenant-relocation problems. These savings were apparently enough to make possible the repairs needed to meet the market. The completed project compares favorably with other, better located projects.

It is surprising to someone not familiar with the Manhattan real estate market to find that apartments as unfavorably located as Turek's could rent for $1,200 to $1,600 a year immediately adjacent to buildings reminiscent of New York's immigrant days. But in Manhattan high-rent and low-rent units live back to back, only faintly concerned with each other's existence. New apartments built recently in the same area rent for more than $65 per room. The important selling feature for a Manhattan realtor interested in the middle-income market is a good building at a good price and near transportation lines. Naturally the more amenities a location has, the more quickly it will rent. If the market demand was weak, however, Turek's project would never have been built.

Fritz Burns's Demonstration

Once-aristocratic Bunker Hill in Los Angeles is located between the northerly edge of the business district and the Los Angeles civic center. It is now a shabby area of mixed uses. What housing still remains is frame, single-family or duplex structures built in the late nineteenth and early twentieth centuries. Although the section cannot be characterized as a slum, it had gone down about as far as it could go.

Fritz Burns was the first realtor to attempt rehabilitation on Bunker Hill. Since he was demonstrating that private rehabilitation can help in renewing cities, in his role as national chairman of the National Association of Real Estate Board's "Build America Better" program, he made no serious attempt at the time to take advantage of the Hill's aristocratic past with prestige rehabilitation.

The first Bunker Hill project involved three unpainted frame houses on solid redwood foundations. The original structures had no plumbing, but subsequent owners had added rudimentary fixtures to the rear annexes. Two of the houses were two-family units and went through extensive remodeling; the third house—occupied by three ministers—was painted only and the tenants left undisturbed.

One of the two buildings had the porch removed and the

entrance remodeled, but otherwise there were no exterior repairs. Both houses were given new baths, kitchens, heating equipment, flooring, backyard terraces, and complete redecoration. Extra pains were taken with the decorative effects in both the backyards and the apartments in the interests of the demonstration. One house was purchased for $7,000 and had approximately $13,000 spent for improvements; the other house cost $6,000 and had $9,700 spent on remodeling. The only interior layout change was to merge some of the rooms to create a more open effect. Apartment rents were increased from $30 per month to $100 per month after the work was completed. The market sought in this project and in later work in the area was the center-city professionals who could walk to work if they chose.[21] The rent return was $200 per month, with the tenants paying utility costs. Burns felt the return on his $20,000 investment was adequate, considering the demonstrative nature of the undertaking.

The first project suggested to Burns that the area was suitable for prestige rehabilitation, since it was close to the center city and had at one time been graced with some prestige. A later project in the same vicinity also involved a detached house of two apartments. The house cost $11,000 to acquire and $17,800 to repair. The completed units rented for $150 per month, half again as much as the earlier project.[22] From a demonstration middle-income rehabilitation project, prestige remodeling on Bunker Hill proved possible and Burns's firm is continuing to remodel homes on the Hill for the upper-income market.

[21] "How to Improve a Neighborhood," *House & Home*, October, 1954, pp. 120–121 (for complete cost figures).
[22] United States Gypsum Co., *Operative Remodeling*, Chicago, 1956, 126 pp. (see p. 21 for complete cost figures).

The Philadelphia Friends' Project

The Friends' self-help housing project is a conscious attempt by a private group to establish a knot of middle-income housing in the midst of a low-rent area—the East Poplar neighborhood in Philadelphia. Directly across the street from the Friends' project is Penn Towne, a state-aided housing project of mixed new construction and rehabilitated middle-income housing. The owners of Penn Towne had to set rent limits within the middle-income category in return for the state's 35 per cent construction subsidy. The existence of Penn Towne enlarged the scope of improved housing in the area, making tenants much easier to find for both projects.

East Poplar had been a stable middle-income neighborhood in the early part of the nineteenth century. The houses were predominantly three- and four-story semidetached brick structures, and views of the area in its prime show blocks of well-tended structures on tree-lined streets softly lit by gaslight. Now, passenger and freight rail lines have cut their way through the area on elevated structures, bringing industrial and commercial uses with them. What housing remains has been converted to small, ill-equipped apartments renting for from $5 to $15 a week, primarily to low-income Negro families. The City of Philadelphia designated the East Poplar area as one of its high-priority redevelopment projects shortly after World War II. The plans call for the eventual demolition or rehabilitation of several square miles, and the Friends' project is only the first small part of this giant undertaking.

The Friends' project was conceived originally to include four square blocks directly north of the 173-unit Penn Towne development and a 203-unit public housing project. Together, the three ventures were to provide a self-sufficient island of improved dwellings capable of withstanding the detrimental influences of the surrounding neighborhood. It was hoped that the projects would have to be less self-sufficient as the larger redevelopment project progressed. Penn Towne and the public housing project were built, but the Friends concentrated on only one block directly north of Penn Towne and adjacent to a Reading Railroad passenger line.

The block on which the Friends' project is located had twenty three-story brick houses, a small ice-cream plant, one structure beyond reclamation, and two small interior lots which were later cleared to provide a small but well-designed interior court. More than one hundred low-income Negro families lived in the structures slated for rehabilitation. The plans called for the twenty structures to be remodeled into ninety-seven units—fifty one-bedroom apartments, twenty-nine two-bedroom apartments, sixteen three-bedroom apartments, and two four-bedroom apartments. The ice-cream plant was to be demolished eventually, but in the interim would continue to operate, yielding an annual rental of $4,800.

The Friends unsuccessfully tried to get families to sign up for 90 per cent of the apartments before the project began. They decided as a first effort, therefore, to undertake the rehabilitation of fifty-two of the ninety-seven units as a cooperative undertaking with the future residents defraying their down-payment expenses either through cash or labor; 800 to 1,000 hours of work would be the equivalent of a 10 per cent down payment, and the final carrying charges would range from $50 to $87.50 per month. Low rents were made possible by a substantial write-down on initial acquisition by voluntary labor,[23] and by long-range, low interest financing

[23] However, the contractor claims it cost him $5,000 in delays while volunteer labor caught up with his professional crews. (See *Quaker "Self-*

obtained under the cooperative housing provisions of the FHA statute.

The average cost of the completed units was $9,300, exclusive of the initial $179,152 land write-down. The land was purchased by the Authority in 1952 for $257,552 and sold to the Friends on June 10, 1952, for $78,400. (This included the ice-cream plant, which has yielded over $20,000 in rent from 1952 to 1957.) The $186,000 project was financed through $100,000 provided by the Friends and a mortgage insured under Section 213 of the FHA statute, running forty years at 4 per cent, held by the Philadelphia Savings Fund Society. The Society of Friends has been defraying the mortgage's $10,000 debt service without depending on the rental returns.

The completed project itself is well designed. Its interior court gives a quiet, pleasant view from the windows of the apartments around it. The project has its own parking lot, leased from the Redevelopment Authority for only $1 a year, which serves as a buffer strip between the houses and the railroad. In 1956 financing was obtained to complete the remaining forty-five units which had stood vacant and boarded up since the completion of the original venture in June of 1953. As a result of these efforts, an entire square block of slum property has been substantially improved through rehabilitation.

The Friends' project might never have been completed without subsidies from the Friends, the Redevelopment Authority, and the City of Philadelphia. Without the land write-down amounting to approximately $1,800 for each of the ninety-seven units, the total unit cost—given the same standards

---

Help" Rehabilitation Program: Philadelphia, American Council To Improve Our Neighborhoods, New York, 1956, 10 pp., for more complete description.)

—would have increased to over $11,000. If the ice-cream plant and its revenue and all other subsidies currently received were removed,[24] the rents would have to be increased at least an average of $50 per month per unit. Putting it another way, the Friends could have paid no more than $3,500 per unit for improvements if rents were kept at the same level and no subsidies were used. Obviously the resulting standards would have been considerably less desirable.

The Friends had hoped that with the subsidy they could provide excellent units to families who had been displaced by the project. However, no families displaced by the project returned to it after the work was done, and only 20 per cent of the units were occupied by families previously living in the neighborhood. Most of the new tenants came from outside the area and have fairly substantial incomes.

The true test of any project is whether it will rent. The Friends project is rented to a highly specialized market. The people living there hold the same principles of cooperative interracial living as the Friends. Apparently even this specialized market has felt somewhat dissatisfied with the neighborhood in which the project stands, although they have been unflaggingly devoted to the project itself. What a less specialized market feels about the area can be found by examining Penn Towne just across the street. The rentals are approximately the same and, the project being larger, has more but not better designed recreational facilities. Yet Penn Towne's resident manager, A. A. Haynes, reported a 20 per cent vacancy rate for 1957.

Haynes thinks better housing in the area cannot sell as permanent homes for the middle-income families. There is

[24] Subsidies include debt payment by the Friends, a tax assessment reduced from $4,800 to $3,200, and the $1 rent for the parking lot.

a very clear pattern of housing decisions in Penn Towne. A Negro family with increased income and a desire for better housing moves to Penn Towne and almost immediately begins searching for a home in mixed and middle-income areas in other parts of Philadelphia. The family wants to own a home but not in a project surrounded by some of the worst housing in the city. The Friends project could have equally bad experience if it were a rental project depending on the general market.

Housing officials in Philadelphia have concluded that redevelopment in the eye of a slum is not sound unless the project is so sweeping that it extends beyond the borders of the slum to a stable community. The housing program has been shifted to conservation areas, with the thought that the slum should be surrounded and then swallowed by redevelopment moving in from improved areas.

Private developers can create middle-income housing in slum areas which possess the same attributes needed for prestige housing. If these attributes are present, however, the sensible investor—like Fritz Burns—will provide prestige housing. This is consistent with the first principle of real estate, that the investor should strive for the most profitable use of the property.

This is not meant to suggest that slums must be left to fester while redevelopment slowly reaches in from outlying areas. We have already seen that under some circumstances modest rehabilitation can be profitable for the investor in slum areas. The most unsanitary conditions of the slums can be removed and better housing can be provided, if either the owner or the tenant is willing to pay a little more for his house. Nevertheless, it is safe to conclude that dwelling units meeting high-standard FHA minimum property requirements are not likely to be successfully provided in the heart of low-rent areas without substantial public or private subsidies.

Conclusions

Opportunities for rehabilitation for middle-income families arise when a gap between existing and potential rents and sale prices allows rehabilitation expenditures averaging between $3,500 and $5,000 a dwelling unit. Middle-income rehabilitators concentrate primarily on functional deficiencies such as plumbing, heating, wiring, mechanical equipment, minor structural repairs, and necessary redecoration. Overcoming obsolescence in design is given secondary consideration provided the expenditures fit the repair budget and will boost the investor's returns. Opening the interior floor plan, removing useless trim, adding built-ins, lawn furniture, or an extra bath usually has appeal for the general market or a ready buyer under contract to pay for them.

The general market for middle-income rehabilitation is comprised of families who are able and willing to pay a little more for their housing. Their tastes are mirrored in almost every advertisement, Sunday supplement article, or entertainment script. They are interested in new things, but their interest is tempered by their ability to pay. Typical middle-income consumers are closely knit families interested in neighborhood amenities. Neighborhood friendship patterns and strong ties to local church or social institutions often hold families with increased incomes in their old neighborhood in a remodeled dwelling. When a roll-over in neighborhood residents occurs, the remodeler can profitably adapt the housing to the tastes and preferences of the newcomers.

In general, rehabilitators report that most of the middle-income consumers are found in the same area as the rehabilitation activity or in similar areas throughout the city. This is only natural when there is little or no disparity between the costs of the rehabilitated units and similar units nearby. Long-term financing with low down payments are needed to attract middle-income buyers for whom ample suburban alternatives are available unless the convenience of the location compensates for the added carrying costs. Adequate financing is usually available for rehabilitated structures located in stable neighborhoods, for families known as good credit risks. However, financing in declining and blighted areas is scarce and carries unattractive terms.

Government's greatest impact on the middle-income rehabilitation field so far has been in the sphere of financing projects in stable neighborhoods. FHA-insured home-improvement loans have been used extensively by contract remodelers in these areas. Similarly, FHA-insured home mortgages and VA-guaranteed mortgages are eagerly sought because of their more favorable terms but are available primarily in the better areas.

More existing rehabilitation opportunities could be utilized in less stable areas with more mortgage funds at more generous terms. Vigorous neighborhood group activity and added community facilities could materially contribute to the stability of declining areas. Government renewal programs can provide these needed factors, but as yet they have not fulfilled their promise. Code-enforcement programs have been the only public activity which has helped in promoting conservation in spite of the fact that housing codes are intended primarily for short-run sanitary improvements in low-rent areas.

Middle-income rehabilitation opportunities are geographically widespread, usually with points of concentration around new community facilities or in neighborhoods where community organizations have revitalized housing-improvement activity. Rising personal incomes, the increased tempo of municipal improvements both publicly and privately undertaken, and the spotlight of public interest on better homes and neighborhoods have caused the rents and sales prices the public is willing to pay for good housing to rise above prior rent levels. Investment opportunities should continue as long as the economy expands or remains stable, with the greatest opportunities lying in those areas where potential rents have risen sharply.

Chapter 4

REHABILITATION OF LOW-RENT HOUSING

Rehabilitation of low-rent housing is inextricably linked with local housing-code enforcement programs. Violation notices, backed by public officials who will go to court if necessary, are directly responsible for most of the low-rent repairs. But code enforcement has indirect effects as well. Many responsible property owners have voluntarily brought their units up to municipal code standards when it became evident through determined public action that the code was written to be enforced. The only form of rehabilitation that has little or no connection with code enforcement is the work of limited-dividend housing corporations.

A majority of the cities and towns in the United States either do not have a housing code or are not vigorously enforcing the code they have. In 1956 only about 150 cities out of nearly 35,000 cities and towns had housing codes, and although this number has certainly increased severalfold, we can still ask why the number is so small.[1] First of all, a vast majority of municipalities are too small to have a housing problem great

[1] *Housing Code Provisions: A Reference Guide for Citizen Organizations,* American Council To Improve Our Neighborhoods, New York, 1956, 36 pp. (p. 5).

enough to justify the expense of administering a housing code. Second, many communities respond to pressure groups who claim building and sanitary codes are adequate for the task. Only a few communities believe it is necessary to write and enforce a new code aimed at the occupancy, facility, and maintenance standards of existing housing. The typical housing code defines a set of minimum standards for the facilities, occupancy, and maintenance for existing units below which no dwelling unit in the community shall fall.

The visual impact of code enforcement programs is affected by the gap between the condition of the existing housing and the stringency of code provisions. In Charlotte, North Carolina, the condition of the existing structures was so primitive that even Charlotte's modest code provisions coupled with vigorous enforcement made permanent, visible improvements in its housing stock. If these same provisions were applied in a Northern industrial city where the housing usually has at least rudimentary plumbing and heating, the change might hardly be noticed.

Although the codes vary from city to city, almost reflecting local differences in the age and condition of structures, the technique of code enforcement and the congeries of associated problems such as relocation [2] and financing are almost universal. Three effective enforcement programs will be discussed and analyzed: those of Charlotte, North Carolina, St. Louis, and Rochester, New York, followed by a discussion of limited-dividend activities.

[2] Relocation problems arise either when the cost of repairs under code enforcement requires a relatively high rent increase or when the housing code is designed to lower the intensity of slum residence. Heavy relocation is usually necessary only where the code standards are high compared to the typical conditions of the existing housing stock.

The Code Enforcement Program in Charlotte

Since the end of World War II, Charlotte had been suffering the pleasant pangs of orderly growth. The population of the city itself increased from 134,000 in 1950 to 155,000 in 1955, while the metropolitan area increased from 196,000 in 1950 to 231,000 in 1955. During the decade following the War, 1946 to 1955, the metropolitan area showed an increase of 56.9 per cent. New industries—some from New England—and complementary commercial growth have been responsible for burgeoning local prosperity. The metropolitan area has seen a gain of 52.6 per cent in its nonagricultural workers since 1945, with a concomitant increase of 182.1 per cent in retail sales. In 1955 alone, thirty new businesses employing 1,500 people were established in the metropolitan area.[3] Civic improvement has been a by-product of prosperity: new schools, highways, shopping centers, improved water and sewer facilities, a modern civic auditorium and arena, added downtown office buildings, and a good-sized residential building boom.

The large number of existing dwellings improved under the enforcement program in Charlotte was greatly facilitated by the community's growing prosperity. Without a rising standard of living for metropolitan-area Negro families who were willing to pay increased rents, it would have been difficult to create the improved environment without causing wholesale dislocations and abysmal overcrowding in the remaining low-rent units. The code enforcement program has done much to better their housing standards and, more important, local

---

[3] Demographic and trade data supplied by the Chamber of Commerce from data collected from the Employment Security Commission of North Carolina and a 1956 survey of buying power in *Sales Management*.

businessmen say that it has had the additional effect of proving that Negro families are able and willing to pay for better housing and better neighborhoods.

Shortly after the passage of the U.S. Housing Act of 1937 authorizing public housing construction, local realtors began discussing means to combat what at the time seemed a threat to their businesses. Local realtors are credited with the conception of an extensive code enforcement program. They were ready to begin by 1939, but the war interfered, and so it wasn't until 1945 that work began on a suitable housing code. The local planning board and housing authority worked with the realtors in shaping the code now in force. The *Charlotte Observer* said of the local rehabilitation program: "The realtors rate a ribbon . . . this thing was their baby." [4]

The enforcement program got under way in 1948. James E. Ritch, a career public servant with thirty years' service in the City Engineering Department, was appointed as Enforcement Director. His report dated June 18, 1956, eight years later, showed that 11,024 units had been brought up to standard (about 20 per cent of the total housing supply in Charlotte) and that an additional 1,661 houses not capable of treatment were demolished.[5] Most of the affected structures were wooden, single-family, detached dwellings on lots measuring approximately 25 by 100 feet. They had four rooms, a front porch, and were supported on brick piles with an air space beneath, a collecting point for rubbish. Most of the houses lacked modern heating or plumbing of any kind prior to the

[4] *A Primer on Rehabilitation under Local Code Enforcement*, National Association of Real Estate Boards, Washington, 1953.
[5] The number of units brought up to standards far exceeds the normal capacities of a two-man staff because the property owners themselves improved many substandard units without formal inspection or violation notice.

enforcement program. Backyard privies were the first target of the drive.

There is no single code enforcement area in Charlotte. The substandard units were built throughout the city, usually behind what had been lovely old mansions now converted to boardinghouses. Some of these shacks were constructed in hollows below the prevailing terrain or along stream beds subject to occasional flooding.

The requirements of the code are simple. Each dwelling unit must have indoor plumbing and electricity; the plumbing is to include a tub or shower, a sink, and a toilet. Weathertight walls and roof, adequate heating, and screens are required. The principal room must be at least 150 square feet, with the master bedroom at least 100 square feet and each additional bedroom at least 70 square feet. The code does not require hot water, painting, or the use of any specific kinds of materials.[6] It is flexible enough to allow liberal interpretations of the provisions, yet comprehensive enough to make a decided improvement in the conditions that existed before its installation.

Ritch was the only inspector for four years after enforcement began. During those four years enforcement methods were shaped, public acceptance gained, and the cooperation of property owners won, and it was primarily through the tact and diplomacy of James Ritch that the program was so successful. Ritch decided at the very outset of the program that it would be difficult to enlist the cooperation of the property owners if he required all improvements completed simultaneously. This was particularly true with the program beginning under rent control. When Ritch checked with the rent-control office he found that 50 cents a week would be allowed for the installation of indoor plumbing, 50 cents for running

[6] Article XXIV, City of Charlotte Municipal Code.

water, 25 cents for electricity, and 25 cents for general cleanup and screens. A $6-a-month increase in rent would barely defray the cost of a complete package of improvements.[7]

Ritch decided that cooperation could be gained most readily if he allowed property owners to make the improvements at a rate they could easily absorb. First, indoor toilets were required, followed by complete bathrooms, and so on, until the full provisions of the code were met. Each property owner could decide on the rate of improvement suited to him, with the full understanding that eventually the code had to be met fully, and as long as he continued working there would be no court proceedings. The degree of cooperation can be measured by the fact that Ritch reports there have been only twelve court cases since the program began.

Selecting toilets as the first target served a double purpose. Ritch began inspecting by car. He had a lot of territory to cover and no help. Outdoor privies were easily spotted, and the owner identified from city records. Notices were served to the largest owners of substandard property first. Thus, even if the notice was on a single property, the owner was warned that it was only a matter of time before all his units would have to be brought up to the same standards. Newspaper coverage was excellent from the very beginning. It was exceedingly helpful to have a sympathetic press telling property owners what was being attempted and making them feel that they were not being singled out for special harassment. Ritch found strong allies, even beyond the members of the Charlotte

---

[7] The average cost of repairs was $750, with the bathroom addition and required plumbing costing between $400 and $500. The allowable rent increases permitted a gross return on the average additional investment of slightly over 10 per cent. The net return was either higher or lower, depending upon the combination of operating costs and financing terms affecting individual properties.

Real Estate Board, when his approach was learned. All but a few property owners gave him their full cooperation. The program moved more rapidly after Ritch acquired an assistant in 1952. As the most arduous part of the program neared completion, Ritch took on the duties of zoning and subdivision controls, while his assistant continued the enforcement program under his direction.

The actual physical improvements made by the program were very uneven. A few property owners went far beyond code requirements, while others barely met the minimum specifications. Exceptional improvements left a square frame house with bathroom added to the rear, a new roof and asbestos siding, new windows and doors, a new kitchen, concrete porch, and the foundations completely enclosed in brick. One property owner was able to do this to a group of houses without displacing any of the original tenants, using a rotating system with one vacant house, and with an increase in rent for each house of less than $25 a month.[8] At the other extreme, minimal work left houses unpainted with exterior repairs showing as visible patches: a hole in the side of a house patched with a packing-crate slat, or a hole in the roof covered with a few cheap shingles. These slapdash jobs were done by property owners with only one or two parcels and little income, or by a few large-scale owners who resented the whole idea of code enforcement. The primary evidence of code enforcement's effects, however, is the universal bathroom addition.

Reinspections have to be undertaken frequently, especially where the work is minimal. This may be the cause of comments that the program has been somewhat overrepresented. Perhaps there is some justification in these charges where the

---

[8] The cost of these improvements varied from about $2,000 to $3,000, depending upon the original condition of the structure.

An example of Charlotte's rehabilitation program.

same house is brought up to standard more than once. However, even without double counting, the environmental improvements through code enforcement are clearly evident.

Another example of what was accomplished in Charlotte.

The following features gave the program the flexibility it needed to be accepted by property owners and tenants alike. First and foremost were the time adjustments liberally allowed to property owners as long as work continued. Second, repairs of a minor nature were often left to tenants. Small patches in sidings or screens which would only take a few minutes and a few pennies for materials did not warrant a formal violation notice. Third, notices were delayed or omitted in cases of real hardship. Fourth, violation notices were omitted where the cause of violation was the tenant's own carelessness. Broken screens are a typical case; if broken after the owner was required to supply them, replacement would not be demanded until new tenants moved in.

Built-in flexibility made the program palatable, but other factors were responsible for its inception and its continuing economic feasibility. The most usual reason given for code enforcement is that a decent housing standard should be maintained for lower-income families. Though this motivation is always present, it can never be the only prime mover behind a really successful program. Somebody has to pay for the improvements, and those bearing the costs want to be shown that the program will produce benefits for themselves. Tenants must be persuaded that the improvements warrant compensatory rent increases (provided they are within their means), and property owners may find that the rent increases and added value justify their remodeling expenditures.

Economic and social motivations mingled in Charlotte in a way rarely duplicated elsewhere. Not only were rent increases readily paid, but the setting for continued economic expansion in Charlotte was enhanced. Further, public housing was officially declared unnecessary by Housing Authority officials in 1955, and some hope of capital gains emerged as an urban-redevelopment program for part of the code enforcement area went into its early stages.

Surprisingly, financing was no particular problem even with average unit costs of $750. Many of the owners held large blocks of unmortgaged property, so that improvements could be financed out of current income, if financing usually obtained from savings and loan associations was not readily available. Many property owners with modest incomes financed the needed improvements with cash borrowed from relatives and friends. Financing would have been much more difficult if higher housing-code standards had increased average repair costs. As it was, costs could be absorbed by rents of about $10 to $20 a month. Application of Philadelphia's standards in Charlotte might easily have doubled that amount.

One of the most striking benefits of the program was the improved housing conditions for Negro families. Many Charlotte realtors had doubted that Negro tenants would be willing to pay added rents before the program began. In fact there was some discussion whether Negro families could be taught to use the modern conveniences. Ritch said he could see how these comments arose, since a walk through Negro areas gave the impression that a greater part of the family income went to television sets, flashy cars, and liquor. If true, it should have caused no surprise, since rising incomes found no outlet in a market singularly lacking in better Negro housing. Negro families had been lucky to earn $30 a week before the war, but by 1948 incomes had risen to an average of $65 to $75 a week while typical rents still hovered between $2 and $5 a week. Consequently, Negro families were able to carry rent increases of $5 to $7 a week without any difficulty.

The evident willingness of Negro families with modest incomes to pay more for better housing has had a profound effect in Charlotte. As old shacks in enforcement areas were demolished, new rental units were constructed in their place to rent for $8.50 to $13.50 a week, plus utilities, for a four-room-and-bath apartment. New home construction for Negro families in outlying areas has also steadily increased.[9] Realtors report a clearly discernible trend in the Charlotte Negro hous-

---

[9] Over 500 apartments and 338 houses were built for Negro families by private investors between 1951 and 1956. And another 1,000 homes were planned for construction during 1957 and 1958. (Data supplied by Charlotte Home Builders Association and its members.)

ing market. The families buying new homes in outlying sections are younger families, while those renting new housing in the enforcement areas are the older families who have become too attached to the neighborhood to move.

What can be learned from Charlotte's experience? Housing-code provisions must bear some reasonable relationship to the tenant's ability to pay. If this is not the case property owners will be unwilling to undertake extensive repairs, banks may be reluctant to provide funds to the property owners, and public officials could have a major relocation problem on their hands when improvements actually take place. Second, careful thought should be given to long-run housing plans for the community. In Charlotte the eventual cost of redevelopment may be increased by the code enforcement program. There must be a balance struck, therefore, between the immediate alleviation of unsanitary conditions and future plans for clearance.

Program flexibility and good public relations ease the acceptance of the program. Flexibility in the form of phased enforcement can substitute for a set of lower standards, but it is of questionable legality unless uniformly applied. Similar effects can be achieved with a high-standard code by concentrating enforcement in areas of relatively better housing with slightly higher-income families than those found in the slums. St. Louis' program takes this direction.

St. Louis Conservation Program

The St. Louis Minimum Housing Standards Ordinance, approved April 20, 1948, controls dwelling occupancy and requires adequate facilities, including sinks, toilets, lighting, and ventilation. It also provides that the owner is required to keep every dwelling unit structurally sound and fit for human habitation.[10]

The ordinance specifies that three official agencies will participate in carrying out its provisions: the Health Division, the Building Division, and the City Plan Commission. A Rehabilitation Coordinating Committee was set up with members from each agency. Its functions were to carry out a housing rehabilitation program, including a field study to determine which neighborhoods were amenable to treatment, selection of neighborhoods, planning the neighborhoods with citizen participation, securing actions by official agencies, and applying enforcement where the minimum code standards were not met by voluntary action.[11] The Building Division, which is responsible for the enforcement of the housing ordinance, would continue to check a completed neighborhood to prevent its return to former conditions.

The Committee divided the city into three classes of areas. Acceptable areas were defined as areas needing no treatment; rehabilitation areas were those declining but in salvable condition; and reconstruction areas were those which could be improved only through clearance. From the very beginning of the program it was decided to do no systematic code enforcement in reconstruction areas but only answer complaints of particularly flagrant violations. Rigorous enforcement in both clearance and rehabilitation areas was beyond the Building Division's budget allowance.

Two pilot rehabilitation areas were selected for enforcement—the Hyde Park and the Cherokee areas—because their

---

[10] St. Louis Housing Survey Report, *Let's Look at Housing*, August, 1953, pp. 4–5.
[11] *Ibid*, p. 13.

residents responded vigorously to advances from public officials. The program got into high gear in early 1955. Immediately prior to the actual start of inspection work a survey of the neighborhoods was undertaken by the Housing Section of the Division of Building and Inspection. This survey covered dwelling conditions not described in census publications, the preferences and feelings of residents about community services, neighborhood cooperation, and possible improvements to increase the desirability of the area.

The findings of the two surveys on neighborhood housing conditions were published in pamphlets, with additional information about the scope of the rehabilitation program and the responsibilities of public and private forces in the work to be undertaken. The booklet for the Cherokee area showed that the section contained 4,813 people living in 1,641 dwelling units contained in 742 structures. The families had an average size of three persons, an annual income of $3,600, and were paying an average monthly rent of $24.88 for an apartment with three to five rooms. Over 90 per cent of the structures were made of brick. Two-thirds of the structures were privately owned, and 26.1 per cent of them needed major structural repairs. Although the houses averaged sixty years of age, most of the units had inside toilets, with only 14.6 per cent of them having toilets on the alley or rear yard and 2.3 per cent having toilets outside. The area has been enlarged three times since the program began and now covers sixty-eight city blocks housing a population of 11,500 persons.

The neighborhood had some excellent community facilities in a park, a playground, a school, and a health center. However, some of the houses had deteriorated badly, with commercial and industrial uses scattered haphazardly throughout the area, and the residential streets carried heavy traffic through

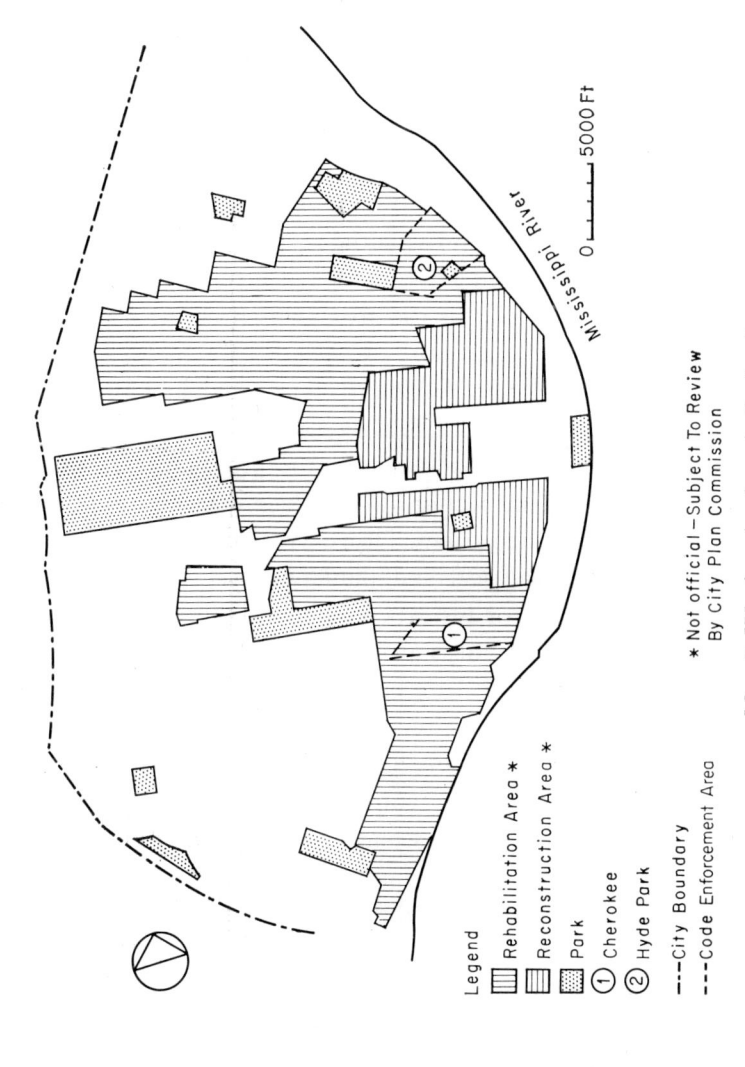

Map 3. Work to be done in St. Louis.

cartways narrowed by street parking. In general the area was quite pleasant, with abundant street trees and some charming, well-constructed houses, most of which were free-standing on lots averaging 33.5 feet in width. The community facilities were well kept and have been improved since the program began.

The city did not take its responsibilities lightly. About $220,000 was spent on improving the park and playground, in addition to budgeting added sanitation collections, traffic engineering, and planning for the area. In return, first-rate cooperation was received from the residents, who spent an estimated $800,000 on repairs and improvements from the time the program began to April, 1958.[12]

Inspections were the backbone of the program. St. Louis had consolidated its inspections so only one housing inspector looked for all code violations. However, if deficiencies were suspected in the electrical and plumbing systems, a special inspector was asked for his expert opinion before a violation notice was sent. The violation notice listed all violations regardless of which code had been broken. In addition, the notices carried a series of "recommendations" for improving the general appearance of the house which were not required by any code and not legally enforceable. They covered such items as painting a fence or seeding a lawn. In the Cherokee area, 76 per cent of the recommendations were voluntarily followed by area residents. If the violations listed in the notice

[12] Data supplied by Monroe F. Brewer, Chief Engineer, Housing Rehabilitation Project. The dollar estimates of expenditures by area residents are from building-permit data and are probably low. See the description (Appendix A) of the demonstration project undertaken by the St. Louis Real Estate Board in the Cherokee area for an example of local repair costs. The Board actually did more than was legally necessary to bring these substandard units to code standards, but unit repair costs averaged $2,120.

were not complied with in 60 days, a second notice was issued. If the work was contracted for or in progress, an estimated time limit would be set for completion, but the owner only received 30 days to comply if nothing had been done. A violator would be taken to a local police court only after he had a chance voluntarily to attend a hearing at the Division of Building and Inspection before an unofficial panel of enforcement people including at least one representative of the violator's neighborhood council. The purpose of the meeting is to obtain compliance through advice and persuasion rather than legal action. Monroe Brewer, Chief of Housing Rehabilitation, is proud of the group's ability to keep the court cases low, thereby keeping public relations with enforcement-area residents high.

The progress report in the Cherokee area from January, 1955, to April, 1958, showed that 7,820 violations were found in 3,729 dwelling units, and 6,791 of these were corrected. Also, 919 of the 1,301 recommendations made to homeowners were followed.

The income, family size, size of units, age of structures, and the percentage of owner occupancy in the Hyde Park area were almost identical with those in the Cherokee area. The average rent of $24.50 differed only slightly. The Hyde Park booklet showed that the area had a population of 6,446 persons in 947 structures or 1,964 dwelling units. The areas contrasted most sharply in the condition of structures. In Hyde Park, 83.4 per cent were in need of major structural repairs. However, this figure is a poor indication of neighborhood character. (The high proportion of structural defects was caused by a sudden windstorm which had swept through the Hyde Park area shortly after the war, seriously damaging the brick structures.) In general appearance the Hyde Park area is quite similar to the Cherokee area, though it has the advantage of a slightly higher elevation on a series of low hills rising from the Mississippi River. Even though the housing is older, wider lots and sloping streets give it a more open appearance.

The progress report for Hyde Park from January, 1955, to April, 1958, shows that 4,677 violations were found in 2,112 dwelling units and that 4,440 of these were corrected. Also, 599 of 1,754 recommendations were followed. An estimated $530,000 was spent by area residents for repairs, and $214,000 was spent by the city for community facilities.

In both neighborhoods housing inspectors used tact and patience. The program emphasized visible improvements because city officials felt success was vital to continuing an expanding enforcement program. The main targets were unsightly sheds, rear-yard clutter, lack of fire escapes for multiple dwellings, and outdoor toilets. Inspectors reported again and again they were able to persuade property owners to do a little more than required in the interests of over-all neighborhood improvement. For example, one inspector was able to persuade a group of property owners to tear down legal, rear-yard sheds after the alley's dilapidated sheds were removed by painting a picture of the sweeping green vista the alley could have with all sheds gone. Concentrated enforcement by inspectors assigned to a particular area brought good results because the inspector became familiar in the neighborhood, and the program he was selling was known and respected. Some of the property owners were spurred on to the point where they spent as much as $3,500 in repairs, although the average spent was $541 in the Cherokee neighborhood and $403 in Hyde Park.

The pilot programs paid off handsomely. Real estate brokers reported that demand had picked up in the two areas, which was later graphically illustrated by about $300,000 worth of new construction, the first in Cherokee since pre-Depression days. Another area, started in 1957, promises to equal the compliance rate of the pilot projects. Two others were selected to begin in the summer of 1958. Like the pilot projects, the three later projects have strong neighborhood groups ready to cooperate with the city.

It is safe to say that these enforcement programs achieve commendable results primarily because they are applied where residents are cooperative and able to absorb improvement costs. The code enforcement program has not been applied to areas earmarked for eventual clearance, in order to avoid added cost of acquisition under condemnation. Moreover, a rigorous application of St. Louis' rather high-standard code in such low-standard areas could cause dislocation both directly through occupancy limits and indirectly through necessary increases in rent.

Waiting for clearance to improve the worst areas may be an extremely lengthy process. In St. Louis, as in other large cities, designated clearance areas contain a high proportion of Negro families with extremely low incomes. Mass relocation would be difficult if not impossible, and the filtering process does not work where community temperament denies even partial integration. Consequently, the normally slow process of redevelopment is delayed even more by the relocation problem. Meanwhile, conditions prevailing in designated clearance areas can only become worse if even code enforcement in the areas is renounced. Some housing officials have proposed a more modest code enforcement program for clearance areas, where sanitary conditions are given the greatest emphasis, and building and occupancy provisions are applied only when no hardship could possibly result.

Reactions to this policy are mixed. Some inspectors claim that residents of the areas will not respond to any treatment. They claim Negroes in the areas would complain of discriminatory practices on the part of the city and tie up any possible achievements in a bundle of accusations. Other inspectors are not so pessimistic. In fact those who have worked in clearance areas are sanguine about achieving results through sympathetic pressure. Monroe Brewer would like to have the funds for enforcement in both rehabilitation and clearance areas, trusting to the discretion of the individual inspectors not to precipitate undue relocation problems. He is convinced that it is possible to remove the worst conditions plaguing the many families living in clearance areas through necessity.

Code Enforcement in Rochester: A Vigorous Sales Program

One of the code enforcement programs receiving wide community participation and accentuating the best features of the St. Louis and Charlotte programs as well as adding others took place in Rochester, New York. The official program began with the appointment of a Rehabilitation Commission in May, 1955, to initiate a plan for housing-code enforcement and to reactivate a then-dormant slum-clearance program.[13] On December 15, 1955, an Executive Director was appointed by the Commission, and one week later a program for code enforcement and neighborhood renewal was adopted.[14] The program proposed centralized, unrelenting enforcement on a "neighborhood at a time" basis. Public officials were to utilize citizens'

---

[13] The operating authority was granted to the Commission by chap. 57.2 of the Municipal Code, adopted Sept. 13, 1955.

[14] *Report of the Rochester Rehabilitation Commission to the City Council,* Dec. 31, 1956.

committees wherever possible. The Commission had a staff comprised of the Executive Director, four housing inspectors, and a senior planner for research on the slum-clearance project.

To aid in these aims the Rochester Home Improvement Action Committee raised $25,000 from local banks, merchants, industries, realtors, and builders, to be used to sell the idea of home improvement to homeowners and landlords. Advertisements were taken in the local papers, and speeches were made by members of the Committee to local citizens' groups. The Rochester Gas and Electric Company initiated the publicity program with the previously discussed demonstration rehabilitation project at the same time the official drive began—December, 1955. The actual inspection work started April 15, 1956.

The people of Rochester were determined to incorporate the best features of other enforcement programs in their own: a forceful public relations campaign, persuasion rather than insistence, and special attention given to low-income families. The speakers' bureau from the Rochester Home Improvement Action Committee, in addition to speaking to local citizens' groups, made continual efforts to convince home builders and contractors that rehabilitation provides business and they should gear their operations to remodeling.

Two wards, the Third and the Sixth, were selected for the first year's program, together with spot checks throughout what were termed "better neighborhoods" in five other wards. About 57 per cent of the dwelling units inspected in the Third and Sixth Wards (which were considered problem areas) needed repairs of some kind. The Rochester problem, however, was less acute than that in Charlotte, where 95 per cent of the dwellings in enforcement areas needed repairs. It was limited even further by Rochester's decision to push ahead with a slum-clearance program in their worst area, and the fortunate presence of vacancies resulting from heavy residential construction. However, even though obstacles to enforcement were few, the large number of violations overcome through immediate voluntary compliance and the small number of cases requiring punitive action indicate clearly that a strong public relations program is of value in code enforcement drives.

Code Enforcement Policies

In Charlotte, St. Louis, and Rochester, the feasibility of rehabilitation from the investors' point of view made eminent sense. In Charlotte any costs of rehabilitation were defrayed through rent increases, allowed by an ability and willingness to pay. In addition, the value of the dwelling units was increased, an increase that could provide some capital gains if the values did not fall as rapidly as the unamortized cost of improvement. Increases in rents and sale prices were equally possible in the other cities.

The balance between housing supply and demand at the time of enforcement and the way in which the program itself affects the balance will determine the level of cooperation the program receives and the amount of dislocation it will cause. It is likely that dislocation will be limited and easily handled when large stocks of housing are vacant. Even if the vacant housing is in worse condition than the occupied units below code standards, consumer resistance will keep the rents for improved units down to a level roughly comparable to the consumer's ability to pay. An exception exists where Negroes have restricted access to the market as a whole.

A definite relocation problem occurs where there are very few vacant units, which will be quickly priced out of the low-income market by excessive demand. Added rent payments resulting from a code enforcement program may cause either further doubling up or a decrease in the consumption of other necessities. Even where supply is limited, it is possible that, assuming a constant but mobile population, relocation would be only a minor problem.

Between the two extremes of abundant supply with consumer ability to pay and a short supply in a market unable to pay for better housing is a vast middle ground which may or may not give rise to relocation problems. Each city has conditions all its own and must decide on the method of code enforcement, independently of discouraging or encouraging news of its effects in other cities having different conditions. When the code enforcement activities in Charlotte are reviewed, the reasons dislocation was not an issue become apparent. New units were added to the supply of housing for Negro families by new construction and downtown conversions. These additions adequately compensated for the units lost through demolition under the code enforcement program. Even more important, families in the enforcement areas were willing to pay needed rent increases. In St. Louis the city officials were aware of the complicated submarkets in clearance areas. Determined enforcement would undoubtedly have caused severe dislocation. The rehabilitation areas selected had a higher vacancy rate, a high proportion of homeownership, and tenants not limited in geographic mobility.

The Economics of Code Enforcement

Thus far the economics of enforcement programs from the investor's point of view have been ignored. In some ways the easiest kind of investor to discuss is the homeowner. Clearly he will absorb immediate repair costs, since his only alternative is to sell at a lower price, compensating the new owner for impending repair costs. If he makes the repairs and continues to live in the house, can the repairs be considered economic? They can if the cost of repairs is equal to or less than the value added to the house as a result of the repairs. In a more limited sense, it would be economic if the cost of repairs were equal to or less than the value lost in the event repairs were not made.[15]

A more difficult question is whether or not it is economic for the owner of rental property to make the required improvements. Before complying with violation notices, the owner can examine a number of alternatives open to him: he may be able to remodel the property for a higher-income market; he can improve the property as required after analyzing the effects of the work on his other holdings; he can sell the property to another private investor without improving it; or he can hold the property vacant, demolishing the structure if necessary, waiting for more propitious circumstances. Each of these situations, moreover, may be modified by a whole set of additional factors, the most important of which is the current condition of the local housing market.

The owner confronted with a violation notice might choose to repair the property far beyond the requirements of the code, if the market made it possible to obtain higher-paying tenants for the property. Code enforcement in areas such as Foggy Bottom or the two sections discussed in central Philadelphia might engender some prestige rehabilitation on the part of investors who had not considered it before. This is exactly

[15] This argument does not take into account alternative investment outlets and further assumes that homeowners look on their home purely as an investment. Also, the altered value of the structure will depend on market conditions, which are themselves affected by the code enforcement program.

what happened in one instance in Philadelphia. The block above the particular properties had been fully rehabilitated, and an adjacent house was in the process of major repairs. The owner began to refurbish the houses for prestige sales after code enforcement became an issue. It is doubtful that he would have done so if code enforcement had not forced his hand, since the houses had been purchased some years before for $400 each and were renting for $40 a month without utilities.

The second situation, improving the property as required, is an alternative only if the property owner has extensive holdings which might be affected by the enforcement drive. One Philadelphia real estate broker, for example, owns about 2,000 low-rent units. His business operation is characterized by a high property turnover rate with only easily maintained properties which draw a high rate of return, held for indefinite periods. The remainder of the property is sold whenever a capital gain is possible. Consequently, a good part of the holdings have not been owned long enough to pay out their initial investment, and selling unamortized properties threatened with code enforcement would diminish working capital. Under these circumstances, it is better to improve those properties in which there is still an investment and to sell those properties where the investment has been amortized.

Leeway in which to execute this maneuver was provided by the City of Philadelphia. Property owners in enforcement areas had convinced the city that tight financing prevented them from improving all their holdings simultaneously. The city allowed them to submit a list of properties below code standards and a schedule of improvements. The city would not crack down on the lack of improvements in the remaining properties as long as owners improved their holdings at a constant rate. Many property owners have invested considerable sums in making not only the necessary improvements but in exceeding the requirements. Many dwelling units in downtown Philadelphia have received full facilities, with complete redecoration included, at a reported cost of between $2,000 and $3,000 per unit. The rent increases have been limited by the market to about $10 per $1,000 added investment, but the properties still yield a satisfactory though lessened rate of return. Mortgages were rarely available, and the entire cost of repairs were undertaken with the owner's equity. Since this tied up working capital, owners were left in a position where they could not take advantage of other investment opportunities.

Selling a property without improvement is often an economic necessity, brought about by a lack of funds necessary to complete the required repairs. However, under certain conditions it may be a wise business decision. If improvement would have the effect of tying up the investor's capital at a low rate of return when more profitable investments were available and if the investor had no money or very little tied up in the building, it might be better for him to sell the property and limit the loss to the difference between the old selling price and a selling price reduced by an amount roughly equal to the cost of repairs.

Of course the original owner only bears that portion of the costs which cannot be shifted by the new owner to the consumer in added rent. For example, if a four-unit rental structure had a value of $4,200 based on a gross monthly rent of $140 and a multiplier of thirty, and $4,000 in repairs would increase the rent to $240 a month, the new value of the building would be $7,200, and the highest potential selling price $7,200 less $4,000 for repairs, or $3,200. Therefore, the original owner of the unimproved property might absorb only

$1,000 of the repair costs if he could find a buyer who would purchase the unimproved structure at the new value, based on its potential rent less the cost of repairs. Obviously if potential rent increases will absorb only a small part of the repair costs or if the future rents are uncertain, the original owner will receive a much lower price for the property, since the new purchaser would be unwilling to absorb any of the repair costs. It is not surprising, therefore, that property values tumble under the impact of code enforcement and that property transfers increase greatly.[16]

The last situation is that in which the owner boards up his property or demolishes it, and holds it vacant, waiting for an improvement in market conditions, a choice that is likely to be made if there is hope of sufficient future revenues or capital gains from a different use of the land that will compensate for the losses sustained during the period of inactivity.[17]

Philadelphia's code enforcement program has interestingly meshed these alternatives. When values tumbled after code enforcement's initial shock, many small holders tried to sell their properties. Many of the properties were purchased by large holders and placed at the end of their improvement schedule. The reason was plain. Large holders are "property rich"; their equity is in their properties and they live off the income. Their incomes would be seriously curtailed if any large block of equity went into remodeling. But if they use part of their income to buy properties still drawing rents, the rents which had determined the higher original value of the

[16] "Code Enforcement Spoils Market for Slum Housing in Philadelphia," *House & Home*, February, 1956.

[17] It is interesting to note that many vacant structures in industrial centers were profitably reopened for residential use during World War II, in spite of their deficient condition.

property, at prices deflated by code enforcement, owners can still schedule enough improvements to satisfy the city without suffering radical curtailment of income.

The discussion demonstrates that very special considerations may be required to reconcile the interests of the investor, the city, the consumer, and the politician who will suffer from the dissatisfaction of the other interests. Without such reconciliation, one of the interested groups may raise obstacles to the enforcement program, and impede, if not defeat, its purposes. Circumstances balance only when the investor can shift the cost to a willing consumer and when dislocated families can readily find housing elsewhere.

What can be done when tenants will not or cannot pay added rents? If there is a high-enough vacancy rate within the part of the market affected by code enforcement, rent increases will be low and dislocation will be manageable. Under these conditions, the property owner may have to absorb a substantial proportion of the costs. In this case there is likely to be organized resistance to the program from landlords. On the other hand, it may be possible to shift the entire cost to the consumers when the vacancy rate is low. Consequently, though the landlords may be satisfied, consumer dislocation may create a problem for the city.

Several approaches to relocation have been used with varying degrees of success. Sometimes the city can provide accommodations in public housing units if the displaced families are eligible for them. Another device is to provide a sum to cover moving costs which, if large enough, can temporarily help pay added rents. Another solution is to minimize the rent increases in return for a series of public concessions which are tantamount to subsidizing the investor. New York State's multiple-dwelling property-tax concession authorizes the city to waive reassessment on remodeled multifamily properties for a period of twelve years and in addition, to reduce the preimprovement tax levy by 8⅓ per cent for a period of nine years, thus absorbing 75 per cent of the improvement cost. An untried possibility is to provide financing for properties improved as a result of voluntary action that will permit an increase in the effective yield on the investment.

Many homes in what are officially designated as the city's worst areas show evidence of real pride of ownership. Many others have been neglected only because the families have not recognized how far deterioration has gone. These families are usually quite willing to make any needed repairs they can afford.[18] The Baltimore Fight Blight Fund found that a majority of cases it handled involved families who wanted to make required repairs but did not know how to go about financing them.[19] Careful rearrangement of family budgets solved all but a few of the cases handled.

A combination of these devices, however, will still leave many problems unsolved. Individuals, unwed mothers, and families without regular incomes may not be eligible for public housing under the present law and may require some form of rent subsidy to obtain units above code standards. Furthermore, even with rent subsidies, many code enforcement officers are hampered by the lack of available alternative accommodations in their communities and fear that an increase in

[18] There is at least one case on record where consumers faced with rent increases resulting from code enforcement objected to government interference in what they deemed a perfectly satisfactory housing situation. "Tenants—Not Landlords—Defy Repair Order in Brooklyn," *Journal of Housing*, March, 1956, p. 104.

[19] William A. Andrews, the Fund's counsel, states that out of 155 cases the Fund handled up to May 2, 1956, only 31 required the Fund's financial backing.

doubling up in neighborhoods untouched by their program may intensify dislocation problems resulting from future enforcement drives.

The cooperation that enforcement programs receive and the amount of dislocation they cause are closely related to the number of vacant units in the community and the resulting distribution of program costs among the government, the property owners, and the tenants.

Limited Dividend Housing: Octavia Hill Association

The limited dividend housing corporation is one type of property owner willing to operate with a low rate of return from property improvement. "Philanthropy at 5 per cent" was at one time common. Prior to the present levels of income taxation, many affluent citizens willingly invested in companies providing housing for the poor and paying dividends at 4 and 5 per cent, although, in total, dividend corporations never accounted for a large share of the housing for lower-income groups. A good example of such operations is provided by the Octavia Hill Association of Philadelphia, which has voluntarily restricted its earnings throughout its life, although chartered as a normal profit-making corporation.

The Association's name comes from an English pioneer in housing. Miss Hill conceived the idea of owning and rigorously maintaining housing for the poor while instilling a sense of responsibility in tenants through her "friendly rent collectors." The rent collectors were always women, who appeared each week under instructions to be firm but sympathetic. Payment had to be prompt or the tenants were asked to leave (with regard, of course, for extreme hardship). There was opportunity for friendly exchanges of confidences and for advice to the tenant on housekeeping methods. Miss Hill thoroughly believed tenants would be willing to maintain their homes properly once they learned how it was done. Even the idea of modest profits started with Miss Hill or, to be more accurate, with John Ruskin, who gave her the first loan with the admonition that unless he was paid 5 per cent she could not expect other men to invest money with her company.

The Octavia Hill Association of Philadelphia was chartered under the auspices of the Philadelphia Civic Club on June 25, 1896.[20] The original founders decided to pay dividends of 4½ per cent for the first two years and 4 per cent thereafter. Twelve thousand shares were authorized at $25 a share. The directors themselves collected the rents in the early days and served on one or more of the five operating committees: finance, new property, office administration, construction and inspection, and rent collecting. It was not until 1901 that a salaried secretary was retained, followed in 1907 by a bookkeeper and in 1908 by the first superintendent.

Three criteria were used for property selection: (1) the property must need repair; (2) it must be economically feasible to make repairs within the low-rent framework; (3) the structure should, if possible, be part of a large-enough group of similarly improved structures to serve as an object lesson for the rest of the neighborhood. The only exceptions to these rules were structures which had been deeded to them without cost or the structures built by the Association. These same general criteria are used by the current directors.

Tenants are selected on the basis of their stability and good

[20] Fullerton J. Waldo, *Good Housing That Pays*, The Harpers Company, Philadelphia, 1917, 126 pp. Earlier efforts included that of the Benevolent Building Association, founded in 1865 to "... provide bright, cleanly dwellings for families of limited earning capacity" (*ibid.*, p. 22), and Hannah Fox, who had worked with Miss Hill in London and helped found the Philadelphia Association.

housekeeping habits. Then, as now, the Association checked with the prior landlords and in many cases present employers. By 1917 this policy had proved its worth. The average length of occupancy was seven years and five months. There were families living in the structures in 1957 who had been in one or another of the Association's dwelling units for over fifteen years, with one family staying for forty-one years.

The Association purchased houses in 1917 for under $1,000 and repaired them to the Association's standards for a fraction of today's costs. Acquisition costs are averaging $1,500 a dwelling unit today, and rehabilitation costs have risen to between $1,200 and $2,000 per unit. Rents have increased from $6 to $10 a month, to $20 to $40 a month, to keep pace with increased investment. In 1917 the Association owned 179 houses, in which 244 families dwelled, and managed another 224 structures housing 460 families.[21] It owned 228 properties and managed 75 properties, housing 305 and 111 families respectively, by the end of 1957.[22] These figures show an actual decrease in the Association's activities. Where in 1917 the Association owned or managed housing for 704 families, by 1957 they housed only 417 families, a decrease of over 40 per cent. Part of the decrease is explained by the Association's policies from 1914 through 1927. Some of the old holdings were sold to help finance the construction of new units. No construction has been undertaken since 1927 because the rents for new units could not be economically supported in low-rent neighborhoods.

The similarity between the operation of the Association fifty years ago and its present operation is striking, but much

[21] *Ibid.*, p. 71.
[22] *Sixty-first Annual Report of the Octavia Hill Association, Inc.*, February, 1958.

has been learned over the years, and the Association has constantly revised its housing standards to keep pace with the changing market. One of the facts facing the Association is that it is in competition with all other housing suppliers. The Association was chagrined to discover in 1956 that 5 to 10 per cent of its units were below code enforcement standards even though its standards were higher than those of surrounding properties. Every effort is being made either to improve substandard units or to sell them for nonresidential uses. A look at its management techniques will show how the Association can operate in the low-rent market.

The Association has fifteen directors, one of whom, the president, Richard Mecasky, devotes almost all of his time to the operation of the Association. The staff includes two office workers, two rent collectors, and the maintenance crew which does all rehabilitation work except plumbing and heating, roofing, and complicated electrical work.

All the structures now owned and operated by the Association were either constructed by the Association or purchased on the open market, except for a few acquired by bequest or gift. Great care is taken to assure structural soundness, and new purchases are rarely made unless they are near existing holdings. There are several major concentrations of properties at the present time. The oldest is found two blocks from the waterfront, in eighteenth-century Philadelphia. About 40 per cent of the Association's dwelling units are within a few blocks of one another in this area. Workman Place has the largest concentration, with 35 dwelling units. The other concentrations are centered around housing constructed by the Association. The Kensington groups, totaling 104 units, are located in the north central area of Philadelphia about three miles from City Hall. Another group of 23 units is located in the northwestern part of the city in Manayunk, an important industrial area of the nineteenth century.

The Association's standards are quite simple. It provides clean, inexpensive dwellings with plumbing and heating, hot water, and electricity. Its standards differ from the city's Housing Code only in the floor area requirements, often unavoidable in older houses. Sometimes the Association cannot provide individual baths for each unit and still meet the rent level which policy dictates, but baths are installed when rising rent levels and physical layout permit it.

Richard Mecaskey is constantly on the lookout for new acquisitions and always makes the initial inspection. The Association's construction committee, consisting of three architects, one of whom is Mecaskey, conducts a more detailed inspection to examine the possibilities for rehabilitation and the condition of the immediate surroundings. It considers potential rents and the estimated repair costs. Mecaskey reports that actual costs are usually within $200 of the initial estimate.

The final decision to purchase is based on the cost figures, weighted to cover contingencies such as undisclosed structural deficiencies. The committee pays particular attention to bulged or cracked walls and the condition of joists and other framing members. Only a few structural defects can be inexpensively repaired, such as a cracked wall over a wooden lintel, which can be corrected with an iron lintel. On the other hand, it is not troubled by a faulty roof or deteriorated windows and doors.

Typical of the Association's improvements are: a three-fixture bath sometimes utilizing second-hand fixtures, a linoleum floor, and composition-board walls. Often the largest room in the dwelling serves as a combined living room and kitchen because, according to Mecaskey, a living-kitchen is preferred by many tenants. Rehabilitation includes structural repairs and installations, repairs to plaster and floors, painting inside and out, and the rooms repapered. The Association occasionally helps tenants obtain the necessary materials to redecorate provided it feels they can complete a creditable job, but has found that the results do not always justify the cost.

The Association's problem is that of maintenance after initial repairs are made. About 20 per cent of the gross rent receipts go to repair and maintenance, including renewals and replacements on existing holdings. Major rehabilitation expenditures are considered capital improvements.

Careful management is the essence of Association policy. The same kind of "friendly rent collectors" used by Octavia Hill in London are used on the Philadelphia properties. Increasing concentration of holdings has minimized unit rent-collection costs and made the collector a familiar neighborhood figure. The rent collector, who is a public relations expert as well as a business woman, is the tenants' direct contact with the Association. Her job begins when she checks the prospective tenant's housekeeping habits, employment stability, and rent regularity. If her advice is solicited, she offers counsel on such matters as garbage disposal, cleaning, and even budgeting after the tenant moves in. The collector will also ask the tenant if he will pay a modest rent increase for any improvement the Association proposes.

Financing has never been a problem for the Association. Enviable financial health coupled with a long relationship with one of Philadelphia's leading banks assures it ready cooperation. Smaller jobs which cannot be financed from current revenue are financed with short-term bank loans. When the volume of these loans becomes large, or when the Association decides to undertake a sizable project, all outstanding loans are refinanced as a single mortgage, with a fifteen- to twenty-year term at the prevailing rate of interest. The Association has always insisted on mortgages with provisions for advanced payment, so that it can repay the loan as quickly as possible.

The 1957 Annual Report clearly shows the Association's financial strength. The value of outstanding stock was $201,950 as compared to total assets after depreciation on real estate of $555,272.60. The gross rents amounted to $115,962.05, with a net profit of $20,802.22 after all expenses including income taxes of an estimated $11,114.77 and depreciation charges of $21,430.67. Of this amount less than half, or $8,078, was paid out in a 4 per cent dividend on outstanding stock, and the remaining $12,724.22 went into an earned surplus account. The Association had a $27,200 mortgage and owed bank loans totaling $40,000 at the end of that year, a small sum compared to its net worth and in light of conventional real estate practice. Its financial position has earned the respect of local bankers. Harold Scott, Senior Vice-President of the First Pennsylvania Company for Banking and Trusts, the bank from which the Association obtains its financing, says that the Association has earned the confidence of his bank, as proven by the fact that no request for financing has ever been denied.

A description of an individual rehabilitation project, however, will give a better idea of the Association's work than do the above figures. Workman Place is undoubtedly the best-known work of the Association,[23] although in a way it is not wholly typical of the Association's activities, because this group of houses not only was a near gift—35 units for $2,500—

[23] Richard Mecaskey wrote a description of the project in an article entitled "Rehabilitation Yields Low Rent Housing," *Journal of Housing*, December, 1955.

but was grouped in such a way that the backyards could form a common open space.

Workman Place is in the oldest part of Philadelphia. Some of the three-room-and-bath houses in the group were built prior to 1754 and two of the houses on Pemberton Street were built in 1748. The Front Street apartments were built later, but built carefully with wainscoted halls, carved balustrades, and solid foundations. A settlement house built in the nineteenth century was not an original part of the group, but its later acquisition permitted the Association to hold a U-shaped group of buildings, with the sheltered portion of the U forming the interior court.

The accounting methods of the Association record all the repairs by groups of buildings without distinguishing the costs of individual units, making an individual cost breakdown impossible. Total funds invested in the project between 1942 and 1956, including the acquisition cost, were $92,481.80. The present value after depreciation is $87,763.26. Average apartment rentals in the project are $38.50 a month, including heat but not utilities, and each of the fourteen houses rents for $28 or $29 a month plus heat and utilities. Annual gross rent for the project is $14,900, with net rent of $5,050 after deducting the approximate 65 per cent operating costs.

The project has a pleasing appearance. Rents three or four times the present levels could be obtained, if further decorating were undertaken and if the project were located in one of the prestige areas. The apartments along Front Street rise three stories from the sidewalk in an almost solid wall. The two wings of the U are made up of small individual structures with private gardens. They have steeply pitched roofs, are quite narrow, and have colonial windows. One side of the U is open to the street because small houses comprising part of the group are on the far side of the street. The other side of the U has a brick wall pierced by what at one time may have been a gateway but is now just a gracefully proportioned opening. The small houses with their tiny garden plots, and the Front Street houses bordered on the rear by their own gardens, surround the court with summertime flowers. The newly planted trees give islands of shade in the black-topped play area. Many of the tenants have redecorated their quarters, leaving the interiors clean but lacking in the refinements of higher-rent dwellings.

Philadelphia's Workman Place—amenities on a low budget.

Speaking for the Board of Directors, President Mecaskey expressed the Association's interest in entering new investment fields, particularly rehabilitation under the auspices of urban renewal. It had estimated the cost of Philadelphia's Southwest Temple rehabilitation project, but found that the acquisition costs asked by the Redevelopment Authority and the standards required would not allow it to charge what they considered an economic rent for the area. The Association has also considered entering the middle-income field, but the directors feel this would be inconsistent with the Association's purpose. Mecaskey reports that the Association believes it must take some vigorous new direction before its role is usurped by public projects and its holdings fall under the redevelopment bulldozer.

Although the Octavia Hill Association is still flourishing, is it doing all it can in the low-rent field and is its approach usable by other groups with similar objectives? The answer to the first question is debatable. A few knowledgeable rehabilitators have said that, given the same starting point, they could easily double or triple the number of low-rent units held by the Association without sacrificing standards. They would do this by mortgaging as heavily as possible and using the funds to purchase more extensive holdings; then, instead of continuing the conservative policy of earned surpluses and depreciation reserves, they would purchase and rehabilitate ever-increasing amounts of property. Other ideas have also been suggested, such as purchasing of related commercial facilities and entering the middle-income field, to plow profits back into the low-rent operation.

It seems doubtful, however, that limited dividend companies could ever gain the backing to make a mass assault on low-rent housing. The few more recent attempts, such as the Powelton Village Development Associates, discussed in the last chapter, and the Washington Urban Redevelopment Corporation following, have limited appeal to investors because of limited dividends. Of the few socially conscious people who had originally been relied upon to underwrite limited dividend companies, many have had their consciences allayed with public housing. Limited dividend activities may become more vigorous if and when public housing dies and if the income tax structure were more conducive to this kind of investment.

The limited dividend corporation illustrates that some housing meeting all the requirements of building and housing codes can be provided at rents comparable to those charged for deficient dwelling units. Furthermore, the provision of such housing can be accomplished without wholesale tenant dislocation.

An Attempt to Reach the Low-rent Market That Failed

The device of limiting profits, however, is no complete guarantee that good housing can be obtained for lower-income families. The potential supplier must have a thorough grasp of what can be provided within a low-rent strait jacket. If too much is attempted, the supplier will have to seek higher rentals than were originally intended, and then, unless his project appeals to a group with the requisite purchasing power, he will meet with limited success.

An example of the dilemma of relatively high standards and limited profits is the work of the Washington Urban Redevelopment Corporation, a private organization established in 1950 with the purpose of rehabilitating and either renting or selling houses in the middle- and lower-income market. Stock was sold in $100 shares with a limit of $1,000 for any one company, and was to pay 6 per cent. Most of the subscribers were Washington home builders and interested companies. The president and director of activities was Herman Schmidt, a Washington home builder whose broad experience in rehabilitation spreads over twenty years.

The first project was undertaken in one of Washington's worst areas. Eight small alley dwellings similar to those rehabilitated for the prestige market in Foggy Bottom were purchased for a price comparable to that of improved land. The houses were located in a row on one side of an alley facing several unimproved structures. Some of the houses were rehabilitated as two-bedroom, living room, kitchen, and bath units at a cost of $4,750 per unit. The rest were rehabilitated as two-family rental units with one bedroom, living room-kitchen, and bath at a cost of $3,750 per unit. The small units rented for $55 a month and the larger units for $77.50 a month, when it became apparent that the cost of renovation did not permit lower rents. The work included the removal of backyard fences, spigots, privies, and sheds, installation of indoor toilets, kitchen sinks, running water and heat, replacement of rotting floors, joists, plaster and wire, ratproofing, and complete redecoration. The end product was a marked improvement, with good equipment supplied and all new plaster and floor coverings.

The work was financed partly by deferred-purchase financing, the owners receiving 20 to 25 per cent of the sale price in cash with the balance due at the end of one year, and partly from the funds of the Corporation. Six to eight months after the work began the units were occupied. Careful tenant-selection methods similar to those used by the Octavia Hill Association were used. In 1953 the project appeared to be successful and the Corporation began to look for new projects and for buyers of the completed project, which they intended to hold on a fifteen-year second trust.

Nevertheless, in August, 1956, it was reported that Herman Schmidt was leaving the rehabilitation business. Two reasons were given: first, he was unable to release his equity from the project by obtaining mortgages; second, he announced, "Rehabilitation is profitable if you don't try to upgrade too much—if you don't do it thoroughly."[24]

What had happened between the time the project seemed so successful and the time Schmidt decided to leave the business? Very simply, vacancies had increased, buyers were not available, financing couldn't be found for either the Corporation or potential purchasers, and the funds of the Corporation remained frozen in the project. Schmidt had trouble keeping the larger units rented because families who could afford rents of $77.50 a month were unwilling to live in a row of houses surrounded by shabby dwellings, inhabited by families who were their economic if not their social inferiors. They had been initially attracted to the units because they were clean, attractive, and reasonable. Initial pleasure was soon overcome by vivid impressions of the neighborhood after dark.

To improve the rental prospects, the corporation converted the two-bedroom houses into two units with one bedroom each. Tenants had to be found, and even a larger number of units than originally planned had to be serviced. Apparently even the solid, dependable tenants originally found to occupy the smaller units were disconcerted by the environment. More and more attention had to be given to the project to assure proper maintenance. When no buyers and no mortgages were found, the Corporation could not increase its activities without selling more stock. Since this proved impossible in face of the incontrovertible facts of the completed project, the last hope for the Corporation to reap a harvest of good will and fair profits disappeared. It is no wonder that Schmidt is con-

[24] *House & Home*, August, 1956, pp. 73–74. Parenthetically, the project will be demolished shortly by the Southwest Washington Redevelopment project.

vinced that a less ambitious approach must be taken in the future—an approach which yields lower rents, lower profits, and lower standards. The project might have worked if the Corporation followed Schmidt's own recommendations made in 1953: "... buy enough properties to assure your purchasers that the new community will be protected." [25]

If the Washington Urban Redevelopment Corporation had been able to purchase and remodel every structure in the alley, and if the alley opened upon an attractive street, or if the Corporation could have purchased and repaired the entire block using the same techniques and appealing to the same income group, it might have had less trouble in obtaining both mortgages and buyers and it doubtless would have had less trouble holding desirable tenants.

How Is Low-rent Housing Improved?

To summarize, existing low-rent housing is being improved by slum homeowners spurred by wage increases, rental-property owners who find it more economic to repair their properties than to sell them at prices deflated by code enforcement programs, and to a minor extent by limited dividend corporations. Tight rehabilitation budgets necessitate emphasis on little more than bare essentials which are durable, inexpensive, and easily maintained, and constant reinspection is needed to maintain early gains.

Code enforcement programs usually make only fitful progress and often bog down in relocation problems and investor resistance, although they sometimes achieve large numerical results. Vigorous enforcement causes property owners who are unwilling to bear improvement expenses to leave the

[25] Herman Schmidt, "How We Do It at a Profit," *NAHB Correlator*, October, 1953 (cost data from the same article).

market. Those remaining are either satisfied with a lower return, hope for higher rewards in the future, or find they can set an improvement schedule so gradual that their incomes are not adversely affected. Stern enforcement programs face two major challenges. Can the city schedule an improvement rate that will have more than a token effect on their low-rent areas? Second, are vacancy rates so low that forcing improvements results in rent increases, causing heavy dislocation?

Although code enforcement programs are primarily stopgap measures to relieve the worst housing conditions in a community, many public officials have said it is far better to push code enforcement than to permit deteriorated housing to fester until time or bulldozers clear the rubble for a fresh start.

Chapter 5

LOCATING AND ESTIMATING REHABILITATION PROJECTS

Although rehabilitation has been undertaken in every type of neighborhood, the motivations, costs, and potential returns differ from project to project. In the same area some investors capitalize on residential rehabilitation, while others promote an entirely different land use, and still others watch for further developments. Each group judges the future market for the land, and estimates the highest net return that might be obtained on its investment.

This premise motivates the investor's judgment whether his estimate of an area's future is right or wrong. If the investor concludes there is a market for units of a given character in a given location, he must then decide whether they can be provided at higher profits by rehabilitation or new construction. Of course, if an investor already owns a fully amortized property in the area, he might increase his yield on investment by selling the property, cleared if necessary, and investing the proceeds elsewhere rather than by providing the new use himself.

Reaching a decision to rehabilitate can be divided into two parts: discovering a market opportunity for rehabilitation and organizing a specific project to meet the demand. The process is complicated by uncertainties in such questions as financing arrangements, property taxes, and miscalculations of remodeling costs and rentals. However, misjudgments in the market demand at least can be greatly reduced if the rehabilitator is able to assess the size and requirements of the future market in different locations throughout the city.

Judging the Future Market

The housing market survey has become a useful tool to the investor, and is equally applicable to new construction and to rehabilitation. Although none of the rehabilitators interviewed had ever undertaken a formal market survey, almost all of them were familiar with its elements in an informal way and supplied themselves with whatever information they could obtain from the local newspapers, utility companies, municipal records, and from other investors who were active in the area of their interest.

Of the nearly sixty rehabilitators from whom case materials were collected, forty-seven were real estate brokers, six were home builders, and only four had no experience in real estate investment before they began working.[1] Obviously the real estate broker's daily business provides him with a constant stream of market information that can be readily applied to rehabilitation analysis. Even the most experienced investor, however, probably will not have enough information to carry him beyond the most immediate and proven investment.

The cost of a broad housing market analysis is prohibitive

[1] The apparent lack of interest on the part of the building profession is likely due to the relatively sustained rate of new construction activity.

for a single rehabilitator, but this difficulty could be overcome by the cooperative action of a real estate board or builders' organization, or the local government may conduct such surveys as a part of its regular planning activities.[2]

SOME ELEMENTS IN A HOUSING MARKET ANALYSIS

A housing market survey collects the facts relating to future housing demand and compares them to the present and potential housing supply. The excess of future demand over future supply indicates the areas of potential housing investment. Among the factors affecting the future demand are population and household trends; changes in the characteristics of the population; shifts in the location of the market; changes in family income; changes in consumer tastes for location; forms of tenure; and unit design. Supply factors include the general characteristics of the present housing stock such as its distribution by size, condition, rent, and value (including a close look at the rehabilitation potential of typical housing types); trends in vacancy rates; changes in the housing stock through new construction, conversion, and demolition; trends in the comparative costs of housing; the future availability of financing; and the effects of government plans, programs, and land-use controls.

Rehabilitators follow some of these market indicators with particular care. Changes in the size of future families when compared to the size of existing dwellings may reveal a market

[2] Two Government Printing Office selections can give the investor an excellent sense of market analysis and were used for materials in this section:
Chester Rapkin, Louis Winnick, and David Blank, *Housing Market Analysis, A Study of Theory and Method*, Washington, 1953, 92 pp.
Housing and Home Finance Agency, *Know Your Local Housing Market*, Washington, 1955, 25 pp. (a highly popularized coverage).

for conversion. Alterations in the travel time from different neighborhoods to employment and recreation centers can create new consumer locational preferences. Changes in family incomes may increase the capacity of homeowners to pay for remodeling or, if incomes fall, increase the demand for small, inexpensive apartments. Trends in consumer preferences for housing styles, interior designs, and household equipment indicate the possible directions remodeling can take. Rehabilitation opportunities grow in number as the cost of new housing increases relative to the cost of existing homes. Finally, government activities are constantly reviewed, particularly Federal credit policies and additions to local community facilities which contribute to area rent levels.

EXAMINING INVESTMENT POTENTIAL

Housing market information, then, gives the investor some indication of the local demands which may make housing investments profitable. He has the opportunity to consider a rehabilitation or new-construction project whenever and wherever there is a difference between existing and potential rent levels or sale prices, for individual structures or neighborhoods.

These differences occur when individual structures physically deteriorate or grow obsolete in design or size and the prices fall below prevailing levels. Conversely, potential rents in a neighborhood can increase because family incomes rise more rapidly than rents, or because families are willing to pay more for remodeled units, as a result of positive improvements in the environment or the pressures of neighborhood groups. An experienced investor will usually consider rehabilitating existing structures to meet housing demands, unless the cost of existing structures can be readily absorbed either by urban redevelopment or the promise of high profits from new construction.[3]

The situations where rehabilitation is clearly suitable or unsuitable are far overshadowed by the bulk of cases where the judgment is difficult to make. Each case must be examined on its merits, recognizing that the success or failure of a rehabilitator only a few blocks away may be inapplicable to the project under consideration.

Rehabilitation in the stable residential areas is explained by the lack of demand for other than the existing residential use and the fact that zoning ordinances may prohibit anything else. Therefore, whatever reinvestment is called for will be for new or remodeled residential structures. Increasing land values will often pull investment toward new rental apartments if there is enough demand and zoning allows them. Remodeling accompanied by allowable conversion will probably prevail if zoning does not permit high-rise construction. Rehabilitating units which have fallen below the neighborhood standards and rent levels of stable areas is a typical investment pattern.

Reinvestment in declining residential neighborhoods often requires a more intensive utilization of the properties. As rent levels in an area fall either absolutely or relatively to rents in areas of new housing, investors find that building new high-density structures and adding units to existing structures are practicable methods of maintaining net income. Returns may even be increased through sensible conversion. Unchecked conversion and reconversion, however, will possibly produce an area of overcrowded dwellings which may easily become a slum.

[3] See Kenneth Kingsley Stowell, *Modernizing Buildings for a Profit*, Prentice-Hall, Inc., Englewood Cliffs, N.J., 1935, 231 pp., for a treatment of investment decisions comparing rehabilitation with other alternatives.

Rehabilitation other than conversion may occur in declining areas, if local families with traditions and memories feel that no other area can offer the same conveniences or neighborhood associations. Philip Shifrin's statement that the best areas for contract remodelers are ones with a strong ethnic or religious consistency supports this contention. Home remodeling, operative remodeling, and rental rehabilitation at the same or slightly higher rent levels are all possible as long as some nucleus of families finds the neighborhood attractive. Sometimes public or private groups can create such loyalties through local renewal councils, neighborhood-preservation groups, or local special-interests clubs directed toward some specific neighborhood problem.[4] Citizen leaders say the resistance to promises held out by such groups will be directly proportional to the basic attractiveness of the area. Public action in the form of added community facilities, better planning, or code enforcement may fill an important role in improving the neighborhood setting enough to stimulate the voluntary home remodeling.

Finally, we come to those transitional areas changing from an obsolete use to one promising higher returns. The most typical are those where low-density residential development is gradually increased in density or changed to commercial or industrial use. Examples of other trends may be cited: abandoned industrial sites being cleared for residential use, or high-density residential structures being replaced by lower densities —a condition which usually involves a subsidy. Changing land uses pose important questions of public policy.

Rehabilitation in transitional areas may either foster the

[4] Note the success of Chicago's Back-of-the-Yards Council in promoting neighborhood improvement on many fronts, reported by Saul Alinsky in *Reveille for Radicals,* University of Chicago Press, Chicago, 1948.

new use, by creating an environment suitable to its growth, or retard its development when owners remodel their properties rather than sell them to new investors. In such cases, there is always the policy question of whether or not to hasten or retard the change by stimulating one or the other possibility with such government actions as strict zoning, tax concessions, low-cost financing, or special community facilities and services.

The Cost-estimating Process

Once the demand for a project has been ascertained, there is no more important part of the rehabilitation process than careful cost estimation. Four basic calculations enter into the estimating formula: the purchase price; remodeling costs (which include the cost of repairs, financing, and merchandising the finished product); profit expectations; and sale price or rents. All four elements are more or less flexible. Profit expectations vary widely with individual preferences, alternative investment opportunities, and motivations. The purchase price varies with the character of the properties, the time of purchase, and the bargaining ability of the negotiator. The repair costs are affected by the character of the structure, the amount of repairs undertaken, the efficiency of the work crews, and the contractual arrangements with specific subcontractors. Sale prices and rents might deviate from prevailing prices in the area, provided the remodeled units are superior to their competitors. Other costs, such as sales expenses and financing, can also determine the final feasibility of the project. With minor modification, the process is applicable to all classes of rehabilitation.

The rehabilitator may work out several alternative projects on paper before he feels he can profitably begin remodeling.

Most operative remodelers consider 15 to 20 per cent of the sale price as a reasonable margin for profit. They will sometimes be willing to accept less if other factors, such as publicity for other business ventures or a sense of public service, are to be considered. The profit decision is reached in a different way by each investor.

PURCHASING A STRUCTURE

The rehabilitator looks for houses in the area of his interest which will minimize his acquisition and construction costs and still have the potentialities he is seeking. The field may be narrowed considerably by his judgment of the market, with possibly only one or two houses considered in his detailed cost calculation.

Factors affecting both supply and demand influence the selection of properties. The market for a particular kind of rehabilitation may require a certain type of neighborhood, but to begin remodeling, structures without prohibitively expensive structural defects must be found in the area. The house to be selected, furthermore, must be obtainable at a price that permits making the repairs necessary to attract the contemplated market.

What may constitute a prohibitive structural defect varies with the level of rehabilitation planned. Each class of rehabilitation and almost every rehabilitator has his own "make or break" repairs. One prestige remodeler will not undertake a project when stairs need relocating. Another, working with middle- and low-income rehabilitation, warns against cracked or bulging walls, a concave roof, or rotted first-floor joists inside bearing walls. And a low-income rehabilitator rarely buys a building needing serious structural repairs of any kind. These rehabilitators have developed a knowledge of local problems and costs, permitting them to shy away from defects implying hidden costs, even when they believe the basic defect is correctable within the budget framework.

An extension of the same problem is that of finding a structure so designed that alteration costs may be kept within the budget. A Philadelphia rehabilitator points out that the typical three-story row house of that city is admirably suited to three- or six-unit conversion because the stairs rise in an enclosed hall with the rooms opening off the hall. Also, interior bearing walls are few, permitting extensive repartitioning at low cost. The high ceilings, moreover, allow wiring and heating ducts to be hung above a dropped ceiling.

ESTIMATING REMODELING COSTS—REPAIRS

Experienced rehabilitators find check lists covering each part of the structure useful in avoiding costly omissions.[5] Very often an engineer, architect, or experienced contractor is hired to verify and supplement the rehabilitator's estimate.

Such a check list may include a general description of the property and its environment, to serve as a guide for project design. Mainly, however, it analyzes the repairs or replacements needed for sewers, wiring, gutters, windows, equipment, plaster, and all other components great and small. Many rehabilitators use a check list specifically devised for their particular projects, which integrate a frequently repeated set of repairs into more generalized categories. The repair list eventually becomes a part of the feasibility work sheet which is used when all the costs are assembled (see Table 1).

Although too much stress cannot be put on the indispensa-

[5] An excellent example can be found in *Operative Remodeling*, United States Gypsum Co., Chicago, 1956, p. 52. The sheets include other needed information.

bility of a good check list, it is no safeguard against the addition of features which will not return their cost in higher rents or sale prices. Therefore, a firm grasp on the design preferences of the future market is absolutely essential.

The Effects of the Work Process on Remodeling Costs

Contractual arrangement, the experience of the crew, and timing can alter the repair expenses. Some remodelers, for example, hold the property at its old rent level before beginning the project, to have it qualify for long-term capital gains tax. Many rental and sales remodelers also delay starting their project while they buy nearby properties in order to benefit from increases in value following the initial rehabilitation.

Almost all the rehabilitators interviewed in the course of the study used their own crews for most of the remodeling work, but usually subcontracted for heating, plumbing, and electrical work. While a rehabilitator must keep his key personnel constantly employed, sometimes at great personal expense, they are trained to his methods and are on call at any time. They are a flexible work force able to meet unexpected complications, which can be inexpensively overcome only by the ready application of varied skills.

Inexperienced investors ordinarily rely on a prime contractor familiar with remodeling work. Even the more experienced rehabilitator may not undertake enough rehabilitation work to justify keeping a steadily employed crew of his own. Still, his experience is usually broad enough to allow him to act as his own general contractor and job supervisor, while his daily supervision assures him of the desired quality and speed of the work.

Many rehabilitators develop a good relationship with trusted subcontractors and depend on their meeting specifications with only minimum supervision. One Washington remodeler is so confident of his "subs" that he outlines the work and then has them send him the bill when it is completed.

Occasionally remodelers steadily employ a supervisory staff that can oversee both a pick-up crew of general laborers and skilled subcontractors. One remodeler pays his foreman a percentage of the profits, in addition to a regular salary, on the tested theory that a profit incentive will bring out the man's best. Finding new recruits for a regular remodeling staff is not the easiest job, because most of the younger mechanics have been trained to only one or two skills and cannot function in the variety of roles a rehabilitation project demands. The older workmen are familiar with the construction methods used on many of the structures they now remodel and thus can anticipate many of the remodeling problems before they arise. A rehabilitator can often find experienced remodeling mechanics left sitting in hiring halls because their age prevents them from maintaining the fast pace of new construction.

SAVINGS IN THE WORK ITSELF

No attempt will be made to give a detailed description of cost-cutting methods in rehabilitation.[6] A few general rules, however, merit special attention. Usually no repair is undertaken if there is the slightest possibility of chain effects. A new living room floor may seem a good way to spend leftover repair dollars, but after the job is done other rooms may require the same treatment.

Two or three structures in various stages of completion permit a rehabilitator with his own crew to keep his men working regardless of the weather.

[6] See *op. cit., Operative Remodeling,* for a detailed discussion.

Rehabilitators can never take anything for granted. Plumbing and wiring may be held together with friction tape, fresh wallpaper may hide crumbling plaster, and "solid" beams may be hollow shells. On the other hand, grimy hardware may have hidden, even antique, value and be less expensive to clean than it would be to replace it, and bricked-up fireplaces and linoleum flooring may hide examples of fine craftsmanship.

The possibilities of large-scale economies are in considerable dispute among rehabilitators. The repetition of similiar construction conditions, in a way which permits economies, rarely occurs because the structures are likely to have been subject to the whims of many owners. Gutting several structures that were originally constructed alike, however, or making a standard set of improvements to apartments that are substantially sound can result in some economies of scale. Little uniformity exists for most rehabilitatable structures, however, and their market prospects are not good enough to warrant providing uniformity with radical gutting.

Other economies and diseconomies exist beyond the scope of the construction process and are related to the size of the rehabilitation firm and its volume of rehabilitation activities. Some of these economies were mentioned earlier. A rehabilitator undertaking a series of sizable projects during the year can obtain economies in the purchase of materials, in constantly occupying his labor force, in merchandising several structures with a single advertisement, in receiving newspaper coverage which will further reduce his selling expenses, and in growing in experience and proficiency with each separate undertaking. Since he is buying in volume, he also has a wide choice of available properties. He has developed ready sources of financing for his purchases; permanent financing for himself and his customers is more easily obtained as his business reputation increases.

It is obvious that the only way to overcome uncertainties and reduce costs in rehabilitation investment is to increase the scope of remodeling activities and learn from whatever mistakes are made. This may offer poor comfort for the fledgling who runs out of money and confidence, before profiting from his mistakes. The use of experienced help is the best way to prevent costly mistakes. While competent advisors and experienced staffs working on a ripe profit margin may not yield the inexperienced investor the same rewards as his more knowledgeable colleague, they will prevent complete failure.

The Feasibility Equation

The determination of feasibility begins when the remodeling estimate has been made and checked. Costs are balanced against the potential sales prices (or rents)—see Table 1—and the rehabilitator goes ahead if the prospective profit is satisfactory. Remodelers will try to pare costs, if the profits seem unattractive, before discarding a project completely, first by offering a lower price for the property, or by eliminating some of the projected repairs, or both. Repair costs will have to be lowered by an amount greater than any resulting decline in possible selling price, if the project is to be safely undertaken.

Special Problems in Cost Estimating for Rental Properties

Cost estimation for rental properties is complicated by the additional element of operating costs: debt service, rental and utility expenses, maintenance, taxes, and janitorial services.

The process is basically identical to estimating on properties for sale, however, because net returns from the project must meet the owner's profit expectations.

TABLE 1. Feasibility Work Sheet

For .... (address)
Original No.
of Units ....
Date of Purchase ...... No. of Units When   Assessment Before ......
Date of Sale .... Completed .... Assessment After ....
Description of Construction Financing ....
Description of Permanent Financing ....

Cost item	Labor cost ($)	Material cost ($)	Equipment cost ($)	Total ($)
Interest on loans				
Building permits and fees				
Architect's fees				
Sales and advertising expenses				
Cleaning and watchman				
Carpentry				
Masonry				
Plumbing and heating:				
Baths				
Kitchens				
Heating				
Other				
Electrical				
Painting and papering				
Plastering				
Roofing				
Property taxes for period held				
Contractors' fees not elsewhere listed				
Allowance for unpaid managerial labor				
Other				

TABLE 1. (*continued*)

For Sales Rehabilitation
Total:
Acquisition cost:
Total investment:
Sale price:
Profit:

For Rental Properties
Total:
Acquisition cost:
Total investment:
Gross annual rent:
Operating expense
 (including real
 estate taxes and
 vacancy allowance):
Net annual rent
 (profit before
 income taxes):

Some parts of the estimating formula are easily handled. Acquisition cost and repair costs are treated in the same manner as those for sales projects. Some of the operating costs can be estimated fairly accurately: janitorial expenses, utility costs, debt service (following a mortgage commitment), depreciation, and a maintenance budget. Less certain, however, are vacancy allowances, rental expenses, and taxes, for all of which rehabilitators usually make ample allowance in order to be on the safe side. Finally, the prospective net profit over a period of years is compared to the investor's expectations, and the decision to proceed or not to proceed is made.

In preparing his repair estimates, the rental rehabilitator has even more reason than the sales rehabilitator to call in an architect or engineer and occasionally an expert to confirm his opinion of housing market conditions. The cost of these services, of course, is levied against the project cost; the larger the investment, the more appropriate a market consultant's and architect's services become to the estimate.

What we have seen is an orderly yet flexible process of approaching the undertaking. In using the four-part formula, estimating errors can be compensated for by using safety margins, which will probably grow smaller as the knowledge and accuracy of the rehabilitator increases with experience.

Chapter 6

THE FINANCING PROBLEM

The variations in financing rehabilitation stem from differences in the location and condition of the properties to be remodeled and the relative economic strength of the rehabilitator. A project undertaken by a commercial remodeler or homeowner with a good credit rating, in a stable neighborhood, can usually be financed by a first mortgage which reflects the completed value of the project and allows advances to finance the acquisition and remodeling of the structure. When a project is located in a declining or blighted area, however, the rehabilitator may be forced to use complex financial arrangements or resort entirely to his own capital.

Though by no means exhausting the possible arrangements, there are three very common ways to finance commercial remodeling in older areas. One, the investor uses 20 to 40 per cent of his own capital supplemented by a mortgage which will later be transferred to the buyer. Two, he assumes whatever mortgage the seller has on the property, supplements this with a construction loan, and after the work is completed, obtains permanent financing for the buyer. Three, he obtains a mortgage at the time of purchase on the property "as is," uses a construction loan for the remodeling operation, and when the work is completed, obtains permanent financing for the buyer. The permanent financing may include junior mortgages if the buyer cannot afford a high down payment.

The process of financing rental rehabilitation is not as complicated. Ordinarily the rehabilitator either buys the building with his own funds, repairs it with a construction loan, and then refinances; or he arranges for a first mortgage with construction advances on the basis of the ultimate value of the property. However, some of the more complicated devices, such as assumed mortgages or an interim mortgage on the unimproved property, might still be necessary.

Homeowners undertaking repairs may finance their improvements with their own capital, with first or second mortgages, or with property-improvement loans. The least costly method of financing for the homeowner is to have an open-ended mortgage, allowing the borrower to obtain additional money up to a specified amount of the original loan. This arrangement, which is usually found in older areas, saves the cost of making a new loan and usually permits a lower interest payment than would be the case with a separate loan.

A rehabilitation project may qualify for several types of financing.

Conventional Loans

Conventional mortgages with interest rates of 5 to 6 per cent running ten to seventeen years with loan-to-value ratios of 50 to 75 per cent represent the type of financing most extensively used by the rehabilitators studied.

In respect to conventional mortgages, state laws may limit the mortgage investment financial institutions may make to a proportion of total assets, fix the loan-to-value ratio of the mortgage, and set the geographic area in which the institution may invest. Such limitations have made it difficult for conventional lenders to finance the one- to four-family homes of modest-income borrowers and large rental projects. The Federal Housing Administration was founded specifically to help in financing those types of structures, by making it possible to bypass state restrictions on the volume and terms of mortgage loans where the loans were insured.

There has been a recent trend towards increased liberalization of conventional mortgages. Federal savings and loan associations are now permitted to make loans up to 80 per cent of value, provided the members of an association approve the move by a majority vote. The legislature of New York State passed a law authorizing mutual savings banks to grant mortgage loans up to 90 per cent of value, but this was vetoed by Governor Harriman. The main advantage of conventional loans to rehabilitators, however, remains their availability. It is significant that over three-quarters of the mortgage recordings during the first nine months of 1958 were conventional loans.[1]

The same trend toward increasing liberalization of terms can be seen in conventional unsecured, short-term loans. They rarely exceed three years in duration but can be obtained in amounts up to $5,000 or more for "repairs or improvements the lender deems acceptable."[2] The interest charge on loans is usually in the form of a discount running from $4 to $8 a year per $1,000 borrowed. Federal savings and loan associations are now able to invest 15 per cent of their assets in five-year unsecured loans, up to $3,500.[3] A few other specialized programs have been instituted by lenders for conventional

[1] Housing and Home Finance Agency, *Housing Statistics*, December, 1958, p. 47.
[2] *Financing Home Repairs and Improvements*, American Council To Improve Our Neighborhoods, New York, p. 7.
[3] Rules and Regulations for Federal Savings and Loan System, 1957 Amendments, Sec. 145.8.

short-term loans. The Banking Committee of Cleveland's Operation Demonstrate, for example, provides eight-year loans over $2,500 at 5 to 6 per cent interest.

In the case of both conventional mortgages and unsecured loans, however, it was largely through the FHA insurance programs that the financial soundness of increased liberalization was proved.

The Federal Housing Administration offers several types of loan insurance to private lending institutions which may be helpful in financing the remodeling of either owner-occupied houses or multifamily rental properties. More than half of the mortgages insured by FHA during the past few years have been on existing homes, many of them remodeled structures.

FHA Title 1 Property Improvement Loans are an important source of rehabilitation financing. In 1957 about 1.1 billion loans were insured, with net proceeds equaling $869 million.[4] However, the loans appear to be mainly on properties in predominantly single-family, owner-occupied neighborhoods. In 1955, 81.6 per cent of the loans were of this class, and of these, fully 37.9 per cent were for additions or alterations and exterior finish, and another 26.5 per cent were for heating and plumbing.[5] It has been stated by some lenders that the FHA Title 1 loan program has had its greatest impact on middle-income, stable, residential areas, although little information is available on this point.

The maximum amount that a homeowner may borrow under Title 1 is now set at $3,500 and the length of the loan

[4] Housing and Home Finance Agency, *Housing Statistics*, March, 1958, p. 70.
[5] Federal Housing Administration, *Amount of Property Improvement Loans, Selected Years and Type of Improvement by Type of Property for Property Improvement Loans*, 1955, tables 86 and 88, AR55-140 and AR55-150, Apr. 16, 1956, and Apr. 13, 1956.

at sixty-one months. If the owner-occupant lives in a structure with more than one unit, he may receive a loan of $2,500 for each dwelling unit up to an amount of $15,000, with a maturity of as much as eighty-five months. The borrower may be charged no more than $5 for each $100 per year up to $2,500, and $4 per $100 per year over that amount.

About two-thirds of the mortgage insurance outstanding is subject to the provisions of Section 203b of the National Housing Act, which insures one- to four-family houses.[6] Loans for rehabilitation under this title tend to be offered on houses in "better" neighborhoods and usually are not granted until the work has actually been completed. Where the mortgage takes effect before the work has been done, the contract stipulates that the final mortgage sum will be extended after completion, but that a certain sum equal to the amount of mortgage permissible on the house as it stands will be insured at the time of purchase. The interest rate (as of the date of writing) may not exceed 5¼ per cent, with an additional ½ per cent for the mortgage-insurance premium.

An owner-occupant may obtain a mortgage in the amount of 97 per cent of the appraised value not in excess of $13,500, 85 per cent of the value between $13,500 and $16,000, and 70 per cent of such value in excess of $16,000.[7] The maximum maturity of the mortgage is thirty years, or three-quarters of the remaining economic life, whichever is less. The nonowner-occupant, the operative remodeler in this case, can receive 85 per cent of whatever an owner-occupant could obtain.

The dollar amount of an FHA home mortgage may be increased to permit home remodeling if the outstanding balance is less than 88 per cent of the first $9,000 and 75 per cent of the

[6] Housing and Home Finance Agency, *op. cit.*, p. 72.
[7] Emergency Housing Act of March, 1958.

amount over $9,000 (but not exceeding $20,000). The amount extended can exceed these limits by a $1,000 excess if the mortgagee is adding a room. These provisions are most applicable to homeowners employing contract remodelers in the outlying and suburban locations.

Insurance of mortgages for multifamily structures (Section 207 of the National Housing Act) is available for new and existing rental projects comprised of eight or more units in detached, semidetached, row, or multifamily structures. The maximum nominal interest rate for mortgages issued under this section was 4½ per cent in April, 1958.[8] For existing properties, insured mortgages may run as high as $12,500 with a minimum of 25 per cent of the mortgage going into property improvements. The duration of the mortgage can be as high as thirty-nine years and three months, but cannot exceed three-fourths of the estimated remaining economic life of the structure. The maximum loan-to-value ratio is 90 per cent.[9]

If the property is not already mortgaged, the full amount of the remodeling costs may be covered under this type of insured mortgage according to FHA regulations. If the project is being refinanced, however, the size of the mortgage is limited to the cost of repairs plus up to 90 per cent of the original fair market value.

The FHA will rarely insure under Section 207 unless the project is located in an area where the valuation will be unaffected by blighting neighborhood influences.

Section 220 of the National Housing Act provides for mort-

[8] Since the market rate of interest on mortgages on multifamily units in 1958 ran between 5½ and 6 per cent interest, FHA rental mortgages sold at a 5-point discount in the secondary market (*House & Home*, April, 1958, p. 105).

[9] Housing Act of 1957.

gage insurance for new or rehabilitated housing in officially designated urban-renewal areas. This section was written separately to give special encouragement to urban renewal. The terms are the same as those under Section 203 except that the loans are made on the basis of an appraised value which takes into consideration not only the value of the property as improved but also the future prospects of the urban-renewal area. FHA field officers are instructed to adhere to the spirit of FHA's property requirements but to allow variations in the actual provisions to suit special situations.[10]

Section 220 can also be used to insure mortgages for rehabilitating or building structures of five or more units in designated urban-renewal areas. The terms are essentially the same as Section 207 above, except that the basis for the mortgage is replacement costs rather than estimated value, and under the regulations the minimum amount of the mortgage that must be devoted to property improvements is 20 rather than 25 per cent.

Although the provisions of Section 220 are most directly applicable to rehabilitation, by October 31, 1958, only forty commitments had been made by the FHA for rehabilitation mortgages under both portions of the Section.[11]

Mortgages for families displaced by government construction can be insured under Section 221 of the National Housing

[10] FHA, Operations Letter 192, July 9, 1956, which discusses "non-assisted" urban-renewal projects, gives as an example the advisability of ignoring the usual minimum property requirements for side yards in renewal areas where a smaller side yard does not appreciably affect the mortgage risk. A full discussion of this flexibility is found in paragraph 404(5) of the FHA's *Underwriting Manual*.

[11] Housing and Home Finance Agency, *Housing Statistics*, December, 1958, p. 65. (However, 810 houses listed under new construction had actually been extensively remodeled.) W. Beverley Mason, Jr., *Digest of FHA Urban Renewal Operations, Dec. 31, 1957*, Feb. 21, 1958, p. 1.

Act. This Section provides for insurance on mortgages for one-family houses built or rehabilitated to aid in relocating families displaced by government construction. The houses need not be built in renewal areas but must be either within the corporate limits of the affected city or in a consenting neighboring jurisdiction. The loans require the determination of a fixed number of units for which the insurance will be available. The amounts of the mortgages are even more generous than those for Section 220, provided the houses built cost less than about $9,335. An owner-occupant can obtain a mortgage of 100 per cent of the appraised value to a maximum mortgage of $9,000 ($10,000 in high cost areas), and a nonowner-occupant can receive 85 per cent of the amount granted to the homeowner. The mortgage, however, can have a term up to forty years or three-fourths of the remaining economic life of the structure. If the remaining economic life of a structure rehabilitated under this title is the same as a similar structure in an urban-renewal area, there is no difference in the mortgage term.

The Loan-guarantee Program of the Veterans Administration.

The Veterans Administration guarantees both mortgages and unsecured loans for modernizing and repairing veterans' housing.[12] Since most of the returning servicemen were without high down payments and many of them had few job skills, the terms of the VA mortgages are very liberal. The VA agrees to guarantee $7,500 of the loan or 60 per cent, whichever is less. A veteran buyer can receive a loan with no down

[12] *Serviceman's Readjustment Act*, 1944, as amended. (See Title 3, Section 500 B, Clause 3 for unsecured-improvement-loans provision.)

payment, a 4¾ per cent interest rate, and a maturity of thirty years. The maturity and down-payment requirements tend to be more favorable than either FHA-insured or conventional loan terms. This has resulted in a relatively heavy use of VA mortgages by moderate-income families for existing homes.[13]

Secondary Markets

The relatively unfavorable position government-insured and guaranteed mortgages occasionally occupy owing to their controlled interest rates is partly overcome by the activities of the Federal National Mortgage Association (FNMA), which was originally established in 1938 under the authority of the National Housing Act, and extensively reorganized by the Housing Act of 1954. Its function is to buy, hold, and sell insured and guaranteed mortgages under a confusing variety of terms and conditions. FNMA is directed by law to buy mortgages insured by the FHA under Sections 220 and 221 at par, and its funds have been increased for that purpose.

Federal Home Loan Bank System

The Federal Home Loan Bank Board (FHLBB) supervises a system of Federal Home Loan Banks in eleven Home Loan Bank districts throughout the country. All federal savings and loan associations must be members, while state chartered savings and loan associations, cooperative banks, savings banks, and insurance companies may voluntarily join. The main function of the Home Loan Banks is to make advances to member institutions to assure their liquidity and to permit

---

[13] Over 70 per cent of the VA-guaranteed mortgages were secured by existing, owner-occupied homes. Housing and Home Finance Agency, *Housing in the Economy,* 1956, p. 14.

their expansion, thus helping to make savings and loan associations the important and dependable source they are for mortgage funds.

Savings and loan associations make the bulk of their loans in the communities in which they are located. They are, therefore, familiar with local conditions. Rehabilitators have looked to savings and loan associations as their primary source of funds, and associations have figured heavily in every major neighborhood renewal project through the country. Chicago's Back-of-the-Yards neighborhood, Washington's Foggy Bottom, and Charlotte's code enforcement areas would not have been restored without the help of these institutions.

The Problems of Financing

In stable neighborhoods, the financing of rehabilitation rarely poses serious problems. On the contrary, financing a remodeled structure in a stable area is usually easier and may carry better terms than financing for neighboring structures not similiarly improved.

Many individual homeowners take advantage of the open-end provisions of their existing mortgage.[14] Others use short-term unsecured loans because of their convenience. Operative remodelers and their buyers may choose between the low equity requirements of a government-insured or guaranteed loan, or conventional mortgages, which, under favorable conditions, may carry lower interest rates. Rental remodelers have the same choices, provided their anticipated returns qualify them for the credit they seek.

The difficulties in obtaining financing grow progressively worse as the condition of the structures and the incomes and

---

[14] Some estimates show that as much as 25 per cent of the existing mortgages have open-end provisions (*Wall Street Journal*, Feb. 4, 1955, p. 1).

potential rents in a neighborhood decline. It is in these poorer areas, with enough sound structures to make them unlikely prospects for clearance, that rehabilitation on a neighborhood scale is most needed. While a few individual homeowners and commercial remodelers in these neighborhoods obtain the financing they require because of their good credit ratings, the bulk of the remodeling projects confront almost insurmountable difficulties. A few specific problems readily come to mind.

Borrowers with low and erratic incomes have never fared well no matter how much their proposals might contribute to the improvement of a neighborhood. Studies of mortgage-lending experience clearly show that foreclosures are most frequent when the owner's income and equity are low.[15] High foreclosure rates are also experienced on rental properties owned by absentee landlords, often the case in older neighborhoods.[16]

Projects involving structures which have become too obsolete to be economically improved or where the work is poorly conceived and badly executed have understandably been unable to gain support. A Boston banker widely experienced with loans on older properties says that encouraging the rehabilitation of obsolete structures is not justified unless the cost of overcoming the obsolescence of design can be absorbed by the potential rents. In most cases potential rents will permit no more than the preservation of the outmoded design and the addition of many small, poorly planned apartments. Although some financing might be extended to make

[15] J. E. Morton, *Urban Mortgage Lending: Comparative Markets and Experience*, Princeton University Press, Princeton, N. J., 1956, pp. 108–109.
[16] Ernest M. Fisher and Chester Rapkin, *The Mutual Mortgage Insurance Fund*, Columbia University Press, New York, 1956, pp. 100–102.

essential repairs, no project involving major remodeling would readily find support.

Finally, and most critically, projects located in areas where the rents have been falling for a number of years usually have difficulty in obtaining financing. In areas such as Foggy Bottom, credit was drastically restrictive until the trend to higher rents was clearly established.

The Need for Financing

If rehabilitation is going to alter the urban scene, it must be made an economically attractive business. To accomplish this, it must have access to credit on terms that are competitive with new construction. It is plain from this survey that this is not presently the case. The problem is essentially one of how to alter the investment situation so that rehabilitators can bid for funds on an equal footing with new-house builders.

A clue to the solution of our problem is suggested by the vice-president of a large savings bank who summarized the position of lenders by saying in substance that where credit analysis did not justify it, lending institutions could not be expected to increase the size and lengthen the maturity of loans. Ample funds, however, would be available for any possible volume of well-located, well-designed rehabilitation projects. He went on to say that if lending institutions were expected to support rehabilitation in declining areas where ordinary risks were not justified, government insurance or guarantees were necessary during the period when it was uncertain that the area would become stabilized. He lauded the urban-renewal program for requiring a contribution of municipal facilities, but warned that a sustained effort to improve and maintain public facilities and services was needed to gain the continued support of lending institutions.

It is clear from his remarks that more funds can be found for rehabilitation by concentrating remodeling activities in areas where there is a good possibility of neighborhood stabilization through government and community action of various kinds. It is equally clear that an increased effort will have to be made by the forces interested in renewal to promote neighborhood stability on an increasing scale if rehabilitation is to have an impact where it is most needed.

Extending Financing Coverage

Many areas have not become blighted enough to qualify for urban renewal and yet are not attractive enough to receive liberal conventional or government-guaranteed financing. There is no intrinsic reason why government insurance should not be made available throughout the city. It would be a relatively simple matter to extend the definition of urban renewal to cover all unstable areas (we shall see in the next chapter that there are other reasons for extending the definition of urban renewal), and at the same time to continue the present FHA policy of modifying minimum property requirements to fit local conditions.

It may also be possible to use FHA Sections 203 and 207 in neighborhoods not designated for urban renewal by making the same kinds of adjustments in the minimum property requirements recommended for rehabilitated homes insured under Section 220. Or the FHA might insure a balanced portfolio of loans of all types under a single title, thus offsetting the normally heavier losses from poorer risks against the prime loans. This would not be an unexpected change, since the separate identification of Section 220 was originally undertaken only to focus "... attention on its objectives ... and enlist ... the interest and cooperation of property owners, local governments, lenders, and builders."[17] The President's Advisory Committee on Housing, when proposing Section 220, argued at the same time for a single fund for all FHA insurance operations on the grounds that it would prevent the anomalous possibility of one fund having to petition the Treasury for help while others were paying substantial dividends.[18]

Some remodelers, however, believe it is unlikely that the FHA will alter its policies, and that other directions will have to be explored to offer protection to lending institutions in the early days of neighborhood revival. A Philadelphia banker has suggested that a simple way to do this would be to have every lending institution dedicate a small percentage of its portfolio to rehabilitation loans in a concentrated area where there is a determined neighborhood spirit.[19] This would increase the amount of remodeling and would also reduce individual risks.

The experience of lending institutions in Chicago's Back-of-the-Yards neighborhood supports the possibilities implicit in this simple proposal. Of thirty-nine lending institutions in or near the neighborhood, thirty-five voluntarily cooperated in an area-wide rehabilitation program. New homes were built and old structures remodeled in an area where rents for apartments in seventy-five-year-old structures were as low as $22 per month. William H. Gleason, vice-president of the Talman Federal Savings and Loan Association, attributed the cooperation of lending institutions to the fact that area residents

[17] The President's Advisory Committee on Government Housing Policies and Programs, *A Report to the President of the United States*, Washington, December, 1953, p. 44.
[18] *Ibid.*, p. 36.
[19] A device analogous to a local Voluntary Home Mortgage Credit Program (see discussion on following pages).

were "... proud of their homes, property, and neighborhood."[20]

A similar idea to reduce the risk of individual lending institutions is at the base of the New York State Mortgage Facilities Corporation, founded April, 1956, and financed by the sale of stocks and debentures to savings banks and insurance companies. Its purpose, however, was directed more to the problem of providing mortgage funds to families, particularly Negro families, who would ordinarily not receive them, than supporting renewal in a particular neighborhood. It is empowered to undertake a program of up to $25 million in loans for the purchase, construction, or improvement of houses in blighted areas. Lending institutions can invest in the stock of the corporation without affecting their present mortgage holdings. As of December 13, 1957, eight mortgages totaling $127,400 had been approved, and twenty-eight rejected because the directors found the properties in poor condition or the rents proposed by the borrower too high.[21]

Risk sharing by private lenders has equal applicability to problem borrowers covered below, and any device used to extend coverage into new areas could be designed to assist in both areas.

Insuring "Problem" Borrowers

Some groups believe that even if the FHA insures all urban rehabilitation loans, lending institutions may be reluctant to buy mortgages from borrowers with poor credit ratings in sufficient quantities to assure neighborhood renewal as long

[20] William H. Gleason, "Fighting Neighborhood Decay," *Savings and Loan News*, vol. 24, no. 9, September, 1954, pp. 28–34.
[21] *Report on Examination of the Mortgage Facilities Corporation, New York City, as of December 13, 1957*, State of New York Banking Department, Dec. 30, 1957 (mimeo.).

as prime conventional and government-guaranteed paper exists in sufficient volume to fill lender's needs. They are convinced that either the special-assistance operation of FNMA will have to be extended, or a new Federal mortgage corporation created to serve these borrowers. An extension of FNMA's activities would in effect make lending institutions intermediary agents servicing loans extended by FNMA to individual property owners.[22]

The need for a new mortgage corporation was stressed by Ira S. Robbins, testifying in behalf of the National Housing Conference before the Senate Subcommittee on Housing in 1957. In referring to a bill introduced by Joseph S. Clark of Pennsylvania to create a nonprofit mortgage company, he said: "We feel strongly that until a new agency is created . . . dedicated solely to the interests of families of modest incomes . . . there can be no progress in this vital area of need." [23]

Several proposals have been made by remodelers to obtain the necessary guarantees for high-risk mortgages from the agencies of all levels of government. The number and variety of their proposals clearly indicate there are enough "unmortgageable" families in many rehabilitation areas to seriously deter area-wide improvements.

Lending institutions have come to recognize that unless they do something about mortgages for families with modest incomes, minority groups, the elderly, single persons, and the heads of large families, government influence in the mort-

[22] See Charles M. Haar, *Federal Credit and Private Housing: The Mass Financing Dilemma* (forthcoming in the ACTION Series in Housing and Community Development, McGraw-Hill Book Company, Inc.), for a full discussion of adjustments in existing credit programs.

[23] *Senate Hearings on the Housing Amendments of 1957*, Mar. 18–Apr. 3, 1957, p. 807.

gage market is bound to increase. In commenting on the legislation advanced by Senator Clark, Harry Held, the vice-president of the Bowery Savings Bank of New York City, said, "The legislation, although defeated this year, represents a challenge to all institutional mortgage lenders and home builders to demonstrate that these segments can be adequately housed and that financing can be provided by private lending sources...." [24] The Voluntary Home Mortgage Credit Program (VHMCP) was one of the solutions cited by Held that institutional lenders have offered as a countermeasure to expanded government influence in the mortgage market.[25]

Whether undertaken under public or private sponsorship, a new lending agency dedicated to rehabilitation mortgages for problem families and neighborhoods would be a useful addition to other financing aids. A study of the function of local mortgage markets, undertaken at the University of California in 1954 and 1955, showed that the support government housing programs received in a community depended on the number, size, and activities of the local institutions. The study found that often a new field of mortgage investment went untapped until one of the institutions invited competition by entering the field. It concluded that:

[24] Harry Held, "Market Observation and Mortgage Lending Challenges," *Commercial and Financial Chronicle*, vol. 186, no. 5680, Oct. 10, 1957, pp. 14–15.

[25] The VHMCP was designed primarily to divert FHA and VA investments from large cities to small urban centers where they would otherwise not be available, and to obtain funds for Negro borrowers. Another proposal was advanced by the National Savings and Loan League and embodied in a bill sponsored by Senator John Sparkman in 1957 which, like the VHMCP, was intended to maintain private control over the mortgage market. It suggested that the government insure only the top 20 per cent of conventional loans to permit lenders to advance more favorable terms to marginal risks.

... the solution to some financing problems may be, not in the direction of modifying interest rates or of establishing secondary markets for mortgages but rather in facilitating the establishment of new types of lending institutions in individual local markets to assist in the attainment of national policies.[26]

Summary

Rehabilitation activities, public and private, continue regardless of any deficiencies in financing. There can be no question, however, that more financing at more liberal terms can expand the scope of rehabilitation activity. The success of any financing scheme to provide these funds, however, will depend on environmental improvements to the rehabilitation area and rigorous enforcement of municipal codes and ordinances. A more basic question facing governments, however, is how to achieve a balance of expenditures for rehabilitation and new construction which will provide better dwellings for slum residents and simultaneously contribute to a permanent housing stock meeting the future needs of a healthy community.

[26] James Gillies and Clayton Curtis, "The Structure of the Local Mortgage Markets and Government Housing Finance Programs," *Journal of Finance*, vol. x, no. 3, September, 1955, p. 375.

Chapter 7

REHABILITATION AS PART OF PUBLIC PROGRAMS

Although it is true that more and more families each year are able to afford new housing, it is obvious that most American families must seek housing meeting their standards of safety and decency within the existing housing stock.[1]

Rehabilitation under local code enforcement programs often brings low-rent units up to existing housing and building-code standards at average costs of $750 to $1,000 a unit, in 1957 prices. Rehabilitation for middle-income families can conserve existing structures at standards which will be applicable for the foreseeable future at a cost of approximately $3,500 to $5,000 a unit. Rehabilitation for upper-income families living in central areas costs between $7,000 to $10,000 or more a unit.

Rehabilitation of sound structures is usually less costly to achieve than new construction on the same site. It can also add to the housing supply through conversion. But the most important role rehabilitation can play is in conserving units

[1] In 1956 the median total income of nonfarm families was $5,221, indicating that more than half of the nonfarm families could obtain mortgages insured by the FHA for new houses within the current price ranges (U.S. Bureau of the Census, *Income of Families and Persons in the United States,* 1956, ser. P-60, no. 27, April, 1958).

on the way to becoming obsolete or substandard. It has been estimated that between 3.9 and 6.4 million dwelling units sink below acceptable standards or are demolished every decade. One expert estimated that, through rehabilitation, fully 400,000 existing units might be saved from destruction or dilapidation each year.[2]

Rehabilitation, then, may figure in public policy as a method of increasing the number of safe, sanitary units and of decreasing the number of units that fall below acceptable levels, with less cost than new construction to both the public and the families occupying the units. But merely preserving the existing pattern of housing is not enough, and the cost of adding neighborhood facilities and lowering urban residential congestion inevitably requires governmental expenditures.

The basic powers employed by governments to accomplish their housing policies are regulatory action under the police powers, condemnation, taxation, credit policies, and direct government subsidies and expenditures. All three levels of government have activities that can affect the location and scope of rehabilitation activity.

Local-government Powers and Programs Affecting Housing

Successful housing programs can only result from familiarity with local housing markets, local housing types, and local community problems. Therefore, the ultimate responsibility

[2] William L. C. Wheaton, "American Housing Needs, 1955–1970," *Housing Yearbook*, National Housing Conference, 1954, p. 23. Wheaton assumes that no substandard dwelling units located in blocks comprised of 50 per cent or more substandard units should be improved. An even larger number of units are physically capable of improvement if housing programs include largely dilapidated blocks.

for framing and coordinating housing policies and programs logically rests with the local government.

Although this has become generally accepted, as the Hearings on the Housing Act of 1957 indicate,[3] local governments have neither the resources nor the powers to undertake the task without the cooperation and support of other governments. This was clearly stated by William S. Slayton, authority on housing conservation:

> The municipal financing problem arises in providing the needed community facilities and in meeting the cost of rehabilitation operations resulting in loss.... These items add up to a sizable sum for a city that wishes to preserve an active program, and with cities hard pressed for funds, a device to produce such funds would be helpful.[4]

Obviously, the "device" Slayton calls for will have to be supplied by either the Federal or state government.

Whether or not we accept the thesis that an unassisted local housing program can achieve only limited gains, there is no question that the local powers can be used more effectively in stimulating neighborhood rehabilitation. Extensions and adaptation of existing powers were suggested by many persons during the course of the study which, taken in aggregate, doubtless involve increased government expenditures. Some of the suggestions touch only parts of the municipal powers and activities, while others are more general and affect not only local programs but the activities of other governments as well.

[3] See *Hearings on Housing Act of 1957* before the Senate Subcommittee on Housing of the Committee on Banking and Currency, for diversified testimony on this point. Note particularly the testimony of Albert M. Cole, HHFA Administrator, p. 220.
[4] William L. Slayton, "Conservation of Existing Housing," *Law and Contemporary Problems*, Summer, 1955, vol. 20, no. 3, p. 455.

THE POLICE POWER

Under its police power, government is called on to protect the health, safety, and welfare of the community. The police power may be exercised to maintain the minimum standards of housing decency, guide and control the use of property, and require improvements on the property to be maintained at the owner's expense in accordance with predetermined standards. The community plan and the various regulatory codes affect in many ways the amount and quality of housing available to fulfill local demands. Codes may correspond to, or be out of step with, the local demand at any point in time, like the zoning ordinance which permits apartment building in an area where no demand for apartments exists. Since codes are not rewritten as often as the housing market changes, many parallels can be found in ordinances of these kinds.

The three most important codes affecting existing structures are the building code, the housing code, and the zoning ordinance. Other codes controlling the operation of properties are the health, sanitation, fire, safety, plumbing, heating, and electrical codes.[5] These codes must be satisfied by the property owner or remodeler, and their variety and complexities often make compliance uncertain and costly.

Many cities, like St. Louis, have already consolidated their enforcement programs by sending one violation notice, which lists all infractions of municipal codes, to the property owner. This procedure allows him to budget improvements on the basis of a single loan and a single repair contract. Certainly there is no reason for cities to refuse to give consolidated in-

---

[5] In many smaller communities the subdivision regulation is often a part of the zoning code, and the various codes controlling the operation of the property are grouped under the building or housing code.

spections, if the property owners want it, because the initial cost to the city for training additional inspectors may be more than compensated by the reduced operating costs.

Building codes deal primarily with the structural safety of newly constructed and remodeled older structures. At the present time few codes have special provisions for rehabilitation, and the minimum requirements of structural safety are applied to new and old structures alike. The nearest thing to a concession to remodelers has been a trend toward flexible standards that govern the final performance of any portion of the structure or the structure as a whole. Performance standards were the reply to builders' dissatisfaction with provisions calling for specified materials or methods, when alternatives could do the job at less expense.[6]

There has been a great deal of discussion about the efficacy of rewriting building codes with special provisions for older structures. Some codes have satisfactorily incorporated such provisions. In other communities the spirit of the building code is met without changing any of the existing provisions by treating repairs and improvements to older properties in an *ad hoc* way. Specific suggestions for changes in local codes are rarely applicable to other communities, and each community must meet the problem in its own way.

The housing code governs the standards of all occupied dwelling units and is the main basis for local code enforcement programs. Most housing codes control the quality and amount of facilities within the dwelling unit, the maintenance of the dwelling and its equipment, and the number of persons living in a dwelling of any given size.

[6] Jack M. Siegel, *Governmental Participation in Urban Renewal;* and National Association of Home Builders, *Housing in the U.S.A.*, Simmons-Boardman Publishing Corporation, New York, 1954, 235 pp. (see Chap. 17).

The ability to pay for better housing is one of the factors limiting effective code enforcement. Communities with poor housing cannot expect to enforce highly exacting codes without causing a sudden jump in rents, and must therefore either adopt a code of relatively low standard or enforce a high standard in easy stages. The process of staged enforcement could be legalized by stipulating that a given level of standards was to be in effect for a fixed period of years and then superseded by a higher level of standards, and so on, until an ultimate level was obtained. This process, by recognizing financial realities, could avoid the stagnation that results from factional haggling over "unattainable" goals.[7]

A few rehabilitators think the provision in some housing codes permitting the razing of unfit dwellings (with the costs acting as a lien against the property) should be the accepted practice. The suggestion arises from impatience with property owners who continue to hold vacant nearby properties. Municipalities where this provision is included in their housing code, however, have shown some reluctance to enforce it because shelter, even though substandard, is lost along with whatever tax revenues the existing structures may yield. Razing, however, may be effectively undertaken where the legal authority exists, vacancies are high, and the tax revenue from slum properties is unimportant.

The zoning ordinance, which regulates the placement of the structure on the lot, the bulk of the building, land uses, and the gradual elimination of nonconforming uses, has been employed for over forty years. Here, too, a recent trend towards performance standards permits the property owners to exer-

[7] Dr. E. R. Krumbiegel, Milwaukee's code enforcement officer, made a similar proposal in the form of a "zoned" housing code, in which different standards would be applied in different parts of the city.

cise originality and inventiveness in the methods used to meet the code. Zoning is one of the main methods of carrying the community master plan into effect. Proper zoning can create and preserve a community setting suitable for continued remodeling activities, or it can aid in speeding the transition from one use to another when an area's demand characteristics change.

One manifestation of the public power which has had an important effect on the housing market is rent control. It was instituted during World War II under special emergency powers when population expanded rapidly at industrial concentrations, causing demand to exceed normal supply. Rents threatened to soar as war workers with inflated pocketbooks bid avidly for housing. Federal rent control, which was begun in 1942, ended in 1947, but many communities chose to continue controls because local demand still exceeded supply, and inflated rents were a hardship to low-income families. By the middle of 1958 almost all cities had abandoned controls. Rent controls have been kept in New York, however, where the demand for low-rent quarters from the growing Negro and Puerto Rican population exceeds the supply of units available to them. It is believed that if controls were removed, many minority families would be priced out of the housing market for standard units.

Yet, in protecting a portion of the housing market through rent control, serious side effects have occurred in the remainder of the market. Rents have remained relatively constant while operating costs have climbed, and the condition of the housing stock has deteriorated rapidly when property owners have reduced their maintenance expenditures to keep up their net returns. Some relief could be gained by undertaking major improvements since the allowable rent increases tended to be proportionately higher for improvements than for simple repair expenditures. Although this allowance occasionally stimulated remodeling, the finished projects were often removed from the low-rent category, reducing even further the supply of these units and intensifying the shortage.

THE POWER OF EMINENT DOMAIN

The power of eminent domain has recently been used to condemn properties for rehabilitation under urban-renewal programs. There is still some question, however, whether the public has the right to condemn the properties of owners who are unwilling to meet the standards of an urban-renewal project, when the plan calls for the property to be used in its original residential use. Owners argue that while the public can require them to meet the minimum standards of the community housing code, it has no right to divest them of their property when refusing to meet a standard higher than that of the housing code.

Litigation may be required in many states before the question is finally decided, but there are already indications that this use of eminent domain will eventually be upheld. Some cases in Illinois pertaining to Chicago rehabilitation projects have supported the use of eminent domain in the project area.[8]

DIRECT GOVERNMENT EXPENDITURES

Among the expenditures by local government are public improvements and housekeeping services so essential to profitable rehabilitation on a neighborhood scale. Many communities now add community facilities mainly in outlying areas

[8] *People ex rel Gutkneckt v. Chicago*, 3 Illinois 2d 539, 121 NE 2d 791 (1954). *Zisook v. Maryland-Drexel Corp.*, 3 Illinois 2d 570, 121 NE 2d 804 (1954) (44 American Law Reports 2d D 1414).

where the demands of new development are pressing. They also tend to reduce housekeeping services in obsolescent areas. This pattern must be modified, and even greater expenditures undertaken for facilities and services in inlying areas, if the existing housing stock is to be conserved and improved.[9]

MUNICIPAL TAXATION [10]

Many economists advocate increased use of the real property tax as a device to stimulate the purposes of planning and public welfare.

In addition to providing revenue, the general property tax on real estate may be used to further the purposes of urban planning and public welfare. For by controlling the amount of taxes to be levied or exemptions to be granted against rights in different types of spatial units, public policy can influence the use of land and effect the distribution of wealth and income.[11]

This attitude has been specifically addressed to rehabilitated property by suggesting that abnormally low assessments on a rehabilitated property as well as actual tax abatements would stimulate rehabilitation by private investors. Tax abatement or exemption has the effect of reducing the operating costs of property, particularly rental property, where any tax saving

[9] Robert Moses, *The Influence of Public Improvements on Property Value*, New York, August, 1953, 16 pp. Also, J. C. Bernard, "Do Public Improvements Create Special Benefits?" *Appraisal Journal*, vol. 13, January, 1945, pp. 20–23.

[10] Although it has steadily declined in importance since the beginning of the century, the real property tax is still the chief revenue source of local governments, having accounted for 58 per cent of local government revenues in 1955 (*op. cit.*, The Tax Foundation, *Facts and Figures on Government Finance*, 1956–1957, p. 174). Actually the dollar revenues yielded by the property tax increased from $624 million in 1902 to $10,323 million in 1955. The tax still represents a share of the operating costs of a property in the neighborhood of 20 per cent.

[11] Ernest M. Fisher and Robert M. Fisher, *Urban Real Estate*, Henry Holt and Company, Inc., New York, 1954, p. 456.

probably will be an addition to the investor's net income and thus may encourage more investment in rehabilitated structures.

Dissenting voices, however, point out two objections. First, the community placing a substantial reliance on the property tax rarely can afford to dissipate any of its vitally needed revenues in tax abatements, which are hard to discontinue and easy to utilize for other purposes. Second, the primary purpose of any tax is to raise revenues in an equitable manner, and using the tax for any other purpose reduces its equitability. For example, if tax exemptions are given to stimulate rehabilitation, local revenues would have to be derived by increasing the levy on the unaffected citizens. In spite of these objections, some governments appear to be using tax abatements to an increasing extent in their housing policies. New York, for example, has a tax-abatement scheme for multifamily properties which allows a partial deduction of improvement costs for nine years, plus a twelve-year freeze on preimprovement assessments.

Some taxing jurisdictions already have established an unwritten policy limiting assessment increases on home improvements in the interests of better housing. This policy has had only limited effect because some increase in the total tax always follows the improvements. If a community can reduce its dependence on the property tax, it might use formal tax concessions as a formidable policy tool for housing improvement.

COMMUNITY PLANNING AND CONTACTS WITH THE PUBLIC

There is universal agreement among commentators on local government's role in rehabilitation that its many activities, public improvements and services, clearance, code enforcement, and tax levies, must be integrated and focused on the local neighborhood by adequate planning and programming.[12] Too often what the community is trying to accomplish is unclear, and its budgets produce conflicts that reduce the effectiveness of public expenditures. These conflicts can only be avoided by a clear program for the community's future, of which the housing program forms a part.

The need for better communications with the public on the part of government is frequently mentioned. The public wants to be kept informed of all government plans. Among the more concrete suggestions for better communications, many private investors speak of the need for courteous, prompt attention from local officials. One rehabilitator has suggested that local governments could employ someone schooled in the realty or building field to interpret local codes and housing programs.

Early public announcement of final intentions as well as these other government devices to promote better relations with the public may not add to the amount of rehabilitation undertaken, but will allow unaffected private projects to go forward on schedule and prevent expenditures on projects doomed to early extinction by public action. Furthermore, a well-informed public is more confident of its government and sympathetic to its programs. Lack of public information invites avoidable opposition to plans that are sprung too suddenly on an uninformed citizenry and are poorly understood.

Even when the local government works at peak efficiency, however, it may still be hampered by limitations in resources and require the support and assistance of the state and Federal governments.

---

[12] William L. Slayton (*op. cit.*) has said, "The coordination of all the functions required in a conservation program necessitates centering authority and responsibility. The precise location is immaterial; but some individual or agency must be given the responsibility."

State Policies Affecting Housing

The states' role in housing rehabilitation and urban renewal is small compared to that of the Federal and local governments but is important nonetheless, and might well become more so. Because local participation in Federal renewal programs is not possible unless the states permit it, the delegation of appropriate powers to municipalities through state enabling acts is one of the important steps that states need to take.[13]

In addition several states have established agencies for the direct support of housing improvement and redevelopment. Illinois and Pennsylvania, for example, have authorized funds for municipalities to use in matching Federal grants. The Department of Public Works and Highways of New Hampshire guarantees local authority bonds as well as offers small capital grants. New York State has probably done the most in housing and redevelopment, with the Division of Housing constructing thousands of low-rent units and making grants to limited dividend and cooperative housing developments.

States can add effectiveness to local renewal and housing programs by complementing existing Federal and local programs. Many cities, for example, will need enabling legislation to allow them to rewrite local codes in order to stimulate rehabilitation, to offer tax abatements if advisable, and to take full advantage of Federal renewal programs. Enabling legislation is also needed to allow formal metropolitan cooperation on problems that go beyond the jurisdiction of the municipality. Similarly, municipalities need the cooperation of their state

---

[13] Two states, Wyoming and Utah, have not permitted their cities to accept Federal aid of any kind, while five other states, Idaho, Mississippi, Louisiana, Montana, and New Mexico, have not permitted their cities to accept Federal urban-redevelopment or renewal aid.

governments in developing new tax sources to meet the added demands of urban renewal. These problems are closely interrelated: "To a considerable extent, the slum problem and our ability to deal with it will depend upon our resourcefulness in resolving the problems of metropolitan area planning and taxation." [14]

In some states clarification is needed on the question of whether holding and foreclosing mortgages by out-of-state corporations constitutes "doing business" within the state. More financial institutions might be willing to spread their investments if the extent of, or immunity from, legal and tax liabilities were clarified.

Lastly, many city officials hope state governments will extend their programs of direct expenditures for metropolitan services, loans for urban improvements including housing, grants for planning and renewal, state housing construction, and their programs in many other fields. They feel states can undertake these tasks by allocating a greater share of the revenues collected in cities to municipal programs.

Federal Government Programs Affecting Housing: HHFA

Since the 1930s the number and coverage of Federal aid programs has rapidly expanded; mortgage, insurance, and aid for public housing and redevelopment were joined in 1949 by grants for urban renewal and in 1954 by assistance for community planning. With the exception of the home-loan guaranty operation of the Veterans Administration, Federal housing activities are administered largely by the constituent

[14] The President's Advisory Committee on Government Housing Policies and Programs, *A Report to the President of the United States*, December, 1953, p. 114.

agencies of the Housing and Home Finance Agency. The Administrator exercises general supervisory authority over the credit policies of the FHA, FNMA, and the Public Housing Administration (PHA). In addition he has direct administration over the Urban Renewal Administration (URA) and the Community Facilities Administration (CFA).

The Administrator also must approve the urban renewal plans and workable programs of communities petitioning for Federal renewal assistance.[15] After the Administrator's approval, the Urban Renewal Administration directs the Federal assistance given to local communities in redevelopment and urban renewal. The renewal or redevelopment plans of the local community must meet the standards set by the URA to qualify for Federal assistance. Urban-renewal technicians in the regional offices of the HHFA assist communities in developing their renewal and redevelopment projects. There were 562 projects outstanding and eight projects completed at the end of 1958.[16]

The Community Facilities Agency, which supervises the public works planning program, and the Public Housing Administration have less immediate significance for rehabilitation than the other agencies. However, in bringing urban renewal and planning to communities where they were not previously

[15] The "Workable Program" provision of the 1954 statute requires that the local community write and enforce adequate housing and building codes, develop a comprehensive community plan, and prepare neighborhood analyses of the areas in which future urban renewal projects are anticipated. It also requires that the community develop a capable administrative organization, have adequate financial resources for a renewal program, have a relocation plan, and that it facilitate the development of citizens' organizations. (Housing and Home Finance Agency, *How Localities Can Develop a Workable Program for Urban Renewal*, December, 1956, 12 pp.)

[16] Housing and Home Finance Agency, *Housing Statistics*, December, 1958, p. 84.

known, the CFA could start a chain reaction increasing the volume of rehabilitation in the future.

Public housing has come to be regarded by some groups primarily as a device to provide housing for families displaced by government action, although its original function is still important. Public housing probably will continue to be an important contributor to urban renewal. Noteworthy is the interest that has been recently expressed in the possibilities of buying and rehabilitating structures for public housing where the authority to do so has been little used in the past.[17] Local officials have shown increasing interest in the lower unit costs of public housing provided by rehabilitation and in the less "institutional" character of the finished product.

On the whole the urban-renewal program still lays too little emphasis on rehabilitation to call forth specific reactions from remodeling investors beyond their desire to obtain the better financing provided by the program as rapidly as possible. Few investors can afford to have their equity tied to a project that may take a year or two to complete. Therefore, to gain the cooperation of the smaller investors, the speed of housing programs will have to be increased.

In 1957, the HHFA took several actions to reduce total project time and provide FHA insurance as quickly as possible.[18] Perhaps the most significant step in this direction was the institution of "nonassisted" urban-renewal projects, which allow the city to designate an area for urban renewal and have investors immediately receive mortgages insured under

[17] See Appendix B, Study 8, The Chicago Housing Authority study of 1946.

[18] The URA suggested several technical amendments to the Housing Act in 1957, intended to reduce the red tape contributing to project delays (*Hearings on the Housing Amendments of 1957*, before a Subcommittee of the Committee on Banking and Currency, Mar. 18–Apr. 3, 1957, p. 142).

Section 220 of the FHA statute, provided no Federal aid for additional community facilities is requested. However, as we saw in Chapter 6, the possibilities of obtaining financing in a neighborhood are increased by vigorous public action.[19] Unless, therefore, the city can afford to make needed additions to community facilities in a "nonassisted" project area, FHA insurance is likely to have limited utility. The Federal government has the power to assist municipalities that have met the challenge of the workable program to add community facilities and eliminate nonconforming uses outside designated urban-renewal areas.

This suggests that there should be a simultaneous reconsideration of the project-by-project approach to renewal that has characterized the movement up to this time.[20] The dual problems of inadequate municipal resources and limited FHA insurance coverage might be alleviated by having the Federal government give general support to the comprehensive renewal program of a municipality without requiring separate approval and supervision of scattered projects within the city.

Federal Tax Policy and Its Effect on Rehabilitation

The effect that personal and corporate income taxes may have on the possibilities of housing improvement will vary with the value of the structure, the size of the investor's in-

---

[19] Guy T. O. Hollyday, Baltimore mortgage banker and FHA Commissioner at the time the Housing Act of 1954 was passed, pointed out that urban renewal and the workable program would permit the FHA to insure loans in what were once high-risk areas because the improvements made the loans secure for both lending institutions and the FHA (see *ibid.*, p. 76).

[20] Richardson Dilworth, the mayor of Philadelphia, in commenting on this point said: "We in Philadelphia have long advocated getting away from the project approach to renewal. I would certainly like to suggest exploration of the possibility of a Federal commitment of some kind to supporting a series of related projects...." (*Ibid.*, p. 598.)

come, and the nature of the credit used to purchase or repair a structure. Since interest on debt is deductible, the cost of the structure is reduced by an amount equal to the interest on the debt multiplied by the owner's tax rate. A family buying a $10,000 house with a twenty-year 5 per cent mortgage for $8,000, for example, would have annual interest charges of about $400. Thus the annual housing cost is reduced by $80 if the family's personal income tax rate is 20 per cent of net income. There have been recent efforts to allow personal income tax deductions for home-repair expenses but as yet they have been unsuccessful.[21]

The effects of corporate income taxes are particularly significant to large-scale rental rehabilitation. Corporate income tax rates are 30 per cent for corporate income below $25,000 and 52 per cent for incomes over $25,000. Corporate tax laws allow both the deduction of interest on debt and depreciation of the cost of the improvements from gross corporate income.

The Internal Revenue Act recognizes three depreciation formulas. The first is the straight-line method, where a sum equal to the depreciable value of an acquired property and to the additional remodeling investment divided by the life of the investment is subtracted each year. Two methods employing accelerated depreciation were introduced by the 1954 amendments to the internal-revenue code, but are applicable only to the value of the improvements and not the total investment. The declining-balance method allows the investor to depreciate the property starting at twice the linear rate and reducing

[21] In 1956 two resolutions were introduced in the House. One would have allowed homeowners to deduct repair expenses up to $500 (H.R. 7172), and the other proposed that 5 per cent of the adjusted gross income be deductible for this purpose (H.R. 4670).

the amount of depreciation each year by an amount equal to the first year's depreciation divided by the life span of the property. The sum-of-the-years'-digits method is computed by multiplying the added investment in the building by a fraction the denominator of which is the sum of the integers and the numerator of which equals the number of years remaining in the depreciation period.

The relative advantages of straight-line over the accelerated-depreciation methods depends on the length of time the investor intends to hold the property. The straight-line method makes the tax higher in the early years but less in the later years than the accelerated methods. If the investor intends to hold the property for its economic life, the straight-line method may be preferred, since his liability would decline as his profits fell. The accelerated methods are preferred by investors who intend to hold the property for no more than a few years.

In spite of these deductions income taxes take a heavy toll from property income, especially when a corporate income tax is paid out of profits which, when distributed, are taxed again at the personal rate of shareholders. The net result is a tendency to limit rehabilitation activity to cases where ownership by individuals or partnerships is feasible. The inhibitive effects on investment make themselves felt time and time again. A simple way to encourage larger rehabilitation enterprise and to improve the profitability of rehabilitation and stimulate further investment would be to allow real estate trusts to have the same advantages as security investment trusts; that is, to permit the net returns to be taxed only once at the personal income tax rate of the trust members. In this way investors could obtain the protection of limited liability associated with a corporation without double taxation on their returns.

Planning for Urban Renewal

Many cities now write their housing programs around the variety of aids offered to them by other governments. Instead, it would be better if they based their program, first, on the future economic needs and aspirations of the community, and afterward sought the support they needed for its execution. Where this latter course is followed, the resulting changes in the structure of the city might produce more durable contributions to its welfare.

Some cities have followed a mechanistic approach to housing planning that tends to lure its users into complacent acceptance of its "scientific" findings. Others have produced plans based on visions rather than reality. A few cities, active in planning for a number of years, have adopted an intermediate policy which uses social-science techniques to detect reasonably clear trends, and then adopts a flexible program consistent with, but not rigidly bound by, the research findings.

Devising a local housing program requires a "realistic" estimate of the community's available housing, its future needs, and a plan to fill the gaps that may be left by inadequate private efforts, with government-sponsored programs which can be rapidly adjusted as the scale of the problem becomes apparent. A realistic survey of housing resources cannot slavishly follow "national" standards that are incompatible with the community's housing conditions. It would, for example, be senseless to consider lots of less than 4,000 square feet as inadequate in New York City, where the standard lot is 2,500 square feet. The standards set by the community for its housing program should also have some relationship to capacities to pay.

Most surveys of housing needs make such adjustments by

applying one set of standards to every house in the city. No hardship results if the selected standards are really minimum, but exceptionally high standards will result in a program with costs which no reasonable community can hope to undertake. Standards which may be fair and reasonable in high-income sections of the community would require such formidable subsidies in low-income neighborhoods that implementing them would be untenable. Current programs must take these differences into account, striving for no more than minimum code levels in one area and for higher standards in an area where residents can afford them.

After housing planners have made their best guess as to what housing resources will be over the next several years if current trends remain unchanged, they should estimate what part of the future needs will be met through natural events: how many units will be lost through demolition, and, of course, how many will be saved by rehabilitation. The estimate of net housing needs, gross needs less those fulfilled, are the raw materials of the final program.

The actual programming begins when the community has at hand a housing survey embracing quantitative estimates of the existing and potential "standard" housing stock in the different neighborhoods of the city, and engineering studies estimating the costs of repairs and probable rents for typical housing in potential renewal areas.[22] The collected facts allow housing officials to estimate for any given area the relationship between housing needs and the probable housing supply resulting from unsupported private action. They can roughly estimate the probable costs, rent increases, and displacement resulting from programs involving different physical standards, and select a

[22] A study is being conducted by Prof. Albert H. Schaaf of the University of California on this topic.

method which might achieve those standards.[23] Conversely, they can estimate what level of repair might be supported by an area's potential rent increases.

Rehabilitation and the Housing Program

For the public official, as for the private investor, rehabilitation is one of several possible treatments of substandard property. The public powers can be used to demolish the building, to permit a new use of the old structure, to produce a new structure which can either serve the same purpose or a new one, or to remodel the old building for the same or a new purpose. A public decision to support one of these treatments of the property is predicated on five basic conditions:

1. What is visualized in the comprehensive land-use plan for the area?
2. How do these plans accord with current market conditions?
3. Will the prevailing market conditions remain operative over the service life of the property?
4. How can public intervention and expense be minimized to achieve a program balancing public aspirations and private plans?
5. Can a program achieving this balance over a given time period be reconciled with the housing goals set for the area?

These conditions assume that minimum government expenditures will result from a program whose housing goals are filled by relying as fully as possible on private expenditures. If

---

[23] The approximate repair costs can be converted into estimated rent increases, to see the displacement effects of the program, by adding the monthly debt service and the desired profit per $1,000 of reinvestment under different assumptions of profit and probable mortgage terms.

this is to be done, the program must accord closely with market conditions prevailing in each private submarket. If the choice is to be realistic, rehabilitation's feasibility will have to be assessed for each block and structure in the renewal area.

Rehabilitation should be accepted as the best method of housing improvement when the existing buildings accord with contemplated land-use plans, when investors find rehabilitation profitable, and when rehabilitation can meet the physical standards demanded in the program at less cost than other available methods. Rehabilitation might be used more effectively if consideration is given to the time element in planning. Policy makers may decide that they want to reach a given level of standards within ten years and that a program stressing renovation will be the least expensive method of attaining this goal within the set time limit.

Clearly the implications of time programming point toward rehabilitation as a flexible housing tool. It can be used to reach almost any physical standard or mortgageable life that policy dictates. However, rehabilitation has inescapable limits. It can rarely achieve the standards of density or design of a new subdivision. Land-use plans which require considerable clearance can raise the average costs of rehabilitated properties beyond costs justified by the end product; thus, fundamental design obsolescence may be much too costly to overcome.

Comparing the Public Costs of Sanctions and Incentives to Make Rehabilitation Possible

The sanctions or incentives selected to implement a given housing program depend on their effectiveness and comparative cost. The questions of where, when, and how many incentives to offer are usually decided by determining the methods that will result in the lowest cost to the taxpayer and still yield the desired results. The effectiveness of different sanctions or incentives will depend on local economic conditions, forms of tenure, and the ephemeral *sine qua non* for any program, "community spirit." No one approach will suit every community's needs equally well.

Whether the device to stimulate rehabilitation by private investors in renewal areas is a tax abatement, a direct cash payment, a land write-down, or an increase in potential rents and sale prices through added community facilities, the cash benefit will have to be at least enough to fill the gap between the rate of return the investor can expect following improvement without help and the going rate of return from rehabilitation projects located in stable, high-rent areas. Any program of incentives planned by a local government should be founded on a bedrock of facts which prove the incentives to be adequate but not excessive to do the job for which they were designed.

Chapter 8

EXPANDING THE VOLUME OF REHABILITATION

Approximately $15 billion dollars is being spent each year to add something over a million dwelling units (including their land) to the total housing supply. In addition, some estimates suggest a like amount is being spent annually to make additions and alterations, and to repair or maintain the existing housing stock.[1] Yet in spite of the strides since 1950 when about 30 per cent of America's dwelling units were dilapidated or without baths or hot water, about 22.8 per cent of all dwelling units and 17.6 per cent of nonfarm dwelling units are still substandard.[2] As the President's Advisory Committee on Housing pointed out in 1953, there is clearly a great need for a vast program of residential rehabilitation.

The present study was undertaken to determine the specific circumstances under which rehabilitation is profitable and to explore possibilities for increasing the investment potential in this field. It was found that rehabilitation is possible when and where potential rents or sale prices for improved units are

[1] These estimates are open to challenge.
[2] *National Housing Inventory, by Location and Condition as of Dec. 31, 1956*, prepared by Miles L. Colean from unpublished data of the 1956 National Housing Inventory, U.S. Bureau of the Census, Aug. 7, 1958.

higher than existing rents or sale prices, and that rehabilitation can be profitable as long as the cost of the repairs made did not exceed the capitalized difference between the existing and potential rents, or the sale price. It was found also that new opportunities for rehabilitation can be created with relative ease by improving the neighborhood setting with added community facilities, by creating consumer interest in maintenance and remodeling, and by lowering remodeling costs to make more effective use of the difference between existing and potential rents.

In spite of this, only a small part of the many existing opportunities for profitable investment are actually being used. Investors tend to regard rehabilitation as a difficult operation with doubtful returns. Unfamiliar with rehabilitation's full contribution to the value of the structure and its neighborhood, lenders restrict or withhold loans on rehabilitated properties. Consumers overlook the assets of existing neighborhoods and the locational and spatial advantages of older houses in their head-long rush to the suburbs. Governments, particularly local governments, fail to make clear-cut decisions as to how, when, and where to use rehabilitation in their local programs.

There is no single device that will greatly increase the investment in rehabilitation. A whole series of interdependent actions by many public and private groups are needed, but the most effective devices will vary with the housing conditions and aspirations of each community. In fact, highly specific proposals are possible only if the facts and figures of the municipality to which the final program will be applied are close at hand. Therefore, the suggestions on the following pages are not intended as a comprehensive or universally applicable program but rather as suggested methods for increasing rehabilitation which might be applied to a large number of communities if they were properly adapted to local circumstances.

Private groups can create a greater willingness on the part of their members to invest in rehabilitation, but without complementary actions by governments to provide the financial and physical setting for rehabilitation, potential investments will never become realities.

Actions by Private Groups

TRADE ASSOCIATIONS

Trade associations in activities related to construction can make a major contribution by educating their members in the potentialities and techniques of rehabilitation. This can be done by preparing and distributing rehabilitation case books and technical pamphlets covering market analysis, design and construction techniques, feasibility analysis, and methods of creating further rehabilitation opportunities in cooperation with other national organizations, neighborhood groups, and local governments.

Building-trade groups should consider the desirability of sponsoring conferences to devise new remodeling techniques and to bring these to the attention of their members. On a long-term basis, intensive research should result in new materials and construction methods, and new management and budget techniques to reduce the cost of rehabilitation. Such research might be sponsored jointly with labor groups, or professional associations such as the American Institute of Architects. The AIA could interest architects in remodeling as a new creative outlet and encourage interest in developing new designs for future buildings which can be inexpensively maintained and readily adapted to changing demands.

Some consideration should be given to establishing greater industry identification for rehabilitators, perhaps through a specialized trade association, as a means of focusing attention on rehabilitation and to provide information about its opportunities and methods.

ACTION BY LABOR ORGANIZATIONS

Almost every rehabilitator who was interviewed complained of the shortage of mechanics skilled in several trades and familiar with the problems of older structures. The need to use labor from several unions appreciably increased remodeling costs because of the inevitable delays occurring whenever a workman ran into a job that was within the jurisdiction of another union. National labor organizations might therefore consider the formation of a special remodeler's union, with its own training program to teach its members remodeling techniques without reference to existing union jurisdictions.

ACTION BY LENDERS

It is essential that lenders find ways to produce an ampler flow of funds than has yet been available for remodeled structures if there is to be any major increase in rehabilitation activity. National associations of lenders should be urged to conduct independent and regular surveys of rehabilitation opportunities as a preface to a program of encouraging their members to invest more extensively in loans for rehabilitation.

Regional or local groups of lenders may find that until they have made enough rehabilitation loans to stand detailed analysis it is safer to pool their risk through cooperative formation of a new mortgage corporation. Any loss occurring on individual loans might then be shared equally by all lenders belonging to the corporation. If risk pools can be established in all urban centers where there is enough capital to make an appreciable contribution to local rehabilitation programs, the experience gained over a period of years may prove that longer-term, lower-interest loans are feasible.

NATIONAL INTEREST GROUPS

National organizations interested in housing improvement can play a major role by convincing consumers of the virtues of older housing and existing neighborhoods. Theirs is primarily a responsibility to inform and educate. Some of the activities they can effectively undertake are:

1. Information on how to organize neighborhood groups to plan environmental improvements and to win the cooperation of the local government and lenders in their efforts.

2. Advice on methods of property maintenance, and promotion of the value of continued maintenance, to protect the resale price or to avert costly future repairs.

3. A series of pamphlets to instruct the homeowner on detecting needed repairs, repair techniques, means of contracting for professional services, and the availability of financing. These manuals can be brought to the attention of the homeowner through local business firms or national advertising.

Action by Government

Government has the twofold responsibility of increasing opportunities for private investment and integrating private investments within its own housing program. The degree of government intervention will ultimately depend upon consumer interest, the cooperation given by private industry, and the extent to which governments can use rehabilitation as a tool for housing improvement.

THE LOCAL GOVERNMENT AND REHABILITATION

How well rehabilitation can serve a local housing program depends upon the levels of achievement the municipality sets for its housing plans. Working with citizen groups and important leaders in the community, city officials must face housing problems frankly and determine: (1) what distribution of land uses, including housing, will best serve the future economy of the city; (2) how and where different groups in the community might be housed and at what standards; (3) what kinds of inducement are required to gain the cooperation of private investors and other levels of government in programming costs; and (4) how can the levels of achievement for each neighborhood be reconciled to standards set by the market. The city's image of the future of the neighborhood, and hence of the profitability of investing in it, must correspond to that held by the speculative investor and the mortgage lender if their full cooperation is to be gained.

Community facilities and services will contribute to the desirability and stability of an area. New or improved schools, parks, transportation, trash collection, and other services will improve the physical environment of the neighborhood, thus increasing its potential rent. A city can use a community-facilities program to direct private investment into areas of its choice. In doing so, the local government must decide whether to concentrate new facilities in a few areas or to distribute them equally and perhaps less effectively over all areas; if additional facilities and services carry them beyond the bounds of existing revenue sources, how to increase tax revenues or obtain aid from other levels of government.

Neighborhood planning will stimulate neighborhood citizen

participation and provide local government with an order of priorities for improvement. A staff planner assigned to work with local neighborhood groups can help articulate neighborhood problems and desires.

This study has shown that a highly exacting code is often unusable in low-rent areas because the cost of meeting code standards may increase housing costs beyond the financial capacities of the residents, thus causing sizable dislocation. Yet local housing officials find a stiff code has great utility in their neighborhood-conservation areas. The local community, therefore, might consider writing a high-standard, "timed" housing code which would stage required compliance in a series of easily absorbed steps. Through this device, enforcement officials can apply minimum standards in low-income areas and at the same time make clear to property owners in better areas that it will be less costly to meet the full provisions of the code immediately, even though they are not required by law to do so.

Local building codes usually make no provisions for the special problems of existing structures. A separate code with flexible performance standards would probably lower the cost of rehabilitation although it would have to be administered with the utmost integrity.

Local government might consider using property-tax abatements to lower the cost of rehabilitation and to expand investment opportunities. Limited assessments or actual tax exemptions should be offered for a short time only and should be well advertised. If the community depends largely on a property tax, however, any concessions may reduce revenues to a point where other desirable community programs will be retarded.

Another stimulus to rehabilitation would be to increase

assessments on properties adjacent to rehabilitated properties, particularly when area-wide improvements produce an undisputed rise in values.

STATE GOVERNMENTS

The fundamental responsibility of state government is to aid municipalities to the limit of their financial capacity and as rapidly as possible provide enabling legislation needed to permit appropriate local action. Such enabling legislation might include the power to rewrite local codes or the authority to utilize Federal housing or renewal aids.

States should offer local governments a variety of tax resources to increase their revenue and reduce dependence on the property tax. They can also return more of the taxes collected in municipalities to the cities either as direct expenditures or as grants-in-aid.

States, working with local governments and lenders, might explore the possibilities of developing a mortgage-facilities corporation on the New York model which could help direct additional credit to neighborhood rehabilitation.

FEDERAL PARTICIPATION

The Federal government can facilitate residential rehabilitation by adjustments in the operations of the several housing programs.

1. *Credit Aids.* The Federal Housing Administration heretofore has not treated the housing market as an entity. Separate programs have been written for different types of housing. The provisions of Sections 203 and 220 of its guiding law are essentially the same, but the former is applied primarily to mortgages on new and existing structures in stable neighborhoods while the latter is reserved for urban-renewal areas.

Since each program is separately accounted for, losses under each section are minimized by insuring only the most promising mortgages. This reduces the utility of both sections to the rehabilitator. If the FHA returned to a single mortgage title, it might encourage the assumption of a wider range of risk because losses would be weighted against the total volume of all outstanding mortgages rather than against only a small part of that total. Furthermore, consideration should be given to what constitutes a reasonable degree of loss in light of the improbability of another depression of the magnitude of that of the thirties.

The FHA should continue its efforts to adjust its minimum property requirements and adapt them to local housing conditions. Also, the application of Section 213 of its statute to the cooperative rehabilitation of existing structures would permit modest-income families to enjoy the advantages of a remodeled structure at lower costs.

The FHA is in a crucial position to help bring better terms and more funds to rehabilitation by insuring lenders against higher risks. If lenders respond to the insurance program, little more is needed to assure a steady growth in remodeling activity. However, if lenders do not respond to the FHA, consideration could be given to expanding the authority of FNMA to purchase mortgages on existing properties substantially improved by rehabilitation.

2. *Urban Renewal.* The study has shown that by and large rehabilitation is less costly than new construction and that maintenance and conservation is cheaper than extensive rehabilitation. Therefore, a simultaneous attack on the housing problems of a complete metropolitan area should be economically less costly in the long run than a piecemeal program

of separate projects undertaken only when an area becomes badly blighted and needs more radical treatment. In spite of the expansion of Federal housing aids, there are still not enough local funds or Federal aids for a comprehensive housing program covering the entire metropolitan area. Furthermore, the degree of preparation and advanced planning which is required for each separate renewal or redevelopment project is out of keeping with its relative importance to the total stockpile of housing. It would seem logical to extend the concept of Federal renewal support to the entire metropolitan housing program. The central city would prepare one housing plan which considers the needs of the entire area and, after its approval, the local field agencies of the URA could work cooperatively with the central city and its neighboring municipalities in the preparation of annual renewal budgets. After their approval by the URA, the Federal share of the net renewal cost could be delivered in a block sum to each city at the beginning of the year.

Although local public housing authorities have always had the permission to purchase and rehabilitate dwellings for low-rent families, they have rarely done it. The Public Housing Administration might consider furthering its efforts to stimulate the use of rehabilitation by local authorities which would not only lower total program costs but overcome many of the social problems associated with large-scale public housing projects.

3. *Tax Adjustments.* Two tax adjustments would stimulate remodeling. First, an exemption in the personal income tax for repair expenditures in excess of a given percentage of gross income would undoubtedly encourage maintenance and remodeling by the private homeowner. Second, in order to

stimulate large-scale rehabilitation, real estate trusts should be exempted from the corporate income tax in the same manner as other security trusts are now exempted.

Many stimulants to rehabilitation require the cooperative action of several groups.

Cooperation is absolutely essential in planning the local housing program and in reaching agreement on the responsibilities of the several agencies and groups concerned. To accomplish this, the chief executive of the municipality might appoint a renewal council or a housing coordinator, and a full-time staff, with the legislative responsibility of devising an acceptable program. The housing coordinator could be one of the existing officials also responsible for general community planning and renewal.

Housing market analyses on a scale never before attempted should become an essential part of every community's housing program. Regional analysis should be coupled with neighborhood analyses where the areas are under special consideration for intensive programs. The city should have the cooperation of remodelers and lenders who will profit from the results.

Summary

The volume of rehabilitation can be increased by providing more financing for rehabilitation, by convincing housing consumers to own and maintain remodeled homes in established neighborhoods, by improving the neighborhood environment with added community facilities and services, and by educating investors and homeowners in the profitability and methods of rehabilitation. The final program will necessarily rely on a variety of tried and untried devices which are based on the decisions and cooperation of many local and national groups.

What are the alternatives to using rehabilitation more extensively in local housing programs? To place complete reliance on new, private construction may accelerate the outward expansion of urban population, producing entirely new city forms replacing existing urban centers. To rely primarily on publicly aided construction in existing urban centers requires an extremely high level of public and private expenditures. Rehabilitation at standards as closely approximating the abilities of local users to pay, without sacrificing a realistic standard of human decency, deserves a larger role in the housing programs of every community.

Appendix A
OTHER CASE MATERIALS

The cases included in this appendix have been collected from questionnaires, interviews, and already published sources.[1] The published sources are given wherever applicable and should be resorted to whenever the reader wants greater detail for a particular case. Published cases are included here either because the sources are not readily available to the reader or because of their particular interest within the context of the study's findings.

The cases are grouped by the three income classes of rehabilitation and under each by the alphabetical order of the cities in which they are found. The reader's attention is directed to Appendix B for an analysis of other rehabilitation studies, past and present, and for other treatments of the included cases.

Upper-income Rehabilitation

CASE 1

The New York Life Insurance Company built high-rent Manhattan House in 1954—an apartment building covering an entire city block at 200 East 66th Street. Across the street from the entrance were ten dilapidated brownstones. Believing these buildings clashed with their project, New York Life purchased and rehabilitated them to guard their larger investment.

The site and structure selections were predetermined by their

[1] It is interesting to note that most of the additional prestige cases come from published sources, while the middle- and lower-rent cases are more frequently derived from questionnaires and interviews. Apparently the shelter press gives more attention to attractive design than to low-cost housing.

199

purpose in rehabilitation. The ten structures were converted into 250 units at an approximate average cost of $9,000 per unit, or $2¼ million. The units ranged in size from one and one-half rooms to four rooms and rented for $87.50 to $185 per month. The usual pattern of investment decisions was cast aside since the project did not have to stand on its own merits but only contribute to the success of the more important investment. Therefore, the costs were fixed by the standards they felt necessary to eliminate the detracting influence of the brownstone structures. Financing was done with the New York Life's investment funds. The apartments were rented in the conventional manner without difficulty.[2] What is interesting in the case is the fact that rehabilitation was successfully used to complement new construction in a high-rent area.

CASE 2

The next two cases illustrate the profits latent in the "worst house in a sound (upper-income) neighborhood." A handsome frame barn was purchased in a suburban Rhode Island town some years ago. An experienced builder bought the structure and converted it to three apartments at a total investment of $24,000. The roof line and eaves were left untouched, but casement windows and a colonial door were placed in the side walls. When the work was done the only reminder of the structure's past was a rooftop cupola surmounted by a weather vane. The house is a white colonial rectangle with dark shutters framing orderly rows of windows.

The market value of the building in 1956 was $30,000 and the net income from the property $2,870 a year, 11.5 per cent of the investment.[3] The repair costs implied by the conversion must have

[2] Jack M. Seigel and C. Williams Brook, *Slum Prevention through Conservation and Rehabilitation*, Subcommittee on Urban Redevelopment, Rehabilitation, and Conservation, The President's Advisory Committee on Government Housing, Policies and Programs, 1953, 142 pp.

[3] *Operative Remodeling*, United States Gypsum Co., Chicago, 1956, p. 37. (There are very few data in this reference and no way to find additional information except through the authors.)

been quite high, making the purchase price necessarily low. The investment hardly seems a gamble. The location allowed the investor to charge rents in the vicinity of $150 per month per unit, and the low purchase price gave him plenty of room to make major repairs. The builder further reduced the risk and costs by acting as his own contractor.

Every neighborhood has neglected houses which can be acquired at a cost allowing some repairs; opportunities to make major changes are rare except in center-city areas. When they are found in outlying neighborhoods the structures have usually been used for some other purpose or been held off the market while they rapidly deteriorated in the hands of an estate or elderly person.

CASE 3

Stanley Epstein has rehabilitated over 2,000 houses in the outskirts of St. Louis in the past twenty-five years. He buys a dwelling in an established neighborhood when the dwelling is far enough below the prevailing market value to allow needed repairs. The illustrative project is a one-hundred-year-old frame house on the edge of St. Louis. The house had deteriorated badly, but its grounds are large and the adjacent neighborhood is stable. It is a two-story structure with a conventional center-hall entrance and rear additions. The project was modernization in the strictest sense of the word. Very few interior space changes were made, except for an added closet and a subtracted cellar stairway. The exterior was painted, some old windows replaced, and the front porch improved. The interior had its utility system overhauled and was completely redecorated. The structure cost $10,000 to acquire and $10,913.33 to repair, and sold for $23,500, yielding a profit of $2,586.67, or 13 per cent on investment.[4]

The case illustrates a simple example of restoring value lost through neglect. It is interesting to note the effects of changes in the level of economic activity on this particular form of rehabilitation. Real estate values are largely predicated on the

---

[4] *Ibid.*, p. 11 (for complete cost figures).

consumer's reaction to comparative quality. Any value a dilapidated structure might be given by supply shortages in a time of rapidly rising prices and consumer demand is quickly lost when the supply shortages are overcome and buying remains steady but not competitive. Therefore the price of deteriorated structures is relatively low after heavy, new construction overcomes supply shortages. This allows the rehabilitator during the height of a building boom to buy and remodel tired houses in neighborhoods of higher value. The opportunity to remodel still exists in a time of depressed prices and oversupply but the amount of repairs is limited if the differential value between the dilapidated structure and its neighbors is reduced. Demand at the same time has fallen to its lowest point, increasing the need for a first-rate finished product to capture whatever demand still exists. This makes remodeling without conversion particularly risky and tends to limit activities almost as sharply as new construction.

CASE 4

Another example of center-city remodeling is the work of Russell Eldridge, a Washington builder. Eldridge remodeled ten small row houses in the Georgetown section of Washington in the early 1950s. The two-story brick houses are only 12 by 22 feet. Two groups of five houses face each other across a narrow alley. The houses had been condemned by the District government shortly before they were purchased for $70,000. Eldridge used his experience as a builder, with the cooperation of a small real estate firm, to virtually rebuild the interiors, meeting local market demands.

Site selection was based on the already advanced rehabilitation effort in Georgetown. The prices paid for the structures were at least $2,000 more than prices for comparable houses in Foggy Bottom [5] and several thousand more than prices in less desirable parts of the city. But the price paid was extremely reasonable for Georgetown and the opportunity to buy ten houses in a group was a windfall.

[5] See section on Foggy Bottom in Chapter 2.

Eldridge employed an architect experienced in Georgetown remodeling. The exteriors were painted white, with a decorative iron railing along the brick stoops. The alley was renamed Pomander Walk, with the center strip between the two rows of houses landscaped with grass and shrubs. The end of the walk was closed off with a low brick wall behind which a well-formed shade tree served as a focal point. The interior design was typical of other projects, with a small kitchen beside the entrance and the remainder of the first floor turned into a living-dining room. The room was given a beamed ceiling, brick fireplace, and a glass door leading onto a brick patio. An open stairway with an iron banister led to the second floor, which had a bedroom, a sitting room which could serve as a guest room, and an interior bath.

The houses lacked basements and none was supplied, so that storage is something of a problem. Every inch of space not used for daily living is closeted or shelved. The absent basement also made heating a problem, but Eldridge settled on four gas heaters for each living unit.

The completed units cost an average of $6,605 for repair, sold for an average of $15,000 each, and by the fall of 1955 had risen in value to about $17,000. Profits averaged $1,400 per unit, or 10.2 per cent of investment.[6] Advanced rehabilitation in the area removed any risk involved in the project.[7]

CASE 5

The Long Island Neighborhood Renewals Corporation bought a twenty-eight-unit, four-story walk-up apartment building in September 1955.[8] The building was only two and one-half years

[6] "Town Houses in Georgetown," *Business of Building*, Late Fall, 1955, p. 6. Also *op. cit.*, *Operative Remodeling*, p. 39 (for complete cost figures).

[7] Other cases can be found in *Rehabilitation as a Business*, Institute of Real Estate Management and the Build America Council of the National Association of Real Estate Boards, Washington, 1954. Note particularly Everett Cook's work in Chicago. His firm makes a specialty of renovating and converting center-city mansions for rents of $150 and up.

[8] "Long Island Builders Set Up Stock Corporation to Finance Rehabilitation," *House & Home*, April, 1956 (unpaged reprint).

old but had thirty Glen Cove, New York, Building and Fire Code violations at the time the Corporation took possession. The prior owner went to jail for 330 days for his repeated offenses.

The Corporation has forty stockholders, all of whom are members of Homebuilders Institute of the National Association of Home Builders. They jointly purchased 1,000 shares at $100 apiece, to bring their combined talents to bear on urban decay.

Since the purchase was the Corporation's first venture they fully expected to take a loss. The Corporation agreed to buy the building and make the needed repairs if the mayor of Glen Cove could obtain a stay of eviction until the work was completed. This was done, whereupon the group bought the structure for $45,000.

The tenants were relocated in an empty resort hotel during the work process. Each of the apartments received a new bathroom, kitchen, and redecoration. The building needed a central heating system because the prior owner had used kerosene stoves in the individual units. The average improvement cost per unit was $3,770, making the Corporation's total investment about $150,560. Where the apartments had rented for $38 to $42 a month without utilities, they now rented for an average of $70 a month including utilities. The Corporation estimates this was an effective increase of about $8 per month. The gross annual rent was $23,520, making a gross return on investment of 15.5 per cent. However, five of the units were vacant in April, 1956, reducing the gross return to about 12.6 per cent.

The Corporation had financed the original project from its own resources (up to $100,000), with additional funds obtained from several contractors who agreed to take $25,000 worth of stock in the project in lieu of payment, and from a construction loan issued by a local bank. Emil Keen, President of the Renewal Corporation, felt conventional mortgages would not permit any increase in profits so that the group attempted to obtain an FHA loan. The local office of the FHA told them that the new-construction standards applied to their structure, making an FHA loan temporarily impossible. The group appealed to the Washington Office of the FHA in January of 1956 to see if they could have the New York Regional Office's ruling changed. No solution had been found by April of 1956, and the Corporation had neither accepted available conventional mortgages of $70,000 to $80,000 nor received an FHA 207 mortgage.

The important lesson of Long Island Neighborhood Renewal Corporation's project according to its stockholders is that corporate action undertaken by experienced builders can get urban renewal off the ground. They are sure that other projects will be satisfyingly profitable and that financing will be eased in the future by careful project selection.

CASE 6

A young sketch artist in Philadelphia rehabilitated a three-story row house near Fitler Square in downtown Philadelphia in 1957. The case history is particularly interesting because he, his artist wife, and their three children moved to their new home from an $11,600 development house in Levittown, Pennsylvania. He had been traveling two hours a day to and from his job in Philadelphia and didn't enjoy it. The family liked the Levittown house well enough but had no intention of making it their lifetime home. They finally decided that a remodeled city dwelling was within their means and would offer several exceptional advantages. First, the journey to work could be reduced to a fifteen-minute walk, saving $45 to $75 a month in transportation bills applicable to the cost of their new home. Second, there would be more recreational opportunities for the whole family, particularly the parents, who could slip off to a movie at a moment's notice. Third, the parents felt the children could gain more by going to school and playing in a city with its heterogeneous population than in a relatively homogeneous suburb.

The family found a tenant for their home in Levittown and purchased their Pine Street home for $8,400. The structure is 16 feet wide and originally had four bedrooms, a living room, dining room, kitchen, and bath. The lot behind the house was 16 by 55 feet, with a tree at the foot of the property. The interior was badly deteriorated at the time of purchase and the exterior had been faced with a stone veneer in some earlier attempt to preserve it.

The work was carried on with the helpful advice of the James Brothers of the Robert J. Nash Realty firm, who had sold the structure to the family. Most of the technical work was contracted, leaving the interior decoration to the new owners. The stone veneer was ripped off, and the brick painted black and the woodwork trimmed in white. The living room had its plaster removed to let the brick serve as a decorative wall covering. An open staircase led to the second-story bedrooms and bath. The third floor was opened out into a single room to serve as the master bedroom with a half-bath. Most of the floors were covered with asbestos tile rather than refinished or replaced. The entire job cost approximately $7,500, bringing the total investment to $15,900. No data covering project financing is available, but if the family's experience was similar to other center-city owners he received an $8,000 to $10,000 mortgage with a fifteen-year term.

The project cannot be judged in purely economic terms since the family's own satisfaction affects the feasibility equation. Apparently it was felt that reduced commuting cost made the new home no more costly than the Levittown house.[9]

The family appear to have moved to the center city more in reaction to Levittown than because of the positive attraction of the center city. The wife is quoted as indicating a continuing interest in rural life. She says their current home is the lightest and airiest house she has ever lived in, and that the city is as quiet as the country. This case gives only slight evidence that families dissatisfied with the packaged suburbs will move to the center city rather than another suburb or stable urban neighborhood more to their liking.

CASE 7

Morton Packman, a Philadelphia realtor, converted a three-story brick row house into nine efficiency apartments for Uni-

[9] Material from an article by Harriett J. Smith in the *Philadelphia Sunday Bulletin*, June 2, 1957.

versity of Pennsylvania students in 1956. Packman began this kind of rehabilitation by accident. He had worked as a salesman for a Philadelphia real estate firm from 1945 to 1953, and after learning the business and amassing some capital he decided to open his own office near the University of Pennsylvania. He purchased a building, converted the first floor into his office, and made the upper floors into residential apartments in order that the resulting rent would pay his office costs, a common practice. Packman was besieged with prospective tenants shortly after the work began. Investigation showed him that the University was unable to house both its graduate and undergraduate bodies in University dormitories, and the students were scattered throughout the area in vermin-infested apartments with few modern conveniences at inflated rents. Packman moved his office into the basement of the original building after converting it into additional apartments. He had completely converted seven other structures by February of 1957 and was looking for more. His remodeling work accounts for about 30 per cent of his income.

Packman confined his activity to within ready walking distance of the University, selecting structures on the basis of their availability and acquisition cost. This example is typical of his work. He purchased a large three-story brick row house and converted it into nine furnished units—three one-room-and-bath units for two students each, and six two-room-and-bath units for three students each. The bath contained pastel tile and a triangular shower stall to conserve space. The larger rooms were partitioned into two sections with a specially built furniture wall. The wall contained two closets, bureaus, bookshelves, and desks.

Packman supervises the whole process from purchasing to management of the finished units. He contracts all the work to the same man who, Packman claims, gives him a price some 25 per cent lower than usual. No partitions are altered in the work since the basic design of the converted structures does not require it. All the rooms open off a stair well and hall located along one side of the building. Most of the bathrooms go into large closets or are specially built in the corner of the room. The furniture wall provides all the closet space a student needs. An example of a typical remodeling cost statement appears in Table 1.

TABLE 1. Approximate Remodeling Costs of Philadelphia Student Apartments

Acquisition cost		$12,500
Remodeling costs:		
Nine baths	$5,400	
Electrical work (200 amps)	1,200	
Six room dividers	3,600	
Plastic tile	1,200	
Carpentry	3,000	
Heating	300	
Masonry	1,000	
Decorating	2,000	
Furniture	5,000	
Miscellaneous (plans, permits, demolition, removal, etc.)	4,600	
		$29,000
		$41,500

Source: Data supplied by the rehabilitator.

The finished apartments rented quickly with no more advertising than word of mouth and a sign in front of the house. The two-room apartments rent for $360 a school year for each of the three students—a total of $1,080 for nine months. The one-room apartments rent for $370 a school year per student—or $740. The total rents from the nine apartments is $8,700, of which 40 to 50 per cent represents operating expenses. The return on total investment is a little over 10 per cent; however, summer rentals increase his returns by 2 or 3 per cent.

The project is financed primarily by personal equity although Packman was able to obtain a first mortgage from a savings and loan association for $10,000 at 6 per cent, for ten years. He also received a second mortgage from a private party of $7,500 at the same terms. He states that better financing would have been obtained if the project were located even nearer to the University.

Packman is a firm booster of code enforcement. He believes that he would have much of his substandard competition eliminated if the code were rigorously enforced. He reasons that many students take units at slightly lower rents even though the units are in much poorer condition than his own. He feels he could compete successfully with any comparably priced units and, if his competition didn't want to make added investments, he could purchase their properties at relatively low costs. Packman's projects are an example of rehabilitation profits found by adapting outmoded structures to current market characteristics.

Low-income Rehabilitation

CASE 8

R. Gordon Tarr, a realtor of Cincinnati, Ohio, rehabilitates from fifty to ninety middle- and low-rent dwelling units a year. He rehabilitated eighty-nine in 1956. The rehabilitation work yields about 20 per cent or less of his income, with the remainder derived from real estate brokerage, property management, appraising, and insurance. His remodeling activities were greatly enlarged after rent control was eliminated. "Until this time, the problems were many in getting a new rental established with rent ceilings in effect." [10]

Most of Tarr's work is done in the West End of Cincinnati where the structures are largely brick three-story tenements from fifty to one hundred years old. Approximately 95 per cent of the residents in the area are Negroes.

The firm selects its projects through a survey of the neighborhood which isolates structurally sound buildings where the repairs can be written off by increasing the rent. A check is then made with the city planning commission to see that the project is not located on the site of proposed improvements. They next check with the owner of the structure, trying to arrange a selling-agent agreement with him, and failing that, a management agreement on the basis of the rehabilitation program they plan. Tarr approaches lenders with the signed agreement, photographs of the

[10] ACTION *Rehabilitation Questionnaire.*

property, before and after pictures of other projects, and a complete estimate of the project's feasibility including repair costs, potential rents, and operating costs. Tarr says financing older properties is greatly facilitated when the rehabilitator is "... able to present a complete plan of the project to the lending institutions and show them completely how ... [the] proposal will work out."[11]

The firm tries to do as much as it can within potential rent-increase limits and, as managers, to set aside a small portion of the income for further improvements when the first set of repairs is paid out—a common practice for rental property managers. John Dwelle of Charlotte says he tries to keep a steady income flowing to the property owners but to hold out enough to cover not only repairs and maintenance but functional improvements as well.[12] The consent of the owner is necessary and can usually be gained if he is made to realize that it safeguards his investment and might even add to the property's value.

Typical improvements to Tarr's properties include better toilet facilities, including at least an inside flush toilet with a tub if the budget permits. The buildings are generally rewired and all requirements of the building and housing code met. Repairing fire escapes and installing and fireproofing stair wells is frequently necessary in this part of Cincinnati. Wooden drainboards or iron sinks are replaced with white enamel sinks, and as much interior and exterior decoration and repairs are made as possible. Repair costs run anywhere from $100 per dwelling unit to $1,000, depending on the initial rents. Top rents in the area run around $10 to $12.50 per room per month, or $55 per dwelling unit. The average number of years to write off costs is anywhere from three and one-half to eleven.

Tarr sees no limit to the work as long as economic conditions continue to create a disparity between existing and potential rents. The only deterrents to increasing the scope of his work are the lack of a trained rehabilitation staff, particularly on the management level, and "a desire to live a little longer. Sometimes this

[11] *Ibid.*
[12] ACTION interviews.

work can be quite exasperating and frustrating, and one begins to wonder if the returns justify the mental anguish." [13]

CASE 9

Flora K. Tierney, a realtor of Louisville, Kentucky, converted two downtown brick structures containing a total of fifty-two rooms to thirty-five two-room and several one-room efficiency apartments in the 1950s. Mrs. Tierney acted as her own designer and prime contractor and subcontracted all the work.

The two eighty-year old houses had been used as Negro rooming houses prior to remodeling. They were converted at a cost of $20,000. The exterior had the cornices and an old porch removed, the rear and porch stairway repaired, and the bricks painted a light cream color. The interior had several partitions installed, some brick walls pierced, and room dividers built in the larger one-room efficiencies to divide the kitchen from the living space. Kitchens, baths, and heating were added when necessary.

Mrs. Tierney undertook remodeling to satisfy local code requirements on behalf of the continuing owner. Therefore the measure of feasibility is whether the rent increases defrayed the cost of the project. Rents increased by over $5,000 ($4,000 on the larger building alone), assuring a rapid payout on investment.

All of Mrs. Tierney's remodeling has been of similar buildings except one small four-room cottage remodeled for a group of women realtors. This last project involved a purchase price of $1,500 and remodeling costs of only $3,000.[14]

An interesting aspect of Mrs. Tierney's work is the profitability of carrying improvements beyond code enforcement levels. The market circumstances permitting it may have been similar to those in Charlotte where a Negro market existed with heavy latent demand and a short supply of better quarters.

[13] *ACTION Rehabilitation Questionnaire.* Cost figures and other supplementary material from R. Gordon Tarr's article in *op. cit., Rehabilitation as a Business.*

[14] Information for this case came from two sources: *op. cit., Operative Remodeling,* p. 38, and *ACTION Rehabilitation Questionnaire.*

CASE 10

John G. Alexander, a Minneapolis realtor, converted a two-family structure into three rental units in 1957. This was his twelfth rehabilitation venture in seven years. Two projects a year account for about 10 per cent of his income, with the rest coming from brokerage, property management, and insurance.

The structure is located in an area of Minneapolis where $60 a month is typical rent and prospective tenants look for clean apartments with functioning utilities but do not expect any extra frills. Mr. Alexander bought the strucure for $3,000 and converted two apartments to three for $5,500, aided by a $3,000 conventional construction loan from a local building and loan association. He receives a gross monthly rent of $2,460 a year.[15]

Alexander says that the volume of his rehabilitation activities could be substantially increased if better financing were available. Specifically he calls for higher FHA limits on the amount of the loan outside renewal areas and an extension of the term.

CASE 11

Label Katz of New Orleans operates a rental business involving over 1,000 dwelling units. He began rehabilitating his properties in 1951—two years before New Orleans began a code enforcement program in August, 1953. Katz has rehabilitated forty to forty-five dwelling units a year since the beginning of his program. The typical monthly rent for rehabilitated units is $50 compared to prior rents in the vicinity of $20 per month.

Most of the structures were frame, single-story duplexes occupied by Negro families. They lacked baths, electricity, and modern kitchens. The houses usually needed a good coat of paint inside and out.

An example of Katz's work is the purchase of two duplex structures for $6,000. They yielded a rent of $80 a month; $9,000 was paid for a kitchen and bath, plus interior and exterior redecoration

[15] *ACTION Rehabilitation Questionnaire.* The case was included in this section because the acquisition cost indicates the property was located in a low-rent area.

for the four units. The rent rose to $240 a month, but Katz sold the buildings for $17,000, a profit of $2,000. The gross return before sale had been over 19 per cent on a $15,000 investment. The new purchaser realized 17 per cent on a $17,000 investment.[16]

Forty dollars a month is a relatively large rent increase. Finding tenants for units with rents far above average would have been difficult if the market were different, but the rent spread in minority areas is much wider than in other markets. It may be remembered in the discussion of conditions in Charlotte that new apartments were constructed on vacant lots in Negro neighborhoods surrounded by relatively low-rent properties.

CASE 12

This is a discussion of two cases in one. Periodically, neighborhood improvement projects undertaken by citizens groups with the sponsorship of a public agency or a national interest group receive wide coverage. Two Philadelphia projects were widely publicized—"Operation Fixup," sponsored by the Philadelphia Redevelopment Authority, and Yardville, sponsored by *McCall's Magazine* with the Planning Commission's help. Today "Operation Fixup" has fallen before the redevelopment bulldozer and Yardville has all but disappeared.

Yardville was undertaken in 1948. It was a backyard project receiving $16,000 and wide press coverage from *McCall's Magazine*. The Philadelphia Planning Commission helped prepare the improvement plans and supervise the project. The alley was paved, private patios were added and partly covered by roof pergolas, garbage cans were recessed, and landscaping and general exterior repairs were made. Fifteen families paid between $75 and $300 each for the repairs beyond *McCall's* contribution.

There was no question involved of economics and no records kept of changes in project property value. Even the satisfaction the homeowners received from the improvements seems to have been short-lived to judge from the project's reversion to nearly its original condition.

[16] *ACTION Rehabilitation Questionnaire.* Also *op. cit., Operative Remodeling,* p. 40.

214　RESIDENTIAL REHABILITATION

"Operation Fixup" took most of 1949. The backyards between two rows of houses were cleared of sheds, fences, and outside toilets. Houses were brought up to code standards and the rear area paved and lighted. Much of the labor and materials were donated by tenants, the American Federation of Labor, and the Redevelopment Authority staff. The project cost $100.62 per house, with the funds supplied by property owners at $50 per house, and $25,000 apiece from the City and the Redevelopment Authority. Francis J. Lammer, Executive Director of the Redevelopment Authority, lauded the results but abandoned hope of carrying out similar programs. As he said,

> Most people were willing, under the stimulus of an organized campaign, to renovate their dwellings. Many were financially unable to do so. Loans made to such people were extremely difficult to collect. The sustained will to maintain the improvement, however, seemed to fail without continued pressure, which seems to require sustained effort by paid personnel, particularly in areas completely surrounded by slums, as these were.[17]

Later, this project was eliminated to make way for a redevelopment project. Lammer's summary fairly well expresses the reasons why most neighborhood-improvement efforts in low-rent areas with constantly changing residents have disappeared after a relatively short life.

CASE 13

Sam Michelson of St. Louis was in charge of remodeling a six-family three-story brick structure for the St. Louis Real Estate Board in 1956. Improvements did not involve conversion. The selected structure was in the Cherokee code enforcement area.

This was a demonstration project, and the repairs made were more extensive than needed to obtain the allowable rent increase. Michelson said many of the windows and doors which had been replaced and some of the new plaster could have been foregone

---

[17] Francis J. Lammer, "Rehabilitation Has Taken Three Forms in Philadelphia," *Journal of Housing*, February, 1955 (also in National Association of Housing and Redevelopment Officials—NAHRO—reprints).

without seriously hampering the total effect. The house was purchased for $12,017, and $12,678.36 was spent for repairs, including a concrete basement, tuck pointing, repairs to roof and gutters, new kitchens and baths for each of the units, new electrical wiring, removal of sheds at the rear of the 100-foot lot, new windows and doors, a concrete stoop, landscaping, heaters for each unit, and complete interior decoration.

TABLE 2. Remodeling Costs of St. Louis Apartment House

Acquisition cost		$ 12,017.38	
Repair costs:			
Hauling	$ 68.00		
Painting and Bondex	315.50		
Steam cleaning	112.50		
Painting and decorating	1,447.00		
Lighting fixtures	40.54		
Carpentry	3,622.72		
Plastering	584.00		
Concrete work	1,365.10		
Electrical wiring	970.00		
Shades and blinds	100.45		
Plumbing	2,225.00		
Floor covering	404.50		
Guttering and downspout	165.00		
Tuck pointing	1,228.05		
Total		12,678.36	
		$ 24,695.74	
Sale price		23,500.00	
		$ −1,195.74	
Net rent collected			
in investment period		1,463.69	
Profit			$267.95

Source: *ACTION Rehabilitation Questionnaire.*

The rents were increased from an average of $32 to an average of $45 a month. The annual net return was $2,805, or 11.4 per cent of the $24,695.74 gross investment. The structure was sold in May, 1958, for $23,500 in cash only ten days after it was offered for sale. Since about $1,500 had been netted in rents since the project began, the demonstration project broke even. If the project had not been for demonstration purposes, however, the work could have been more carefully limited and the profits from sale substantially increased. As it was, the project proved to local property owners that remodeling in a code enforcement area could allow a satisfactory return.

Summary

The foregoing were some of the cases not included in the main body of the manuscript. Those not included in the text or in this appendix were either too incomplete to be useful or too outdated to serve for comparison with contemporary market conditions.[18]

[18] There are two groups of cost figures deliberately excluded from the text. The first is the feasibility estimates made by local redevelopment authorities where the projects have never proven themselves under market conditions. (The techniques employed in these studies are covered in Appendix B.) The last group of cases covers the feasibility of enforcement programs from the local government's point of view. These show the costs of the programs and official estimates of the program's effects in reduced municipal service costs for enforcement areas, increased tax revenues, and the new investment made by private investors to comply with the code. In general, every community reporting such figures finds that the returns to the community in permit fees and added taxes alone cover the costs to the community of enforcing the code.

Appendix B
STUDIES OF THE ECONOMIC FEASIBILITY OF REHABILITATION

In the eighteen studies which follow, spanning the twenty-seven years from 1931 to 1958, are found lively presentations of private and public attitudes toward the feasibility of housing rehabilitation.[1] Each study was prompted by at least one of the following objectives: promoting economic recovery, slum clearance, emergency housing needs, or the idea of profitability. Pump-priming preoccupations which continued through the 1930s were parent to and joined by slum-clearance studies (which called for a program similar to urban renewal) around the time the Housing Act of 1937 created the U.S. Housing Authority. Slum clearance became the primary study emphasis until the sharp economic decline of 1938 reinstated an interest in housing remodeling as a way to facilitate economic recovery. But the recession was brief and economic recovery forgotten as soon as World War II began. The National Housing Agency promoted rehabilitation as a sound method of meeting the emergency housing needs of war workers.

[1] Four of them appeared in the thirties, six in the forties, and nine thus far in the fifties. This by no means exhausts all the studies written which mention remodeling as a part of a housing program. There have been several other studies undertaken in recent years with funds provided by the URA under Section 314 of the Housing Act of 1954 for which the reports have not yet been completed. It is believed that the studies discussed adequately represent all those in this field.

The postwar prosperity once again gave emphasis to the role of rehabilitation in slum clearance, which bore fruit with the Housing Act of 1954. The most recent publicly undertaken rehabilitation studies are businesslike in character and designed to facilitate local urban-renewal programs by proving the profitability of private investment in remodeling. These have been joined by private studies promoting rehabilitation utilizing public policies and public incentives as a profitable business investment.

The studies are arranged chronologically, and each is described and its purpose, methodology, historical significance, and conclusions discussed.

Study 1 *The President's Conference on Home Building and Homeownership*

December 2–5, 1931, unpaged (thirty-one committee reports—twenty-five fact-finding and six correlating)

The Conference was held in Washington when the worst of the Great Depression was still to come. Its aims were to suggest methods for reviving the stricken building industry and stem the rising tide of mortgage defaults.

Among the twenty-five fact-finding committees was the Committee on Reconditioning, Remodeling, and Modernizing. Their 68-page report was in three parts: a factual report to the Conference, a popularized version of its findings to serve as a basis for public promotion, and a bibliography of books and articles on remodeling as well as a home-improvement check list. Actually this report was not based on formal study but upon the opinions, knowledge, and experience of the participants, who represented government bureaus, trade organizations, shelter journals, colleges, and interested civic organizations. The report, therefore, is mainly comprised of a series of very general judgments and suggestions to which the entire committee subscribed. The committee emphasized improvements undertaken by the homeowner in its stated aims (p. 7):

(*a*) to foster the interest of the homeowner in reconditioning, remodeling, and modernizing;

(*b*) to guide the homeowner in the proper and economical way to recondition, remodel, and modernize his home;
(*c*) to analyze the problems involved in improving the home;
(*d*) to find helpful solutions of the problems and state the conclusions.

Its philosophy in fulfilling the purposes of the report was stated (p. 6) as follows:

If, therefore, home life is to be rich and alluring, it is not enough that houses be periodically reconditioned, as factory buildings are. Nor is it enough that they be equipped with such modern equipment as represents the major advances between the pioneer homes of our forefathers and those that best serve us today. Instead, to safeguard the financial and social investments already made, it is often the part of wisdom, especially during periods of slack employment and when materials are relatively low in cost, to remodel as well as modernize homes. Home improvement is, as the president has indicated, necessarily "a more or less continuous process, if American standards of living are to be maintained."

The Committee on Reconditioning, Remodeling, and Modernizing concluded (p. 12) that:

After a careful study of available data the Committee wishes to stress the fact that a great number of homes over the country could be materially improved by constructive modernizing plans; often by changes involving minor expense. It is also noted that delay in making needed improvements frequently results in the homeowners' suffering much more than is necessary for depreciation of their property.

The report covered room-by-room improvements in a house which would materially improve its appearance, functioning, and marketability. It noted the problem of obtaining financing but listed methods which were felt to be readily accessible to homeowners. And finally, the check list systematically covered those points most vulnerable to obsolescence and decay. The coordinating committee which recommended legislative adjustments to further the ends of the Conference made no recommendations for remodeling aids.

It was left to another committee of the Conference to discuss rehabilitation's role in relieving urban blight—the Committee on Blighted Areas and Slums. The size of this report alone, fifteen pages, is enough to indicate the relatively cursory attention the topic received. The findings begin to suggest the possibility of Federal participation in urban renewal (p. 4):

> The great difficulty in the reconditioning of either individual buildings or groups of buildings is for the owner to secure the necessary money to carry out the improvement.
>
> Reconditioning will greatly improve many neighborhoods and it is a most important factor in the treatment of slum districts. There are, however, certain areas where the general conditions are so bad that complete demolition and large-scale operations are necessary.

The idea of redevelopment, though very much alive, was not yet housebroken enough to take part in the government family of services.

CONCLUSIONS

The two conference reports are helpful as a guide to the history of rehabilitation but offer little in the way of specific policy recommendations.

The Committee on Reconditioning, Remodeling, and Modernizing, however, partly fulfilled the fourfold purposes of the Conference by giving homeowners some information on remodeling. But little care was taken to provide the homeowner with methods of judging the economic soundness of his investment, apparently with the thought that making "home life rich and alluring" was not a matter of dollars and cents. It is hard to determine exactly what effects the Conference had on subsequent remodeling investments, but certainly the report contributed to the continuing public interest in rehabilitation both as an investment and as a way of improving the private home.

Study 2 *Modernizing Buildings for a Profit*

> Kenneth Kingsley Stowell, Prentice-Hall, Inc., Englewood Cliffs, N.J., 1935, 231 pp., illustrations and plans

Stowell was a practicing architect at the time he wrote this study, deriving a large share of his practice from remodeling residential and commercial structures. He discussed the subject with a series of documented case studies showing "before" and "after" pictures and plans. He treated the economics of the business with a cost analysis of a completed project including acquisition and repair costs, an operating statement, and in some cases where remodeling was the final choice, analyses of alternative treatments of the property. In short, it was the most thorough treatment of rehabilitation as an investment that had been published to date, covering not only residential sales properties as operative remodeling, but residential and commercial rental properties as well. His case studies included higher-cost private homes, apartments, a hotel, retail outlets, and office buildings (see Table 1).

TABLE 1. Cost Study Based on Making a Proposed Alteration *

Investment:			
Present book cost	$30,800		
Cost of alteration	23,000		
Total cost		$53,800	
Gross rent	7,680		
Expenses	4,578		
Net rent		$ 3,102	
Return (5% on $23,000)			$1,150
Amount available for amortization			1,952

* Stowell, p. 15.

Stowell listed six factors influencing modernizing (p. 4): the needs of the community or neighborhood; the competition to be met, both present and future; the occupancy and vacancy history of the present building and its competitors; the financial structure of the present building, with the profit-and-loss history; the plan, design, and present physical condition of the property and its equipment; the various possible plans of improvement in outline form. The first factor is the most important, Stowell said, and the potential investor should always ask himself: "Is the building needed in this community and neighborhood?"

He gave four ways to increase profits through rehabilitation: increasing tenancy; raising the rate of rental, either by making the space more desirable for its original use or by changing the use to a type for which there is a demand; adding rentable areas through replanning and utilization of waste space; and decreasing the operating and maintenance costs (p. 14).[2] The first six factors, then, were used to determine the need for modernization and the last four factors to determine the form remodeling should take.

Stowell always compared several alternative treatments of a property to see which would offer the highest net return. He suggested design techniques which would most effectively increase a structure's sales or rent potential. The design suggestions were made on a room-by-room basis with special treatment to major interior and exterior components. He used a check list as a guide to his design tour.

CONCLUSIONS

This excellent businessman's book included subjects of contemporary importance. The treatment was limited to the profit potential in remodeling middle- and upper-income properties. Stowell's concern for the neighborhood environment was entirely one-sided, stressing its effect upon the value of the property under consideration and ignoring the effects of the improvements upon the neighboring properties. The book discussed events isolated in space and time without reference to the individual investor's other holdings and business needs.

There was no discussion of economic or social conditions which could set the stage for added profits through remodeling. The implicit assumption throughout the book was that the Depression and the natural crumbling of physical and economic values attendant upon age were the reasons behind new investment considerations. Public programs for community facilities, slum abatement, or planning and zoning, and private speculation

---

[2] Obviously point three is subsumed under point one, since using space previously wasted increases tenancy whether an entirely new tenant is obtained or an old tenant contracts to use the additional space.

on increases in general property values following a few local rehabilitation projects had no place in the text.

However, considering that Stowell was writing for a market of prospective clients, drawing upon his own experiences and those of other architects, the coverage was ample. His interests were limited to rehabilitation projects where an individual architect would ordinarily be employed and, therefore, lower-rent properties or series of spatially related properties considered over an extended period of time were not treated in the book. What Stowell covered was covered well, with the major contribution being his cost-analysis sections, in which remodeling was treated as only one of several alternative investment possibilities.

Study 3 *Urban Blight and Slums*

Mabel Walker, Harvard City Planning Studies, Harvard University Press, Cambridge, Mass., 1938, 442 pp., illustrations, maps, and diagrams. See particularly Chap. 8, "Rehabilitation of Blighted Areas," by Henry Wright and Chap. 16, "Common Problems in Rehabilitation Procedures," by Ira S. Robbins

This work reversed earlier approaches to rehabilitation by promoting rehabilitation as a device to eliminate slums. The book's definition of rehabilitation (p. 191) is what is today called urban renewal.

Rehabilitation means the restoration of an area in a manner consistent with good city planning, so that it becomes an economic asset rather than an economic liability.

The conditions to be created may involve the elimination of nuisances, obsolete structures, a new use to which the area is to be put, the type of structures thereon..., the use of existing structures, remodeled buildings, or new buildings,...

Remodeling was considered as only a part of the total treatment needed to raise a slum to an acceptable neighborhood. The decision to rehabilitate rather than replace a structure was to be made on the basis of its structural soundness and the ability of the remodeled structure to fit into the master plan for the area. The authors voiced concern over a total remodeling program which, though it might keep the costs of structural improvements to a minimum, would do little to reduce the building coverage and population densities of slums.

The authors concentrated on broad housing policies. They listed and discussed alternative approaches to good housing for the masses (p. 423): using government subsidies to reduce housing cost for one-third of the nation's families (over 10 million urban and rural families, or about 40 million persons); raising the level of incomes; and lowering the cost of housing.

Miss Walker chose among them (p. 424):

> ...the creation and rationalization of a large-scale home-building industry which can meet the people's housing needs, and strict governmental regulations concerning planning and building with a vigorously enforced condemnation and demolition policy and a reformed tax system.

CONCLUSIONS

The treatment of the topic was intentionally broad, and the details of any phase of the slum-elimination problem faded into the broader canvass of the study. Placed in a historical setting, the study's conclusions can be viewed as a natural outgrowth of preceding events. Slum clearance had begun with the Public Housing Program of 1937, but the progress was distressingly slow and amount of clearance minuscule. A dynamic new approach was sought by planners, and some of the leading figures in the slum-clearance movement found the Harvard Planning Series an excellent sounding board for their views.

The final conclusions were meant to be provocative rather than definitive. No attempt was made to detail proposed legislative programs to guide municipal and Federal legislators. Nor did the study delve into rehabilitation's economic feasibility or the problems inherent in the business. Its contribution to the general literature of rehabilitation is as a paving stone on the road leading to municipal code enforcement and Federal urban-renewal programs.

Study 4 *Report and Recommendations of the Committee on Old Housing to the Citizens and Housing Council of New York*

June, 1938, 22 pp., plans and maps

This small study was published about the same time as the Harvard Planning Study and covered the economic feasibility of rehabilitating old-law tenements in New York City.[3] Where the Harvard Study was policy-oriented and general, the New York study was highly specific, covering only one type of structure in one city.

The Committee estimated that it would cost about $7,500 to purchase an old-law tenement and $7,500 to remodel the structure to sound community standards. The rents following project completion were estimated at $6 per room per month, or a maximum of $3,600 annually. Operating expenses including vacancy allowances were estimated at $2,406, yielding a 6.8 per cent net return on investment. The Committee concluded that rehabilitation was economically feasible and that projects should be undertaken on an entire-block basis to ensure a compatible environment for the improved units.

CONCLUSIONS

The results of their study served little practical usefulness as a solution to New York's slum problems. The feasibility of one project does not necessarily prove that the process could be repeated indefinitely. It would be impossible to estimate the

[3] A much more complete series of studies suggesting block-by-block rehabilitation under the corporate management of the collected property owners of each block appeared in the publication *Land Usage*. This monthly bulletin reported the "highlights of district and community rehabilitation studies by the Land Utilization Committee of the New York Building Congress." (*Infra.*, vol. 3, no. 1, January, 1936, p. 1.) The Committee included Arthur C. Holden, Ralph Walker, Harold S. Buttenheim, and Ira S. Robbins. Their concept of rehabilitation can be seen in Ira S. Robbins's work in the Harvard Planning Series (reported above), published two years later.

total number of structures amenable to the proposed improvements without complete market data to estimate the total demand for rental units in the price range, quality level, and location of the old-law tenements. However the report is one of the earliest studies suggesting rehabilitation for a specific group of low-rent dwellings. Many of the current studies under Section 314 of the 1954 Housing Act are undertaken on the same basis. They recognize that the final answer to the feasibility of rehabilitation has to be sought in the light of local market conditions and not on the basis of community desires unsupported by economic realities.

Study 5   *Investigation of Concentration of Economic Power*

U.S. Temporary National Economic Committee, Hearings, Part Eleven, "Construction Industry," 1940, pp. 4933-5593. Also *Final Report*, "Investment in the Housing Industry," 1941, 435 pp. (see pp. 285-296)

Housing rehabilitation became a part of the report only because Arthur W. Binns, Philadelphia realtor and rehabilitator, was interviewed by the Committee. His contribution signified a growing interest in rehabilitation as a political and social tool in the hands of the business community and not just as an investment outlet. The hearings, held in the summer of 1939 with testimony published the following year, were intended to seek out instances of monopolistic or oligopolistic concentrations of power which were interfering with the free play of American business.

The report's section on the housing industry dwelt primarily on the problems of new construction, including a lengthy discussion of Public Housing. Binns testified (p. 5357-5377) on the ability of rehabilitation to provide low-rent units at lower costs than public housing. Although it was received with apparent interest, it did not figure in the conclusions and recommendations of the Committee.

Binns began by stating he had been involved in the rehabilitation of over 1,000 dwelling units both as an owner and as a rental-property manager. He said that families with annual incomes under $1,200 were unable to buy a home and had to seek their housing in the rental market. Binns estimated that 20,000 to 30,000 houses in large metropolitan areas could be purchased for $500 or less and said (p. 5359):

We have been able by sound methods of management and engineering to provide houses at not over $1,500 per home, complete cost, with all modern facilities, at rentals of between $4 and $5 per room in order to provide housing at approximately 25 per cent of the cost proposed by the USHA—to provide a shelter rent less than the USHA, to pay taxes every inch of the way, and to pay a good return [about 10 per cent of investor's capital] on private moneys invested.

Binns suggested the reasons why more rehabilitation work was not undertaken for the lower-rent families were that the typical investor lacked the courage and vision and the real estate and building industries allowed their labor forces to lie idle part of the year. Also, helpful financing for low-rent properties was not available and real property taxes had become confiscatory.

In cross-questioning, the members of the Committee asked Binns what he felt the Federal government could do to facilitate his rehabilitation role. In response to the question, Binns said that he hoped to obtain some form of FHA insurance for low-rent remodeled properties.

The *Final Report* of the investigation included only twelve pages on the "Investment in the Housing Industry," relying on two technical monographs (33 and 8) to cover the more detailed problems arising in the building-material and supply and the construction industries. The *Final Report* gave great weight to the need for more public housing as the only practicable solution to the problem of housing low-income families (p. 296): "An expansion of the USHA program... would in no sense constitute a threat to the private building industry, which does not provide for the lowest-income group." Absolutely no mention was made of housing rehabilitation as a possible method of meeting low-income needs.

CONCLUSIONS

Binn's claim that taxes and mortgage terms made extensive rehabilitation exceedingly difficult lost much of its weight after he stated that he had rehabilitated over 1,000 units with profits averaging 10 per cent. More important, however, low acquisition costs of the properties resulting from tax liens was a situation peculiar to Philadelphia during the Depression. Normal times would increase acquisition costs and rents, lifting remodeling projects beyond the reach of many low-income families. It was not until "normal" times and the acceptance of rehabilitation as a public-policy tool that the financing Binns requested was finally proposed to be extended to the rehabilitator.

Study 6 *Waverly—A Study of Neighborhood Conservation*
Arthur Goodwillie (for the Home Loan Bank Board), Washington, 1940, 97 pp., illustrations and plans

The Depression found the Home Loan Bank Board, through the Home Owners' Loan Corporation, in possession of countless properties through mortgage foreclosure, and so the Board instituted a policy of remodeling and selling its holdings to close out its books (p. 6).

During the first 5-year period of its existence, it (HLBB through the HOLC) spent or directed the expenditure of approximately $120 million for the repair of more than 640,000 properties. In the course of this tremendous rehabilitation operation, it learned that the utilitarian and investment value of a depreciated residential structure in a reasonably good neighborhood can usually be restored at a cost somewhat less than the amount thereby added to the value of the subject property.

The HLBB decided to attempt a neighborhood conservation program employing its experience in rehabilitation and testing the theory that (p. 5)

> ... except in those sections where early transition to commercial use is clearly indicated, coordinated and properly directed neighborhood action will practically always serve long to postpone serious decline and by so doing will preserve the integrity of family life, will maintain the community's character and standards, will save much that is valuable in its economic resources, and will long continue it as a civic asset.

Waverly was a declining area lying 2½ miles from the center of Baltimore. It had been a section of large estate homes during the early nineteenth century but was built over with small homes in the last half of the century. Most of the 1,629 buildings were about fifty years old at the time of the study. Seven thousand persons lived in the 98.8 per cent of the structures which was devoted to residential use.

Several reasons were given for selecting Waverly as a test area: it was close to Washington and the results of the program could be closely followed; it was also an area of single-family homes similar to the tenure of the current market; a downward trend was just beginning and could be observed on many of the neighborhood's blocks, partly as a result of the slum to the south of the neighborhood, which was exerting an undesirable influence. Unless the incipient decline was checked, Waverly, too, would become a slum.

The study began with a field survey conducted from March 15 to August 15, 1939. The owners in the area were asked 132 questions covering the type and condition of structures and the socioeconomic characteristics of neighborhood residents. In this latter category were questions on the residents' attitudes toward a neighborhood group and toward added expenditures for needed improvements. Physical planning was complemented by fiscal planning covering the methods of financing individual home improvements and the added tax costs of needed community facilities.

Goodwillie and his staff estimated that about a hundred structures needed remodeling to restore the area to sound condition. The actual estimates of rehabilitation were reported for all buildings as a group using "total" repair costs and "total" value added by improvements. These totals were derived from case studies of selected neighborhood houses and from the experience of the HOLC. The costs of exterior remodeling and replanning were set at $150,000 for the entire neighborhood. Most of the structures needing reconditioning were privately owned, making the criteria for economic feasibility the increase in residential values after improvement. The resulting estimate appears in Table 2.

TABLE 2. Exterior Reconditioning (Residential Structures Only) *

"As is" appraised value	"As reconditioned" value	Estimated cost of reconditioning	Increase in value over cost	Per cent increase over cost
$1,024,035	$1,303,830	$149,022	$30,773	20

* Goodwillie, p. 35.

Goodwillie estimated the same return to owners would result from suggested interior repairs. In short, if Goodwillie's proposals were followed, owners should have been able to realize a 20 per cent profit from the immediate sale of their homes after the project was completed.

The HOLC remodeled fifteen properties in Waverly shortly after the report was completed as examples for the neighborhood; the properties cost an average of $663 to repair and their estimated value rose by $797. Yet nothing ever became of the program. An article in *House & Home* [4] stated:

> Waverly, a 75-year-old former village of cheap houses, deteriorated to a rock-bottom slum by 1950, even though the steeple of St. John's Episcopal Church preserved a half-dingy dignity amid the surrounding blight. The 23-acre neighborhood, two miles north of Baltimore's City Hall, became one of the nation's first Federally aided redevelopment projects. It cost over $1.5 million to rebuild, now contains 24 apartment buildings (and) several recreation centers.

CONCLUSIONS

The Waverly study was one of the first examples of an economic study of rehabilitation on the neighborhood level. Its approach, like later renewal studies, blended planning principles with the financial analysis designed to show that loans were available and that the market response could prove itself in added value.

[4] "Neighborhood Identity Saved One Area from Blight, Lack of It Rotted Another," *House & Home*, November, 1957, p. 51. It is important to note that the neighborhood referred to as Waverly in this article is only the southern portion of the Waverly in the Goodwillie report.

The *House & Home* article, however, quoted James Rouse, a Baltimore mortgage broker, as saying that Waverly failed as a renewal effort because the neighborhood was not ". . . given shape and definition by natural boundaries like parks, playgrounds, schools, hospitals, public buildings, and—most important of all —highways. . . ." If Rouse's explanation is accepted, the Waverly study, in spite of its social survey, did not penetrate into the social values of the neighborhood to engender citizen response. Also, no attempt was made to suggest added community facilities or to integrate the Waverly plan with the plan for the remainder of the city. The authors plucked Waverly out of Baltimore and planned it as if the neighborhood were unconnected with its surroundings.

However, the study added the concept of a neighborhood market in analyzing the feasibility of a rehabilitation project. Also, it recognized the need for adequate sources of financing and the presence of a sound plan to improve the neighborhood environment.

Study 7 *Building a Better Boston*

> Boston City Planning Board, vol. 1, 1941, 57 pp., maps, plans, and tables. Also, *A Progress Report on Reconstruction*, vol. 2, May, 1943, 54 pp., maps, plans, and tables; and *A Progress Report on Reconditioning*, vol. 3, January, 1946, 81 pp., maps, plans, and tables

The first three volumes discussing rehabilitation in Boston outlined the entire study's approach and analyzed the conditions existing in Boston's South End, an area containing mostly brick row homes densely clustered along relatively narrow streets. While the structures were physically salvable, they needed considerable improvement.

The concept of rehabilitation employed in the study (vol. 1, p. 1) was the same as that used in the Harvard Planning Series Study of 1938.

Rehabilitation may involve any of the following media: removal of unfit and outworn buildings, repair of sound structures, rearrangement of streets and services and replanning the area to create an environment marked by greater openness and amenity.

Any reconditioning or redevelopment in the area was to be jointly sponsored by the city and private industry. Property owners were to repair or replace their buildings with loans from local lenders, who would exercise financial control over the project along with the State Board of Housing. The city was to maintain planning control over the entire effort, integrating any improvements in the local area with their master plan for the entire city.

The third volume in the series was released fully five years after the publication of the first volume [5] and was "an investigation into a method of procedure and not a recommendation of a specific project to be carried out exactly as detailed" (vol. 3, p. 6). This study proposed a private redevelopment corporation which was to undertake the actual rehabilitation and discussed the corporation's expenditures and receipts. It outlined the role the city should take and the estimated annual municipal expenditures and receipts in the area before and after the project, and made a statement of the legislation to implement the proposed procedure.

The Dwight-Hanson area discussed in the study contained 132 structures, of which 39 per cent needed minor improvements including the repair or partial replacement of plumbing, heating, roofing, and trim redecoration. Sixty-nine per cent of the structures needed major repairs including new plumbing, heating, roofing, electrical wiring, structural repairs, and complete redecoration. The rear yards of the blocks were to be cleared of fences to form central courts. The neighborhood was to continue its original use as a rooming-house area. The building-code standards were to be met only in spirit in the interests of the repair budget; for example, shared bathrooms were to be compensated for by placing a wash basin in every room. A higher level of rehabilitation was considered, but estimates proved it to be too costly and it was dropped from the analysis.

[5] The second volume appeared two years later and analyzed a plan to reconstruct two sections of the South End.

Local realtors informed the Planning Board that the potential rent increases following improvement would be from $5 to $10 a month per unit. The Planning Board then estimated that 250 persons paying $2 a room per month would be replaced by 240 persons who could pay $6 to $6.50 a room per month. They anticipated no difficulty in renting the completed units.

The cost balance sheet for the redevelopment corporation assumed that the amount of stock sold would be equal to the total investment minus the sum raised from lenders (p. 53). The corporation was to receive an 80 per cent mortgage on total project costs. The total project was to cost $1,170,537, leaving a net investment of $234,107. The profits before taxes and after interest payments on outstanding stock were estimated as $4,358, or 1.9 per cent of net investment (see Table 3).[6]

TABLE 3. Profit on Boston Rehabilitation Project

Total project cost	$1,170,537	
Mortgage (80% of cost)	936,430	
Net investment	$ 234,107	
Current profits before taxes (after deducting operating expenses including interest of 4%, or $9,364, on outstanding stock)	$4,358	(1.9%)

At the time of writing, corporate income taxes were still at their wartime high, and the Planning Board was pressed to make ends meet once the taxes were paid. Its taxable income was the sum of the 4 per cent stock dividends ($9,364), current income ($4,358), and the capital gain through depreciation reserves ($14,579 for principal payments on mortgages). Of $26,301 taxable income, about 39 per cent, or $11,212, would have to be paid in taxes. This left a paper profit of $16,981, or 6 per cent, on its outstanding stock but not enough cash to pay interest on the outstanding stock. While the business part of the project looked unfavorable, the Planning Board found the city's yield

---

[6] The proposed repairs would cost approximately $777 per capita.

from project completion quite satisfactory. The area would still cost the city $94,871 more than it yielded in taxes, but this was a saving of $22,593 over the cost of the unimproved area.

The city's diminution of losses and the private redevelopment corporation's profits before tax were added to approximate the total economic worth of the project. This came to $30,210, which the Planning Board apparently thought was inadequate since it reminded readers that the social profits in improved dwellings compensated for any deficiencies in the economic profits. It concluded that if the original land use of a neighborhood were to continue, repairs were in order, but if the use were to change, reconstruction was more desirable. Nothing was done with the proposals.

CONCLUSIONS

The Boston study added one very important ingredient to rehabilitation feasibility studies. It planned neighborhood improvements on the basis of a community-wide plan which kept the neighborhood in rooming houses rather than altering it to meet the needs of a more generalized population. Another interesting feature of the study was the use of prospective rent estimates to reduce the proposed repair schedule to make the project more attractive to private investors.

Study 8   *The Slum . . . Is Rehabilitation Possible?*

    The Chicago Housing Authority, Chicago, 1946, 37 pp., maps and photographs

    The Housing Authority sought the answer to three questions:

    Is rehabilitation of a slum area physically possible?

    Is rehabilitation of a slum area under private ownership economically sound?

    Will rehabilitation of a slum area by the Housing Authority provide housing for low-income families more economically than new construction?

    The study compared privately sponsored rehabilitation with rehabilitation on new construction undertaken by the Public

Housing Authority.[7] An average block in the middle of a slum was studied in depth. The survey included both physical conditions and improvements, and questions covering family composition, income, tenure, and attitudes toward the community. An architect made the cost estimates, and a sociologist assessed the effects of the improvements on the local residents.

Two distinct levels of repair were considered in the analysis: first, the cost of raising the condition of the units to standards set by the Chicago Municipal Code; and second, the cost of complete modernization to standards comparable with new construction. The physical survey revealed that 96 per cent of the structures were in need of major structural repairs including such items as leaning walls, unsafe foundations, and sagging floors or ceilings. The demographic portion of the survey showed that slightly less than half the families in the area had incomes in excess of $2,000, with an average family income of $1,950. The attitudes toward the neighborhood expressed by the residents indicated that only 93 families out of the 351 households would move from the neighborhood if they could obtain better housing. A little more than 36 per cent of the tenants in the area said they were willing to pay up to $8 more a month for their housing, while the remaining households said they either could not pay more rent or were paying too much already.[8]

Cost estimates for minimum repairs (code standards) were passed over quickly in the report and were not included in the comparative estimates. The modernization estimate was very thorough. The resulting units were to compare favorably with new construction.

The Housing Authority planned small, efficient units in keeping with the demand for the neighborhood. Sixteen of the seventy-five

[7] Housing rehabilitation undertaken by local housing authorities was eligible for a loan of 90 per cent of construction (rehabilitation) cost and an annual contribution not exceeding the Federal interest rate plus 1 per cent (P.L. 412). At the time this report was written the annual contribution equaled 3½ per cent of construction cost.

[8] The group willing to pay more rent were spending 15.4 per cent of their incomes on rent, and the other families were spending slightly more than 20 per cent.

structures were to be eliminated, thirteen because of physical condition and the rest to reduce extreme land crowding. The remaining structures would contain 220 two-and-a-half to four-room dwelling units. The costs of improvement ranged from $1,350 to $4,300, with the average cost resting at $2,500. The average gross monthly rent was estimated to increase from $31 to $42.50. These rents coupled with the proposed demolition would require approximately 40 per cent of the existing population to move elsewhere.

Neither the minimum nor maximum improvement program appeared attractive to an investor. Returns on the structures in their unimproved condition ranged from 3 to 41 per cent, averaging approximately 13.5 per cent. Minimum standards through compulsory enforcement would reduce the average returns to about 6.5 per cent, and about one-sixth of the property owners would suffer a loss or have their returns cut to less than 1 per cent.

It was estimated that the returns to a private owner obtained by rehabilitation to new-construction levels would not be enough to cover expenses, and they would incur an average loss of 7.5 per cent. The Housing Authority, therefore, gave greater attention to meeting housing needs with public housing provided through rehabilitation under existing or newly proposed legislation [9] or through new construction. Its criterion of feasibility was low rent. The method by which the Housing Authority could reach the lowest rents was the most desirable treatment of the properties.

The total cost of providing rehabilitated units under existing legislation averaged $4,000 a unit, requiring a rent of $43.75 before the annual contribution. The Federal stipend would lower monthly rents by $11.75 to $32 per unit a month. The new bill would have provided a contribution of $15 per unit, making the average unit rent $28.50 a month. If the site were cleared and new units constructed, the average cost to provide a unit would be $6,400, requiring a rent of $43.25 before contribution. But the

[9] The proposed legislation, which was enacted in modified form in the Housing Act of 1949, was the Wagner-Ellender-Taft Bill (sec. 1592) which would increase the annual contribution to 4½ per cent.

higher unit cost would increase the Federal contribution to $18.75 per unit per month, and this contribution coupled with lower operating costs would bring the unit rent down to $25.50 per month (p. 24, Table 6).

The conclusions were automatic. Rehabilitation by private owners would cause major dislocation and be highly unprofitable. Rehabilitation by a public authority would lower rents and hence displacement, but the environmental standards would be low. Open spaces resulting from the program would be too broken up to use in a sensible scheme of added community facilities. Therefore (p. 25),

> Complete razing of the area and the erection of new dwellings under public ownership and subsidy would result in an average rent of about $25 a month. Buildings would be modern and attractive and would be planned for the best possible land use. This makes obvious the conclusion that modernization of slum buildings is neither profitable for private owners nor the economical way of providing subsidized housing under government ownership.

CONCLUSIONS

The study's estimates of modernization's feasibility was thoroughly but unimaginatively covered. The incontrovertibility of its analysis broke down when the public provision of housing entered the chain of argument. We were told how many families would be displaced and what losses owners would suffer if the housing was modernized by private efforts, but there was no estimate made of the net family displacement under any of the three public housing proposals, nor were the demands on the public purse contrasted with private profit yields.

Selecting a method of providing shelter to low-income families purely on the basis of the lowest rent, even though the method is the most costly one available, displays a limited approach. The study might have contributed more if it had asked how the greatest number of above-standard units could be provided at the least possible cost, with rents suited to low-income families.[10]

[10] In spite of this study, Chicago is one of the few cities to employ rehabilitation in their public housing program.

Study 9 *New Houses from Old: Your Guide to Home Remodeling*

R. R. Hawkins and C. H. Abbe, McGraw-Hill Book Company, Inc., New York, 1948, 558 pp., illustrations

There have been many books published as guides to the repair and improvement of private homes. Most of them discuss the physical signs of housing deterioration and what steps a homeowner can take either to correct the deficiencies himself or to contract for their elimination at minimum expense. If there is any discussion of the economic feasibility of home improvement it is usually a few brief comments on the added value created.

This book was a good example of these works. Hawkins was the Chief of the Science and Technology Division of the New York Public Library and Abbe was an architect, and their backgrounds facilitated a thoroughgoing discussion of the mechanical and design problems inherent in home improvement. The book's treatment of rehabilitation cost analysis, however, was discursive, giving no cost studies to document the authors' opinions.

The authors asked (p. 3): When is rehabilitation justified; how do you judge the need for rehabilitation; and how do you carry out a remodeling program? They declared that not only does housing improvement add immeasurably to the homeowner's satisfaction but also that it can be profitably undertaken as an investment.

Remodeling to increase the rental or sales value of a house is often very good business. Banks, insurance companies, and other agencies that lend money on houses resorted to remodeling on an extensive scale during the Depression of the 1930s to make foreclosed houses rentable or salable.

The authors warned homeowners, however, to rely on real estate experts rather than attempt remodeling without guidance.

If the house in question is one that you rent to others or one that you offer for sale, you will want a dollars-and-cents answer and it should be relatively easy to obtain from bankers, contractors, and real estate men in the community.

The authors then pointed out (p. 7) that rehabilitation must be economically feasible for homeowners because:

Architects, who are always in a position to compare the relative costs of new buildings and remodeling, often remodel old houses for their own use.

The soundest discussion in the book covered the structural danger signals and the signs of design obsolescence which reduce the value of a house. They cautioned investors and homeowners (p. 42) to "... get the advice of an architect or builder before committing yourself to the extensive remodeling of any house." The answer to the third question—how to do remodeling—was implied in the earlier comments. They tell us that "successful remodeling is based on good ideas" and conclude (p. 144) that "if remodeling is going to be extensive and if you have no more than the average person's knowledge of house construction, the right answer is that you should employ an architect."

CONCLUSIONS

The study provided a thorough guide to the mechanical and design probems in remodeling older houses but failed to deal adequately with the question of investment feasibility from the homeowner's point of view.

Study 10 *Slum Prevention through Conservation and Rehabilitation*

Jack M. Siegel and C. William Brooks, Report to the Subcommittee on Urban Renewal, Rehabilitation, and Conservation, of the President's Advisory Committee on Government Housing Policies and Programs, November, 1953, 143 pp.

The Siegel and Brooks report supported the urban-renewal concept in the Housing Act of 1954. The report contributed along with other Subcommittee reports to the scope and imaginativeness of the recommendations found in the final report. The published materials covered rehabilitation activities in a number of cities emphasizing public-policy aspects of the work. The conclusions of the report (pp. 2–3) summarized the authors' findings and opinions. Each of the conclusions was supported by one or more examples from the authors' case book.

1. The feasibility of structural rehabilitation varies with the type of architecture and construction involved. Many old buildings have hidden defects not ascertainable on cursory inspection.

2. Minimal rehabilitation of individual structures as a result of law enforcement cannot fundamentally change the character of a slum neighborhood.

3. The cost of rehabilitation which has produced structures that compete with new construction is beyond the means of slum dwellers.

4. The cost of unsubsidized thorough rehabilitation (reconstruction) is often equal to that of new construction.

5. Rehabilitation work requires close supervision and a wide variety of skills.

6. Rehabilitation must be carried on over a wide enough area to produce its own environment.

   a. It must be carried on in pursuance of a plan which provides for environmental improvements beyond the structures themselves.

   b. The power of eminent domain appears necessary to acquire sufficient area at a reasonable price.

7. Rehabilitation of high-density multiple dwellings in slum areas is usually not feasible for the following reasons:

   a. The rents required are beyond the reach of slum families.

   b. Total coverage is usually too high to provide amenities for family living.

   c. If obsolete and inadequate street patterns and public utilities remain, the area itself will still retain slum characteristics.

   d. If the density is substantially reduced, a significant relocation problem is involved.

8. Financing of rehabilitation is difficult because of the problem of estimating the mortgageable life of the structure and the uncertainty surrounding the future of the area.

9. Even buildings outlive their usefulness. Large slum areas have deteriorated to the point where clearance and redevelopment are the only answer. Housing must be provided at all price levels slum dwellers can afford to pay.

10. Minimum rehabilitation in blighted areas may tend to perpetuate rather than eliminate slums.

CONCLUSIONS

The report clearly indicated the conflicting interests of the public and the private investor. Circumstances can be seen under which rehabilitation would be unsound from a public-policy viewpoint but would offer substantial profits to a rehabilitator. For example, the authors pointed out that the rehabilitation of high-density dwellings in a slum area was not feasible because the units would be beyond the reach of slum families. However, there may be a profitable market for rehabilitated dwellings in a slum area for families with higher incomes provided the units are in or near a patch of prestige dwellings. The authors supported their point by saying that the coverage is "too high to provide amenities for family living" and that obsolete street patterns will assure that the area retains its slum characteristics. These statements again may not apply from the viewpoint of an upper-income market for whom the needs of children are unimportant and obsolete streets are quaint rather than objectionable.

Also, there are a few points upon which this present study would expand. For example, Siegel and Brooks concluded that code enforcement cannot fundamentally change the character of a slum neighborhood. While this is largely true, the present study has suggested that occasionally there is a demand for new residential or commercial construction in an area once the worst housing is razed or improved under code enforcement. Code enforcement, furthermore, can assure community groups in conservation areas interested in making fundamental neighborhood changes that their modest efforts will not be short-circuited by large blocks of dwellings which do not even comply with minimum standards.

The statement that the costs of thorough rehabilitation are "often equal to that of new construction" is quite true when new suburban construction and rehabilitation on high-priced center-city land are compared. But duplication of an existing structure through new construction on that same site has to include the costs of demolition and site preparation, which are rarely if ever included in rehabilitation involving reconstruction.

The Siegel-Brooks report exercised a crucial role in the field of rehabilitation. Its conclusions supported the proposals of the Subcommittee later enacted into law. The urban-renewal legislation requiring a major contribution of the local community in a workable program is foreshadowed by the Siegel-Brooks recommendations calling for area-wide improvement planning in addition to structural improvements. The FHA 220 mortgages came as a response to the Subcommittee's findings that mortgage financing for new construction or rehabilitation in blighted areas was almost impossible to find. But the report and the ensuing legislation did not fully reconcile the conflicting relationship between private investment opportunities and public policies.

Study 11   *Conservation—A Report to the Conservation Committee of the Metropolitan Housing and Planning Council by its Conservation Study Staff*

3 volumes, Chicago, 1953

The study included a summary of current thinking on the topic of neighborhood conservation, several examples of neighborhood conservation in cities throughout the country, a plan and program for neighborhood conservation, and rehabilitation costs for typical neighborhood units.

The report analyzed a specific neighborhood project from a broad conceptual viewpoint, emphasizing the larger economic questions of rehabilitation. For example, in commenting upon the renovation of Georgetown in Washington, they concluded (p. 122) that this was not true conservation because "The amount of money expended probably could not be justified in purely economic terms." A little later (p. 124) they commented that "Rehabilitation of structures in slum areas which may be cleared is contrary to good planning."

A few structures were studied in some detail. They were selected "... for their susceptibility to desirable physical changes within a plausible economic structure" (p. 192). The actual studies were undertaken by some faculty members and students of Harvard University, an architectural firm, the Conservation Study Staff, and the Michael Reese Hospital Planning Staff. The structures for which rehabilitation estimates were made were as follows:

1. A three-story mansion containing twenty-one rooms and three baths, built about 1925 on a lot 100 by 160 feet. This was planned as a two-family home with the costs set at $10,300 per unit.

2. A fifty-year-old row house containing thirteen rooms and two baths. This was to be left as a one-family home at a cost of $11,400.

3. An apartment containing six flats of eight rooms and three baths. This was to be converted to seventeen apartments at a total cost of $54,000.

The report gave no indication how these costs were apportioned among repairs, acquisition, financing charges, and overhead, but they were doubtless computed because without them there could be no reasonable conclusion about the feasibility of rehabilitation as part of the final plan.

CONCLUSIONS

The report shows a conceptual similarity to the Siegel-Brooks report. The conservation program outlined for Hyde Park–Kenwood is essentially an urban-renewal plan embracing both rehabilitation and new construction within the context of a neighborhood plan calling for substantial environmental improvements. Like the Siegel-Brooks report, it argued the public interest and describes the opportunities for private investment in the context of a broad renewal program.

Study 12 *Urban Redevelopment Problems and Practices*

Coleman Woodbury (editor), University of Chicago Press, Chicago, Ill., 1953, 525 pp. (See particularly pp. 315–401, William L. Slayton, "Urban Redevelopment Short of Clearance.")

The Urban Renewal Study conducted by the University of Chicago under the direction of Coleman Woodbury spanned several years. It served as a contemplative summary of urban renewal and redevelopment in the same way as the Harvard Planning Series volume edited by Mabel Walker in 1938. Several years had passed and new facts were added reinforcing the earlier conceptions of urban renewal. This later report emphasized clearance more heavily than the earlier report, which is to be expected, since federally sponsored redevelopment had become a part of the public effort with the Housing Act of 1949 and construction activity was at its all-time peak.

The earlier notions of mixed clearance and rehabilitation come through most clearly in Slayton's contribution on rehabilitation, reconditioning, conservation, and code enforcement. Enforcement programs in Baltimore, Milwaukee, Kansas City, and Chicago—three area-renewal studies and one actual project—were analyzed and discussed. The studies were Goodwillie's Waverly study, the Boston City Planning Board's Dwight-Hanson study, the Woodlawn Conservation study in Chicago, and the American Friends Project in Philadelphia. Slayton concluded that code enforcement programs should be used to supplement redevelopment programs, selecting the form of enforcement on the basis of program needs. He recommended (p. 388) concentrated area enforcement for reconditioning, conservation or growth districts, and complaint referral or routine enforcement through permits for other areas.

His findings on the question of area-wide rehabilitation were less conclusive (p. 389):

> Nearly all the subject matter discussed in this part of the URS has suffered in times past from too loose and sweeping generalizations. For example, we have been told that police power measures or regulations have failed or that enforcement is all that is necessary to do away with slums. Both publicly and privately sponsored rehabilitation needs further study. The objective should not be to displace other necessary ways and means to decent, livable cities but rather to find out, under the condition of each urban locality, what their redevelopment activities short of clearance can reasonably be expected to accomplish, and then to see that they play their parts in well-planned and well-administered local redevelopment programs.

CONCLUSIONS

Slayton's work opened new directions for publicly sponsored code enforcement programs. Slayton suggested that code enforcement could effectively be applied to substandard housing in areas containing predominantly standard dwellings, thus forcing recalcitrant landowners to take part in at least minimum neighborhood renewal. Furthermore, he expressed interest (p. 353) in Dr. Krumbiegel's suggestion, which "... has broken new ground in proposing graded sets of maintenance standards for areas that vary in housing quality." Milwaukee has never enacted the suggestion because of its questionable legal strength, but the idea of a zoned housing code conforms to current housing theories of trying to raise or maintain existing standards in every neighborhood regardless of its basic condition.

Study 13 *Feasibility of Rehabilitating Certain Residential Structures*

Urban Renewal Administration (report of a field trip to Kansas City, Mo., Attucks Project No. UR Mo. 3-1), 1954, unpaged, illustrations and plans

The Attucks study was undertaken because questions were raised about the feasibility of rehabilitating some of the buildings scheduled for clearance in the project area. Two staff men of the Urban Renewal Administration conducted inspections in nine buildings on May 18 and 19, 1954. Then conferences were held with local FHA officials on the probable repair costs and future rent scales.

Special circumstances in Missouri made the criteria of economic feasibility somewhat inapplicable to the rest of the nation. "The Missouri State Enabling Act does not permit the acquisition by condemnation or negotiation of dwelling structures for resale to others for rehabilitation" (p. 2, in "The Problem"). Therefore rehabilitation was possible only if the present owner of the structure were willing to undertake the repairs needed to achieve project standards.

The costs reported in the study included only the appraised and assessed value of the structure and the current rent levels. The URA compiled repair costs and then asked the owners if they would be willing to make the suggested repairs. The project standards were considerably above the Kansas City code standards. Since seven of the nine structures examined were near or below minimum standards, the estimated repair costs far exceeded minimum compliance costs. Only two structures were close to project standards, and these were the only two structures where the owners expressed a willingness to rehabilitate.

The seven structures deemed unsuited for rehabilitation were all returning a relatively high income, and rehabilitation would have reduced rather than increased net returns. For example, the owner of four of the test structures was realizing a 35 per cent gross return on their appraised value (p. 11, comments under Katz). Potential rent increases on the remodeled units would have had to be extremely high before current owners could have realized a return as high as that on the unimproved units.

CONCLUSIONS

The study was probably inspired by the interest in the newly proposed urban-renewal law. At this early stage, public officials are asking whether rehabilitation can achieve new-construction standards and still pay an attractive return, rather than seeing if the attainable standards of rehabilitation are sufficient justification for public expenditures.

In the Attucks project, the question asked by the Urban Renewal Administration was not fully answered. It may have been possible to remodel several of the dwellings successfully to their project standards if the units were acquired by condemnation and sold to a fresh investor with no profit preconceptions formed by past experience. However, the prohibition of condemnation made the study's conclusions a satisfactory response to the problem posed by the URA for this particular project.

Study 14 *Operative Remodeling*
United States Gypsum Co., Chicago, 1956, 126 pp., illustrations and plans

Operative Remodeling was written by the publications department of the United States Gypsum Co. with the cooperation of the National Association of Home Builders as a service to the "New Face for America" program. The book limited its discussion primarily to sales remodeling with heavy emphasis given to middle- and upper-income work. However several cases of the repair and sale of rental properties are given.

This is a book for builders in language a builder can understand. It covers the whole process from the selection of a likely project to the final financing and sale. The authors give their greatest attention to problems of design and construction, using illustrations and diagrams prepared by experienced architects. These are the most valuable sections in the book from the builder's viewpoint. The designs suggested in this section are calculated to add sales value to typical obsolete houses and the construction solutions are meant to keep remodeling costs at an absolute minimum.

The book shows some influence of the twenty years of urban-renewal thought. The authors tell us (chap. 2) that the neighborhood "is the first key to remodeling profits." They highlight the absolute necessity of nearby community facilities for higher sales prices and accept the role of public urban renewal. For example, they ask (p. 32), "Is there likelihood that it [the neighborhood of the project] will be designated an urban renewal area? If so, how can the rehabilitator's individual project tie in with the larger effort?" The authors also look with hope towards the FHA 220 program for badly needed help in financing (p. 29). "FHA has taken another long step forward in recognizing the needs of remodeling and rehabilitation projects through the provisions found in Secs. 220 and 221 of the Housing Act."

The authors, however, do not lose sight of their primary objective: telling builders how to make money in remodeling private homes. Other considerations take second place. The book begins with a series of case examples of profitable remodeling largely for middle- and upper-income families. The few examples of low-rent rehabilitation are drawn from Memphis, Louisville, and New Orleans, where profits in low-rent work are permitted by the low mobility of the minority groups which keeps a ready market for better housing in low-rent areas.

Case studies are followed by a description of the remodeling process with suggestions at each step of the way. The chapter on buying and estimating gives the four-part formula (purchase price plus remodeling cost plus profit equals sale price) and a check list to be used in estimating the project's feasibility. The chapter on design provides architectural solutions for thirty- to fifty-year-old detached homes with obsolete designs. The chapters on construction cover inexpensive methods of repairing structural defects and replacing plumbing and wiring. The chapter on merchandising and selling the completed project covers methods of advertising and pricing. The discussion of pricing includes a suggestion that a rehabilitator involved in large-scale projects could effectively use housing market analysis in deciding the market for his product.

The book concludes that there is a real need for urban renewal in the United States and (p. 126) that "All is in readiness for a broad advance on the problem by an army of builders—fired with civic spirit and motivated by honorable possibilities for personal gain. All America is waiting for the attack."

CONCLUSIONS

Operative Remodeling does not cover rental rehabilitation, rehabilitation by the individual homeowner, or the special problems of rehabilitation under local code enforcement. The authors have intentionally concentrated on that form of rehabilitation with the greatest appeal for the homebuilder—sales rehabilitation in the profitable middle- and upper-income neighborhoods. They have attempted to persuade trained builders to contribute their talents and resources to the conservation of the existing stock of housing.

However, the book has its shortcomings. It fails to suggest how builders can develop and carry out a sound neighborhood-renewal program in cooperation with local officials. While the book mentions the neighborhood as the key to rehabilitation profits, the possibility of a private neighborhood-redevelopment corporation, the need for financing, and the advisability of seeing how "the individual project ties in with the larger effort," it never weaves these strands into a logical plan for neighborhood renewal using available government supports.

The book might have helped a broader builder audience if the design suggestions had included row houses, semidetached units, and multiple dwellings instead of concentrating on detached frame dwellings. Also there were no design suggestions given for treating groups of houses as a whole; how to unite backyards, treat the parking problem, or integrate street designs.

The book, however, is the most complete postwar work on private remodeling. It gives evidence that an increasing number of housing investors and their professional organizations see the public necessity and potential profitability of urban renewal.

Study 15 *How to Profit by Rehabilitation Real Estate*

    Mary Warren Geer, Prentice-Hall, Inc., Englewood Cliffs, N.J., 1957, 207 pp.

Miss Geer has been active in the real estate business since 1931. She has written extensively of her experiences in the *National Real Estate Journal*, the *California Real Estate Magazine*, and a book entitled *Selling Home Property*.[11] Miss Geer says in her latest book that she followed Peter Turchon's lead and began rehabilitating properties during the Depression.[12]

Miss Geer begins her book, which is directed to other realtors, by reminding her fellow professionals (p. 5) that "Our country would blossom brightly if the real estate people became interested in helping their neighbors make the right kind of improvements in their properties." She goes on to say (p. 12) that re-

[11] Prentice-Hall, Inc., 1951.
[12] Mentioned by Robert Douglas Baer, "How Tired Properties Can Be Reconditioned to Sell at a Profit," in the *Boston Sunday Globe*, Jan. 19, 1958, p. 25a, from *How to Profit by Rehabilitating Real Estate.*

habilitation pays quite well. "The effort you put into rehabilitation can, if you prefer, take all your time. It will pay you handsomely."

After telling of several instances where investors have profited from rehabilitation, she points out that while new houses are clean and maintenance free, older homes are in neighborhoods where the buyer knows exactly what kind of community facilities and neighbors he will have. The old-house buyer will be able to see whether the ground has settled or if faults built into the house have been painfully neglected or corrected by previous owners. Miss Geer declares it is the realtor's responsibility to reduce the faults of older homes through rehabilitation. Rehabilitation, she says (p. 34), can "... provide them [the buyers] with more for their money in older property."

Miss Geer says that while financing most older properties is difficult, a remodeled property in a sound neighborhood "... will then have become eligible for strong financing at higher prices" (p. 41). She feels that it is the duty of realtors to convince prospective sellers that remodeling would facilitate the sale (p. 48). "Financing is available to bring property up to its highest and best use. Our job is to channel as much of that financing as we can to this end."

Five essentials to rehabilitation are listed (p. 84): a property you know is really a good buy for rehabilitation; a comfortable cost setup; a sensible location for the extent of work being done; willingness to work for a small profit; and complete confidence in a successful outcome for everyone involved in the undertaking.

The house selected for rehabilitation should be well located and structurally sound. Miss Geer advises the rehabilitator to get help in judging the structural condition (p. 113): "The architect or building contractor can detail the proper and economical correction and make a fair estimate of the cost." She also suggests (p. 115) thinking of new uses for the property in keeping with land-use trends for the neighborhood. "The important thing to keep in mind is this: you are money ahead when you instigate the rehabilitation to which the whole property is best adapted."

Several chapters are devoted to the discussion of latent opportunities for profitable rehabilitation such as conversion, interesting buyers in property improvement, and trade-ins. Miss Geer finds the profits in remodeling flowing from an increase in general property values as well as the direct rehabilitation profit. She concludes by advising realtors (p. 194) that:

> When you, a familiar and respected real estate man or woman, make sense on more enjoyable and better use of property—when you can explain and demonstrate new value in old property—then you become the person to see for personal pleasure and money gain through rehabilitation.

CONCLUSIONS

Miss Geer provides a simple and personalized account of rehabilitation as a business. She also gave several convincing arguments why a realtor should take part in rehabilitation activity; however, the book is singularly lacking in details. Cost estimating and construction problems are avoided by advising the rehabilitator to depend upon an architect or building contractor. The design features which appeal to varying income groups are apparently assumed knowledge for the readers because, beyond a warning to undertake no repairs which do not make a positive addition in sale price, there is only the most general discussion of design. Financing problems which trouble so many rehabilitators in all but middle-income rehabilitation projects in stable residential areas are passed over by saying that extensive remodeling makes financing simple. Those limitations result from her apparent belief that rehabilitation makes the most sense both financially and from a policy viewpoint when it is undertaken in stable neighborhoods having a high proportion of homeownership.

The direction of her book limits Miss Geer to only those aspects of rehabilitation which concern the small project rehabilitator. The book was designed for the remodeler who works house by house. There is no mention of organizational techniques and problems involved in remodeling on a project scale. There is only scant reference to government urban renewal or code enforcement programs. Finally, there is no attempt to view rehabilitation as only one of several alternative treatments of the property, although this is implied in the concept of highest and best use.

The book cannot compete with the clear detail of *Operative Remodeling* or the public-policy orientation of the Siegel-Brooks report. However, the book gives a simple message—simply put by a realtor with broad experience in the rehabilitation field. Its main purpose and major value is in making real estate professionals conscious of the rehabilitation business.

Study 16 *West Side Urban Renewal Study*

Prepared by Brown and Guenther, architectural consultants, for the City of New York. Preliminary Report, Aug. 15, 1957 (multilithed)

The study was undertaken with a demonstration grant from the Urban Renewal Administration to the City of New York. Its purpose was to determine the feasibility of rehabilitation in a pilot urban-renewal area in the Nineties on Manhattan's West Side.

There are 387 structures in the eight-block pilot area: 152 old-law tenements, 179 brownstones, 13 new-law tenements, 9 elevator buildings, 19 religious and educational structures, and 15 commercial structures. A representative sampling of each class of residential structures was examined for three levels of rehabilitation standards. The investigation includes an assessment of physical condition, architectural designs for each level of standard, and a thorough cost estimate. The cost estimate includes the acquisition cost, repair costs, operating costs, changes in rents and assessments, and the effects of either a write-down in acquisition costs, tax concessions, or both. Fifteen per cent profit is assumed as the minimum amount needed to attract investors to the project.

The potential rents and final feasibility conclusions are determined with the aid of local real estate consultants. The final conclusions suggest that 157 brownstones and 52 old-law tenements could be profitably rehabilitated to the "minimum" standards and pay a return as high as 16.2 per cent as equity for the brownstones and 35.71 per cent on the old-law tenements provided FHA Section 220 financing were available.[13]

Brown and Guenther outline the first two stages of two alternative ten-year plans for area renewal, one to emphasize rehabilitation and the other new construction. The new-construction proposal is estimated to cost $4,572,800 more than the rehabilitation proposal and would return $127,682 more to the city in taxes each year (part 4).[14] The consultants make no effort to suggest that one proposal was better than another.

CONCLUSIONS

The Brown and Guenther study is a good example of the locally based rehabilitation study. The report, however, does not tell the reader unfamiliar with New York why various physical standards were chosen, what evidence was present to justify the assumed rent increases, and how the area-improvement plan fits into the general plans for the entire city. Sparse information is an obvious consequence of concentrating attention on the feasibility question for a specific area and a specific group of buildings.

The report also fails to include some investigation of investor and lender interest in the project, although this may have been informally done during the course of the study. A sample of potential investors at this stage of project programming might save the city considerable difficulty when the land is put up for sale at the last stages of project execution. The Zisook report

[13] The minimum improvement standards emphasized repairs and supplementation rather than replacement for the utility system of the structures. Only limited changes in interior spatial arrangements were to be made, and the redecoration included only patching for plaster and floors. The entire operation was to cost approximately $3,750 per dwelling unit for the brownstones and $3,600 per unit for the old-law tenements.

[14] These figures cover the pilot area only. It is estimated that the redevelopment proposal for the entire area would return $1,424,811 in taxes compared to $1,312,500 for the rehabilitation proposal. (The 1957 yield was $853,300.) (*The New York Times*, Apr. 23, 1958, pp. 1 and 29.)

appearing in Study 17 adds this analysis by having a builder interested in developing the area undertake the initial study.

Study 17 *A Survey of the Rehabilitation Possibilities in the Hyde Park-Kenwood Urban Renewal Area*

Chicago Community Conservation Board and Zisook Construction Company (under Federal Advance Planning Contract, unpublished); materials from a speech by David Zisook, NAHRO St. Louis Conference, Oct. 22, 1957; and the preliminary *Report of the Feasibility of Rehabilitation*, Chicago Community Conservation Board, David Zisook, and Zisook Construction Company, Inc., 1958, 43 pp.

The study was undertaken after the Chicago Community Conservation Board had prepared preliminary plans for the Hyde Park–Kenwood area. The study intended to establish standards for determining the appropriateness of rehabilitation as against clearance, to determine the degrees of rehabilitation most suited to designated types of structures, and to determine the profitability of varying degrees of rehabilitation in light of general area improvement.

The Zisook Construction Company examined 150 structures selected as representative of the housing in the renewal area. Rehabilitation is divided into five categories:

1. Structural reconstruction—reconstruction or replacement of the basic safety elements such as foundations or beams.
2. Functional remodeling — overcoming obsolescence by changes in floor plans and occupancy.
3. Mechanical replacement—replacing the "operating guts" of the building including wiring, plumbing, and heating.
4. Modernization—repairs and replacements designed to offset aesthetic obsolescence.
5. Site alteration—improvements to the immediate environment of the structure such as parking facilities and landscaping.

The study concludes that rehabilitation commonly involves some of all five forms of remodeling, with the heaviest expenditures made for mechanical replacement and modernization. Site alteration cannot be made by a single rehabilitator working on a small project but must wait for a full-scale attack on the area, said Zisook. The site alterations which accompany urban renewal make it economically possible to rehabilitate many more structures in an area than if the environment of the proposed rehabilitation project were untouched. However, even with urban renewal some structures must be eliminated. "In these cases the cost of remodeling and renovating would be greater than the cost of demolishing and constructing new." Others would have to be demolished to make way for neighborhood facilities.

Zisook's approach to the actual feasibility question is one of an experienced property manager. "Because such a decision in its basic aspects is an economic one, as a property owner and manager I know the first question the owner and investor will ask is whether enough net income can be produced to result in a satisfactory return on investment." The least costly rehabilitation projects employ as much of the old structure as possible but "In order to produce rehabilitated housing with long-term economic life it is essential that the obsolete, deteriorated, and substandard features be remodeled, altered, repaired, and otherwise improved so as to achieve housing environmental appeal."

The actual cost studies employ physical standards designed to ensure mortgageability for a thirty-five-year term with future rents and values based on the improved neighborhoods. Mr. Zisook reaches twelve basic conclusions in his study.

1. In a vast majority of cases the rehabilitation of basically sound residential structures is economically feasible.

2. In order to induce equity capital and finance into the rehabilitation of housing, it is essential that such rehabilitation produces housing which is economically feasible, with the exception of single-family homes and owner-occupied apartments. (These last categories need the least repairs.)

3. Existing environmental inadequacies must be corrected as a precondition for private investment in area-wide property improvements.

4. Since a given environment is a product of community forces, it is necessary and proper that the improvement of that environment be undertaken as a community responsibility. (Public sponsors.)

5. Rehabilitation should be limited to buildings that are in good

structural condition. (Structural improvements imply primary and secondary costs which cannot be justified by return on investment.)

6. Structures that are not marketable by virtue of obsolescence should be excluded as objects for rehabilitation.

7. It is essential to conserve as much of the existing value of a building as is reasonably possible. (The rehabilitator's taste should not influence construction decisions based on market factors.)

8. The imposition of modern floor plans upon existing interiors should be avoided. (If the existing floor plan is so obsolete and undesirable as to require extensive remodeling, the structure should be demolished.)

9. Improvements generally must be designed to add new values rather than to replace existing ones.

10. Conversions and deconversions of existing living units create conditions which generally would exclude them from a privately financed rehabilitation program.

11. Expenditures for code compliance add very little to value. Expenditures for deferred maintenance alone add very little to value.

12. The feasibility of large-scale rehabilitation is dependent upon the availability of long-term financing.

CONCLUSIONS

One of the main conclusions reached in the ACTION Rehabilitation Study was that locally oriented studies based on local conditions, problems, and standards were the only way to determine the economic feasibility of an area-wide rehabilitation project. To the Chicago Metropolitan Housing and Planning Council Report of 1953, which covered the same area, Zisook adds a real estate investor's point of view. His knowledge of the local market makes it possible to reach more conclusive decisions on project profitability. Where the earlier study made no compromise with project standards, Zisook is willing to investigate the possibility that the standards set by potential rents are not too greatly different from the standards set as a desirable goal before his investigation began.

The Zisook study approaches what is needed for local rehabilitation studies intended to stimulate private investment, but because it is a local study the conclusions drawn by the authors cannot be applied to other areas. Several conclusions (5, 6, 10, and 11) reached above were based largely on local conditions and would have to be carefully reviewed if the study method was applied to another area where different conditions prevailed. Major structural repairs, conversions, and adding value through code enforcement are all possible in other areas under different market circumstances.

In spite of its limited applicability, the Chicago study will add valuable methodological information on locally based feasibility studies when the findings after publication are either supported or overturned by actual rehabilitation experiences.

Study 18 *The Feasibility of Rehabilitation*
Albert H. Schaaf (director).

This study is being conducted by Prof. Albert H. Schaaf of the University of California, Berkeley, and is jointly financed by the University's Real Estate Research Program and a Section 314 grant from the Federal government. The study is directed toward an analysis of various conditions under which rehabilitation may be feasible and the economic effects and policy implications of such conditions. The analytical results are being applied to data gathered in three residential areas in Oakland, California, in order to estimate the quantitative effects of various approaches to rehabilitation and develop a survey method designed to predict the feasibility and possible outcomes of rehabilitation in a given area.

CONCLUSIONS

Although the study has not progressed to the point where it can be adequately analyzed, the study promises to contribute to public and private groups alike interested in housing rehabilitation under urban renewal.

Summary

Investment potential more than housing theory is the main emphasis in recent rehabilitation studies. The potentiality of rehabilitation as a part of a unified housing and planning program apparently has been fully accepted by housing planners. The question is no longer whether rehabilitation deserves inclusion in a unified housing plan for a community but precisely how and where it will be used.

The contemporary urban-renewal program, so akin to proposed rehabilitation programs in the 1930s, should assure an almost continuous stream of locally based rehabilitation studies, many financed by the HHFA. The future student will have a rich mine of information which he can synthesize into a firm groundwork for his own research.

REHABILITATION BIBLIOGRAPHY

Background to Rehabilitation

American Housing Statistics: Condition, Supply and Demand, American Council To Improve Our Neighborhoods, New York, April, 1955, 28 pp., tables.

Bauer, Catherine: "Three-way War in Housing: Lender v. Builder v. Reformer," *The Reporter*, June 22, 1954, pp. 18–21.

Bernard, W. C.: "Do Public Improvements Create Special Benefits?" *Appraisal Journal*, vol. 13, January, 1945, pp. 20–23.

Blank, David M., and Louis Winnick: "The Structure of the Housing Market," *Journal of Economics*, May, 1953, pp. 181–208, diag., tables.

Brown, Samuel Lovitt: *The Elasticity of Demand for Housing*, Georgetown University Library, Washington, 1951, 177 pp., diag.

Burchard, John E.: *A Method for Analyzing the Economic Distribution of Shelter*, The Albert Farwell Bemis Foundation, Massachusetts Institute of Technology, Cambridge, Mass., June, 1940, 25 pp.

Colean, Miles L.: *American Housing: Problems and Prospects*, The Twentieth Century Fund, Inc., New York, 1944, 466 pp., tables, charts, graphs.

———: *Renewing Our Cities*, The Twentieth Century Fund, Inc., New York, 1953, 181 pp.

———: "The Realities of Real Estate," *Architectural Forum*, vol. 102, no. 4, April, 1955, pp. 125–127.

Dewhurst, Frederic J., and associates: *America's Needs and Resources*, The Twentieth Century Fund, Inc., New York, 1955, chap. 7, pp. 196–231, illus., maps, tables.

Downs, J. C.: *Principles of Real Estate Management*, 4th ed., Institute of Real Estate Management, Chicago, 1954, 475 pp., illus., bibl.

Fisher, Ernest M., and Robert M. Fisher: *Urban Real Estate*, Henry Holt and Company, Inc., New York, 1954, 502 pp.

Grebler, Leo, David M. Blank, and Louis Winnick: *Capital Formation in Residential Real Estate: Trends and Prospects*, National Bureau of Economic Research, Inc., and the Institute for Urban Land Use and Housing Studies (to be published).

———: *Experience in Urban Real Estate Investment*, Columbia University Press, New York, 1955, 277 pp., diag., tables.

———: *Housing Market Behavior in a Declining Area: Long-term Changes in Inventory and Utilization of Housing in New York's Lower East Side*, Columbia University Press, New York, 1952, 265 pp., maps, diag., tables.

———: "New Indications of the Housing Market," *Appraisal Journal*, vol. 18, no. 1, January, 1950, pp. 54–62, tables.

"Housing," *Law and Contemporary Problems*, vol. 12, no. 1 (entire issue), Winter, 1947.

Housing and Home Finance Agency: *Know Your Local Housing Market*, 1955, 25 pp.

Husband, William H., and Frank Ray Anderson: *Real Estate Analysis*, Richard D. Irwin, Inc., Homewood, Ill., 1948, 576 pp., graphs, tables.

Lipstein, Benjamin: *The Role of Residential Conversions in the Housing Market*, Columbia University, 1956, 172 pp. (typewritten Ph.D. dissertation).

Mayer, Harold M.: "Current and Prospective Population Trends—Some Real Estate Implications," *Appraisal Journal*, vol. 23, April, 1955, pp. 212–224.

National Housing Committee: *The Housing Market*, Washington, Dec. 3, 1947, 32 pp.

Rapkin, Chester, Louis Winnick, and David M. Blank: *Housing Market Analysis, A Study of Theory and Methods*, Housing and Home Finance Agency, Division of Housing Research, 1953, 92 pp., illus., bibl.

Ratcliff, Richard U.: "The Problems of the Used House," *Proceedings of the Annual Educational Conference*, University of Michigan, April, 1939, 32 pp. (Michigan Business Paper #5).

"Social Policy and Social Research in Housing," *Journal of Social Issues*, vol. 7, nos. 1 and 2 (entire issues), 1951, bibl.

Stowell, Kenneth Kingsley: *Modernizing Buildings for a Profit,* Prentice-Hall, Inc., Englewood Cliffs, N.J., 1935, 231 pp., illus.

Tannenbaum, Judith: "The Neighborhood: A Social-Psychological Analysis," *Land Economics,* vol. 24, November, 1948, pp. 358–369.

Vignan, Fred K.: *Crisis of the Cities,* Public Affairs Press, Washington, 1955, 155 pp.

Walker, Mabel (and others): "Urban Blight and Slums," *Harvard City Planning,* ser. XII, Harvard University Press, 1938, 442 pp., illus., maps, diag.

Wickens, David: *Residential Real Estate,* National Bureau of Economic Research, Inc., New York, 1941, 305 pp., tables.

Wheaton, William L. C.: "American Housing Needs 1955–1970," *Housing Yearbook,* National Housing Conference, 1954, pp. 5–23.

Woodbury, Coleman (ed.): *The Future of Cities and Urban Redevelopment,* University of Chicago Press, Chicago, 1953, 764 pp.

———: *Urban Redevelopment Problems and Practices,* University of Chicago Press, Chicago, 1953, 525 pp.

Historical References

Boston City Planning Board: *Building a Better Boston,* vol. I (of 3 volumes on the subject of rehabilitation in Boston), 1941, 57 pp., maps, plans, tables.

———: *A Progress Report on Reconstruction,* vol. II, May, 1943, 54 pp., maps, plans, tables.

———: *A Progress Report on Reconditioning,* vol. III, January, 1946, 81 pp., plans, maps, tables.

Chicago Housing Authority: *The Slum ... Is Rehabilitation Possible?* 1946, 37 pp., maps, plans, illus.

Chicago Metropolitan and Planning Council, Conservation: *A Report to the Conservation Committee of the Metropolitan Housing and Planning Council by Its Conservation Study Staff,* 1953, 345 pp., illus., plans.

Federal Housing Administration: *Four Decades of Housing with a Limited Dividend Corporation,* 1939, 108 pp., tables, diag.

Goodwillie, Arthur: *The Rehabilitation of Southwest Washington as a War Housing Measure,* Home Loan Bank Board, Washington, 1943.

———: *Waverly—A Study of Neighborhood Conservation,* Home Loan Bank Board, Washington, 1940, 97 pp., illus., plans, tables.

Gould, E. R. L.: "Economics of Improved Housing," *Yale Review*, vol. 5, May, 1896, pp. 8–30.

Hawkins, R. R., and C. H. Abbe: *New Houses from Old: Your Guide to Home Remodeling*, McGraw-Hill Book Company, Inc., New York, 1948, 558 pp., illus.

Housing and Home Finance Agency–Urban Renewal Administration: *Feasibility of Rehabilitating Certain Residential Structures*, Report on Field Trip to Kansas City, Mo., Attucks Project MO. or MO.–3–1, unpaged (multilithed).

"Modernizing Number," *Building Age*, vol. 51, no. 1 (entire issue), January, 1929.

The President's Conference on Home Building and Home Ownership, December 2–5, 1931, Washington, 1931.

Report and Recommendations of the Committee on Old Housing to the Citizens' Housing Council of New York, June, 1936, 22 pp., maps, plans (mimeo.).

Waldo, Fullerton J.: *Good Housing That Pays*, The Harpers Company, Philadelphia, 1917, 126 pp.

Rehabilitation Cases and Comments

"A 'Basket Case' Gets New Life," National Association of Home Builders, *NAHB Correlator*, vol. 8, no. 1, January, 1954, pp. 208–209.

Brethren Brotherhood Service, Inc.: *Rehabilitation of the Brotherhood Pilot House*, Housing Bureau, Baltimore City Health Department, Baltimore, 1952, 4 pp.

Build America Better Committee of the National Association of Real Estate Boards: *Modernizing Homes for Profit*, Washington, 27 pp., illus.

Chicago Community Conservation Board: *A Survey of the Rehabilitation Possibilities in the Hyde Park–Kenwood Urban Renewal Area*, 1958.

Conklin, Groff: "The Builder Makes a Profit on Rehabilitation, *NAHB Correlator*, vol. 8, no. 10, October, 1954, pp. 13–15, illus.

"The Contract Remodeler," *Ohio Builder*, vol. 4, no. 5, May, 1956, p. 10.

"Example of Rehabilitation," *House & Home*, vol. 8, no. 12, December, 1955, pp. 44–46, illus.

"First Round Won in Slum Fight," *Electrical World*, Oct. 8, 1956, p. 47.

Geer, Mary W.: *How to Profit by Rehabilitating Real Estate*, Prentice-Hall, Inc., Englewood Cliffs, N.J., 1957, 207 pp.

"Housing Rehabilitation," *NAHB Correlator*, vol. 7, no. 10, October, 1953, pp. 2–25.

"How to Estimate Modernization Jobs," *Practical Builder*, vol. 10, October, 1955, p. 20.

Institute of Real Estate Management and The Build America Council of the National Association of Real Estate Boards: *Rehabilitation as a Business*, Washington, 1954, 99 pp., illus., tables, plans.

"Lone Slum-clearer Makes Money; Mr. Binns of Philadelphia Turns Rundown Properties into Profitable Investment," *Business Week*, Dec. 9, 1939, pp. 32–33, illus.

"Long Island Builders Set Up Stock Corporation to Finance Rehabilitation," *House & Home*, vol. 9, no. 4, April, 1956, pp. 75 and 82, illus.

"Look Behind the Dirt and Find a Gold Mine," *House & Home*, vol. 5, no. 10, October, 1954, pp. 106–108.

McCord, Paul: "Saving Old Houses Profitably," *Freehold*, Feb. 1, 1940, pp. 97–102.

Mecasky, Richard: "Rehabilitation Yields Low-rate Housing," *Journal of Housing*, vol. 12, no. 12, December, 1956.

"Modernization Issue," *Architectural Forum*, vol. 93, no. 4, 1950.

"Modernization Issues," *House & Home*, vol. 4, no. 4, October, 1953; vol. 5, no. 10, October, 1954.

National Association of Home Builders: *Housing in the U.S.A.*, Simmons-Boardman Publishing Corporation, New York, 1954, 235 pp., illus.

"Old Houses Make Desirable Apartments in Montclair, New Jersey," *American Builder*, vol. 69, June, 1947, pp. 118–120.

"Philadelphia Cure; Clearing Slums with Penicillin, Not Surgery," *Architectural Forum*, vol. 96, no. 4, April, 1952, pp. 112–119.

Quaker "Self-help" Rehabilitation Program in Philadelphia, American Council To Improve Our Neighborhoods, New York, April, 1955, 12 pp.

"Remodeling Tips from the Nation's Top Remodelers," *Popular Mechanics*, vol. 106, no. 4, October, 1956, pp. 170–171.

Schmidt, Herman: "How We Do It at a Profit," *NAHB Correlator*, vol. 7, no. 10, October, 1953, pp. 10–16.

Shifrin, Philip: "How I Sell Modernizing to Home Owners," *Practical Builder*, vol. 20, no. 10, October, 1955, pp. 4–7.

Shinner, E. G.: *Arresting Slums through Private Enterprise*, The Shinner Foundation, Chicago, January, 1956, 35 pp.
"This Is Not a New House...It Just Looks Like One," *House & Home*, vol. 10, no. 5, November, 1956, p. 126.
"Town Houses in Georgetown," *The Business of Building*, Late Fall, 1955, p. 6.
Operative Remodeling, United States Gypsum Co., Chicago, 1956, 126 pp., illus.

The Mortgage Market

Babson, R. W.: "Remodeling Houses," *Commercial and Financial Chronicle*, vol. 174, Oct. 18, 1951, p. 1490.
Financing Home Repairs and Improvements, American Council To Improve Our Neighborhoods, New York, 1956, 13 pp.
Fight-Blight Fund, Inc.: Baltimore, American Council To Improve Our Neighborhoods, New York, 1956, 10 pp.
Gillies, James, and Clayton Curtis: "The Structure of the Local Mortgage Market and Government Housing Finance Programs," *Journal of Finance*, vol. 10, September, 1955, pp. 363–375.
Hoagland, H. E.: *Real Estate Finance*, Richard D. Irwin, Inc., Homewood, Ill., 1954, 515 pp.
Home Mortgage Lending, American Bankers Association and American Institute of Bankers, New York, 1953, 420 pp., bibl., illus., tables.
Mortgage Financing for Properties Available to Negro Occupancy, National Urban League, New York, 1954, 13 pp.
Morton, J. E.: *Urban Mortgage Lending*, Princeton University Press, Princeton, N.J., 1956, 187 pp., tables, graphs.
Outhwaite, Stephenson: *Home Improvement Loans under FHA Title I for the Investment Portfolio of Savings Banks*, Graduate School of Banking, Rutgers University, New Brunswick, N.J., June, 1955, 47 pp., tables, biblio.
Ross, T. H.: "Effect of Mortgage Financing on Real Estate Values," *Appraisal Journal*, vol. 21, April, 1953, pp. 203–210.
Schechtee, Henry B.: "National and Local Mortgage Market Structures," *Housing Research*, no. 4, October, 1952, pp. 9–22.
U.S. Senate Committee on Banking and Currency: *Mortgage Market Problems*, hearings before subcommittee, Nov. 28–29, 1955, Washington, 1955, 168 pp., tables, charts.

The Consumer

Agan, Tessie: "Housing and the Family Life Cycle," *Journal of Home Economics*, vol. 42, May, 1950, pp. 351-354.

Ashley, Everett E.: "Mobility and Migration as Factors in Housing Demand," *Housing Research*, no. 6, October, 1953, pp. 1-7.

Beyer, Glenn H.: *Housing and Journey to Work*, Cornell University, Agricultural Experiment Station, Ithaca, N.Y., August, 1951, 19 pp. (Bull. no. 877).

Bureau of Labor Statistics and the Wharton School of Finance and Commerce: *Study of Consumer Expenditures, Incomes, and Savings: 1950*, University of Pennsylvania Press, Philadelphia, 18 volumes, 1957.

Cornell University Housing Research Center: *Houses Are for People*, Ithaca, N.Y., 1955, 85 pp.

Fuller, Robert S.: "Changing Characteristics of Dwellings," *Appraisal Journal*, vol. 21, October, 1953, pp. 555-559.

Ramsey, Duane V.: *What Some Slum Dwellers Want in Housing*, Henry Street Settlement, New York, July, 1935, 10 pp.

Stephen, Frieda, and Joseph Palmer: *The Pattern of Expenditures for Non-farm Residential Repair and Maintenance*, Department of Commerce, Construction Division, Washington, 1946, 67 pp., illus., tables, diag.

"Tenants—Not Landlords Defy Repair Order in Brooklyn," *Journal of Housing*, vol. 113, no. 3, March, 1956, p. 104.

Rehabilitation and the National Government

Bloomberg, Lawrence N.: "The Role of the Federal Government in Urban Housing," *American Economic Review*, vol. 41, no. 2, May, 1951, pp. 586-598, illus., charts.

Colean, Miles L.: *The Impact of Government on Real Estate Finance in the United States*, National Bureau of Economic Research, Inc., New York, 1950, 171 pp., biblio.

Housing and Home Finance Agency: *Annual Reports*, charts, tables.
———: *Housing in the Economy: 1956*, 1958, 44 pp.
———: *Housing Statistics* (monthly).

Morton, Walter: *Housing Taxation*, University of Wisconsin Press, Madison, Wis., 1955, 262 pp.

The President's Advisory Committee on Government Housing Policies and Programs: *A Report to the President of the United States,* Washington, December, 1953, 377 pp.

"Redevelopment Issue," *Journal of Housing,* vol. 14, no. 10, October, 1957 (a series of articles appraising the progress and future of government housing and urban-renewal programs).

Rouse, James W., and Nathaniel S. Keith: *No Slums in Ten Years,* A Report to the Commissioner of the District of Columbia, Washington, 1955, 51 pp.

Siegel, Jack M., and William C. Brook: *Slum Prevention through Conservation and Rehabilitation,* Subcommittee on Urban Redevelopment, Rehabilitation, and Conservation, President's Advisory Committee on Government Housing Policies and Programs, Washington, 1953, 142 pp.

"Slum Clearance and Urban Renewal," *NAHB Correlator,* vol. 8, no. 10, October, 1954, pp. 2–40, illus.

Temporary National Economic Committee: *Investigation of Concentration of Economic Power,* Hearings, Part II, Construction Industry, Washington, 1940, pp. 4933–5593.

Wheaton, William L. C.: *The Administration of Federal Housing Programs,* unpublished Ph.D. dissertation, University of Chicago, 1953.

Young, Michael, and Peter Willmott: *Family and Kinship in East London,* Free Press, Glencoe, Ill., 1957.

Rehabilitation and the State and Local Government

Barnhart, Gilbert R., in collaboration with the American Society of Building Officials: *Housing Codes,* Housing and Home Finance Agency, Washington, 1953, 55 pp., tables.

Bloom, Murray Teigh: "One Way to Stop Slums," *National Municipal Review,* vol. 45, no. 2, February, 1956.

Brewer, M. F.: "Enforcement of Housing Standards in St. Louis," *American City,* April, 1955, pp. 117–118.

Brown, Harry G. (and others): *Land Value Taxation around the World,* Robert Shalkenbach Foundation, 1955, 216 pp., illus., charts.

Buehler, A. G.: "The Capitalization of Taxes," *National Tax Journal,* vol. 3, December, 1950, pp. 283–297.

Buttenheim, Harold S.: "Real Estate Taxes That Stimulate Improvements," *Michigan Municipal Review,* April, 1957.

"Chicago Starts a Pilot Block Rehabilitation Project," *House & Home*, vol. 5, no. 2, February, 1954, pp. 39–40.

"Code Enforcement Spoils the Market for Slum Housing in Philadelphia," *House & Home*, vol. 9, no. 2, February, 1956, p. 61.

"Conversion Control and Neighborhood Conservation," *Northwestern University Law Review*, vol. 48, no. 5, November-December, 1953, pp. 599–608.

Cornick, P. H.: "Evaluation of Alternative Basis for the Property Tax," *American Journal of Economics and Sociology*, vol. 13, October, 1953, pp. 57–69.

Creighton, Roger L.: "Rethinking Urban Redevelopment; the Viewpoint of a Small City," *Journal of the American Institute of Planners*, Spring, 1953, pp. 95–102, illus.

Housing and Home Finance Agency, Office of the Administrator, Division of Law: *Comparative Digest of the Principal Provisions of State Planning Laws Relating to Housing, Slum Clearance, and Urban Redevelopment*, 1951, 80 pp.

How Localities Can Develop a Workable Program for Urban Renewal, Housing and Home Finance Agency, 1957, 12 pp.

Johnson, Ralph J.: "The Requirements of a Good Housing Ordinance," *American City*, June, 1955.

——— and Roy O. McCaldin: *Evaluation of Housing Law Enforcement in Housing Rehabilitation*, Department of Public Health, Education and Welfare (Public Health mono. no. 4), 1954, 34 pp., tables, maps, graphs.

Kreitzer, Donald J.: *Urban Redevelopment and Rehabilitation in Columbus, Ohio* (University Microfilms Publication No. 12,175), University of Ohio, Columbus, Ohio, 1955, 262 pp.

Lammer, Francis J.: "Rehabilitation Has Taken Three Forms in Philadelphia," *Journal of Housing*, vol. 12, February, 1955, pp. 47–50.

Massachusetts Department of Public Health, Division of Sanitary Engineering: *Housing Rehabilitation, an Administrative Guide to Community Action*, Boston, 1954, 34 pp., bibl., illus., charts.

McDermott, John: *Operation Fix-up*, Philadelphia Redevelopment Authority, 1952, 12 pp. (mimeo.).

McDougal, Myres S.: "Municipal Real Estate Taxation as an Instrument for Community Planning," *Yale Law Journal*, December, 1947, pp. 219–242.

Moses, Robert: *The Influence of Public Improvements on Property Values*, New York, August, 1953, 16 pp. illus., maps, plans.

"New Orleans Begins Job of Housing Rehabilitation," *American City*, vol. 69, no. 4, April, 1954, pp. 112–113.

Oster, Robert M.: *Municipal Housing Codes in the Courts*, American Council To Improve Our Neighborhoods, New York, 1956, 21 pp.

A Primer of Rehabilitation under Local Law Enforcement, National Association of Real Estate Boards, Committee on Rehabilitation, Washington, 1952, 68 pp., illus.

Rapkin, Chester: "The Role of Real Estate Taxes in the Investment Experience of Real Property," *Appraisal Journal*, vol. 22, October, 1954, pp. 486–496.

Redevelopment of Blighted Residential Areas in Baltimore, Condition of Blight, Some Remedies and Their Relative Costs, Baltimore Commission on City Planning, 1945, 102 pp., maps, diag., tables.

Report of the Rochester Rehabilitation Commission to the City Council, Dec. 21, 1956, photos, maps, charts.

Rhyne, Charles: *Demolition, Vacation, or Repair of Substandard Buildings*, National Institute of Municipal Law Officers (The Institute), Washington (Report No. 111), 1945, 86 pp.

St. Louis Housing Survey Report, *Let's Take a Look at Housing*, August, 1953, 54 pp., maps, charts, tables.

Silverman, Leon: "Municipal Real Estate Taxation as an Instrument for Community Planning," *Yale Law Journal*, vol. 57, no. 219, December, 1947.

Slayton, William L.: "The States and Urban Renewal," *State Government*, vol. 27, October, 1954, pp. 203–204, 215–217.

"Taking the Profit Out of Slums," *House & Home*, vol. 9, no. 2, February, 1956.

INDEX

Alley Dwelling Law, 9, 12
American Council To Improve Our Neighborhoods (ACTION), *American Housing Statistics: Conditions, Supply, Demand*, 2
    consumer study with *Fortune* magazine, 5, 41–42
    Federal Credit and Private Housing, 160
    Housing Code Provisions, 85
    rehabilitation questionnaire, 4–5, 130
American Institute of Architects (AIA), 188

Back-of-the-Yards Movement, 48n., 134, 154, 158
Baltimore Fight Blight Fund, 113
Binns, Arthur, 3n.
Board for the Condemnation of Insanitary Buildings, 9
Boston, Massachusetts, 62–70
Breckenridge, Gaston L., 53–55
Brewer, Monroe F., 100–101, 104
Britt, Edward, 14
Building code, 166–167, 192
Bunker Hill, Los Angeles, 75–76
Burns, Fritz, 53, 75–76, 81

Camac Street Area, Philadelphia, 31–34
Campbell, John, 35–38

Charlotte, North Carolina, 86–96, 106
    Charlotte Observer, 88
    code enforcement, 86–96
    Home Builders Association, 95n.
    Real Estate Board, 91
Clark, Joseph S., 160–161
Code enforcement, 83, 107–113, 127–128, 164, 168
    Charlotte, 86–96
    Columbus, 71–72
    Philadelphia, 108–111
    Rochester, 104–106
    St. Louis, 96–104
Cole, Albert M., 165n.
Colean, Miles L., 186n.
Community Facilities Agency, 176–177
Conventional mortgages, 146–148

Dilworth, Richardson, 178n.

East Poplar Area, Philadelphia, 77
Farr, Newton, 52, 55–57
Feasibility equation, 141–144
Federal Home Loan Bank Board (FHLBB), 153
Federal Housing Administration (FHA), 44, 46, 55, 72, 81–83, 147–153, 157–159, 161, 176–178, 193–194

Federal Housing Administration
(FHA), Section 213, 79
Section 220, 35, 151–152
Section 221, 71
Title I, property improvement loans, 43, 50, 148
Federal National Mortgage Association (FNMA), 153, 160, 194
Fitler Square Area, Philadelphia, 26–31
Foggy Bottom, 9–25, 44
Green's Court, 11
Hughes Court, 11–14, 16
Snow's Court, 11, 16–19
Renewal Area, 22
Restoration Association, 21
Friends (see Society of Friends)
Funk, Jacob, 9

George Washington University Urban Renewal Area, 22n.
Georgetown, Washington, D.C., 8–10, 39
Gleason, William H., 158
Goodwillie, Arthur, 4n.

Havens, John, 52, 71–72
Haynes, A. A., 80
Held, Harry, 161
Hollander, Milton, 32–33
Hollyday, Guy T. O., 178n.
Home Building Association, 14
Home Modernizing Bureau of National Industries, Inc., 3
Home Owners Loan Corporation, 2
Homes, Inc., 62–68
Housing codes, 85–86, 96–97, 166–168, 181–182, 192

Housing and Home Finance Agency (HHFA), 49n., 131n., 147n., 165n., 175–177
Hyde Park, Chicago, 55
St. Louis, 101–102

Income tax, corporate, 179–180, 196
personal, 179–180, 195

James, Earl, 30

Kenwood Area, Chicago, 55
Klavans, Elmer, 52, 57–59
Krumbiegel, E. R., 168n.

La Grossa, Charles, 31–32
Limited dividend corporations, 85, 114–124
Los Angeles, California, 75–76

Manhattan, New York, 73–75
Manning, Mrs. Halsey, 28–29
Mecaskey, Richard, 117–118, 120n., 122
Mortgages, conventional, 146–148

Nash, Robert J., Realty Co., 30
National Association of Real Estate Boards, "Build America Better," 75
National Housing Conference, 160
New Hampshire Department of Public Works and Highways, 174
New York City, 73–75
New York State, Division of Housing, 174
Mortgage Facilities Corporation, 159, 193
Norris, Charles, 11–15

Octavia Hill Association, Philadelphia, 114–124

Philadelphia, Camac Street Area, 31–34
code enforcement, 108–111
East Poplar Area, 77
Fitler Square Area, 26–31
Octavia Hill Association, 114–124
Penn Towne, 77–78, 80–81
Powelton Village Development Association (PVDA), 59–62, 123
Redevelopment Authority, 77–79, 81, 123
renewal, 35
Society of Friends, 53, 77–82
President's Advisory Committee on Housing, 1, 158, 186
Public Housing Administration, 176, 195

Real property tax, abatements, 171–172, 185, 192
assessments, 171–172, 193
Relocation, 86n., 106, 112–114
Rent control, 169
Ritch, James E., 88–90
Robbins, Ira S., 160
Robitscher, Dr. and Mrs. Jonas B., 11, 16–22
Rochester, New York, code enforcement, 104–106
Gas and Electric Company, 52–53, 105
Home Improvement Action Committee, 105
Rehabilitation Commission, 104–105

St. Louis, Cherokee Area, 97–103
code enforcement, 96–104
Hyde Park Area, 97–102
Minimum Housing Standards Ordinance, 96–98, 100–101
San Francisco, Telegraph Hill, 35–38
Savings and loan associations, 154
Schaaf, Albert H., 182n.
Schmidt, Herman, 124–127
Scott, Harold, 120
Shifrin, Philip, 49–50
Siegel, Jack M., 167n.
Slayton, William S., 165
Snow's Court, Washington, D.C., 11, 16–19
Society of Friends, Philadelphia, 53, 77–79, 81
Suburban Life, 3
Sutton Place, New York, 8

Telegraph Hill, San Francisco, 35–38
Turchon, Peter, 52, 62–70
Turek, Harry, 52, 73–75

United States, Housing Act of 1937, 88
Housing Act of 1957, 165
Senate Subcommittee on Housing, 160
Urban renewal, 21–25, 35, 44–46
Urban Renewal Administration (URA), 194–195

Veterans Administration guaranteed mortgages, 68–69, 83, 152–153, 175
Voluntary Home Mortgage Credit Program, 161

Washington, D.C., 11–14
  Foggy Bottom, 9–25, 44
  Georgetown, 8–10, 39
  Northwest Section, 57–59
  Urban Redevelopment Corporation, 123–127
  urban renewal, 21–25
  Zoning Board of Appeals, 20

Wheaton, William L. C., 164n.
Wiland Corporation, 12, 14
Williams, David, 28–29

Young, Brinton, 28

Zoning ordinances, 166, 168–169